THE
CHILDREN'S
ANNUAL
A HISTORY AND COLLECTOR'S GUIDE

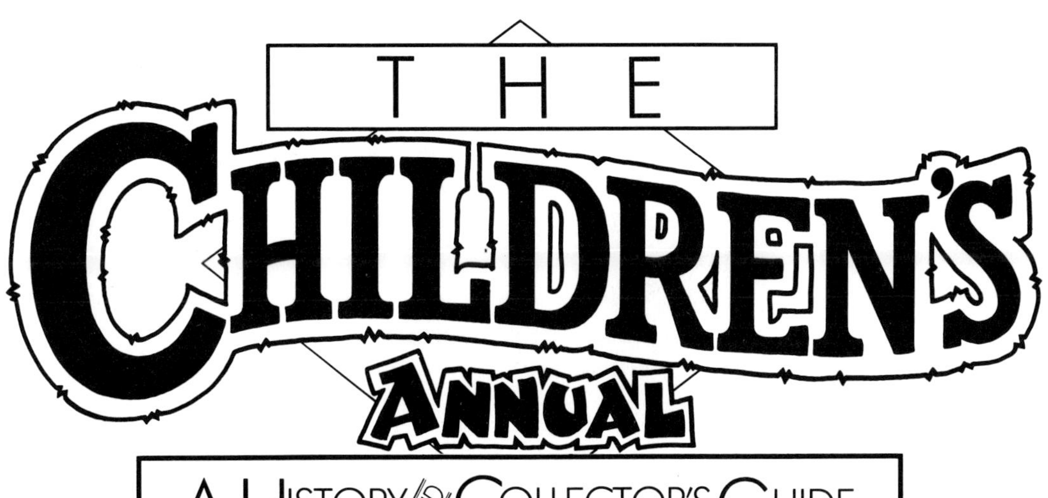
THE
CHILDREN'S
ANNUAL
A HISTORY AND COLLECTOR'S GUIDE

ALAN CLARK

Boxtree

For Laurel, Justin and Ben...

Acknowledgements

All the illustrations reproduced in this book come from the author's own private collection, and are reproduced as historical illustrations to the text. Grateful acknowledgement is made to the publishers and their original artists without whose contribution this book would not have been possible. The author is especially indebted to the following for permission to reproduce copyright material: Solo Syndication Ltd (for the Daily Mail); IPC Magazines; Fleetway Publications (Amalgamated Press and Odhams); BPCC PLC; Express Newspapers PLC; Collins Publishers; Oxford University Press Ltd.; Blackie & Son Ltd; World International Publications; BBC Books; Macdonald & Co.; Gerald G. Swan (Alan Clark); DC Comics/ National Periodicals; all material originally published by D.C. Thomson & Co. is reprinted by kind permission of D.C. Thomson & Co. Ltd.
Although every effort has been made to trace the owners of copyright material, in a few cases this has proven impossible and the author takes this opportunity to offer his apologies to any copyright holders whose rights have been unwittingly infringed.

Other books by Alan Clark

The Comic Art of Roy Wilson
The Comic Art of Reg Parlett

The author is also editor and publisher of *Golden Fun*; established in 1974, this was the world's first magazine devoted to British comics, story papers and annuals.
Send SAE for details from:
Golden Fun, 24, Arundel Road, Tunbridge Wells, Kent, TN1 1TB.

Front cover: Illustration by Roy Wilson (1900–1965) from *The Funny Wonder Annual* 1939.

First published in Great Britain in 1988
by Boxtree Limited

Designed by Groom & Pickerill
Typeset by Tradespools Limited, Frome, Somerset
Printed and bound in Italy by
IPE Amadeus, S.p.a., Rome
for Boxtree Limited, 36 Tavistock Street,
London WC2E 7PB

British Library Cataloguing in Publication Data

Clark, Alan
The children's annual: a history and collector's guide.
1. Children's annuals in English – Lists
I. Title
016.082

ISBN 1-85283-212-6

Contents

Introduction

Annuals for children have been published for more than one hundred and fifty years, and collected for almost as long. Collecting began in earnest in the late nineteenth century when publishers of periodicals such as *Chatterbox, The Boy's Own Paper* and *Chums* stockpiled each and every issue and published them, bound, as a complete volume just prior to Christmas every year. Sales were buoyant and the tradition continued. In due course, enthusiasts who hankered for complete sets made sure that their bookshelves contained every annual that was published for the periodical concerned. Those who started late often had to pay a premium for a missing and comparatively scarce back edition: hence began 'collectors' prices'.

The publishing explosion which began in the 1870s led to the thousands of titles which have been published to date. Today, annuals are collected more widely than ever before, and prices, fueled by the easy credit of the 1980s, have reached unprecedented levels. Recently as much as £700 has been paid for a single edition which would have been valued at £5 fifteen years ago. On the other hand, there are still bargains to be had: many annuals can be purchased for several pounds, or, in some cases, just a few pence.

One of the delights of collecting annuals is not only that they are widely available either from secondhand bookshops and specialist dealers, but also that it is still possible to find bargains at a local jumble sale (although, admittedly, the chances of this have been considerably reduced in recent years). And collectors cut across all boundaries, well-to-do and not so well-off; young and old.

There is a particularly useful aid that has been compiled for the collector. It is the (privately published) *Catalogue of Boys and Girls Annuals* by W.O.G. Lofts and D.J. Adley, two diligent researchers who have spent countless hours at the British Museum and at their typewriters to produce a comprehensive listing of thousands of titles and the years in which editions were published. This is highly recommended for all collectors and can be purchased from A. Cadwallender, 47, Athol Street, Gorton, Manchester, M18 7JP.

The enjoyment to be gained from collecting is immense. People collect for different reasons. Some do it for personal nostalgia, seeking out the books they had when they were children; others regard annuals as aesthetically pleasing and full of social interest. Furthermore, annuals provide a convenient means of collecting a comic title when a set of weekly issues (possibly running to thousands) would be almost unobtainable.

If collecting for investment, the buyer must consider how much of the price has been fueled by nostalgia rather than aesthetic appeal. The former must be approached with caution. Nostalgia runs in cycles: annuals such as the *Boy's Own Paper* and *Chums*, once relatively valuable, are worth comparatively little today. As generations of collectors disappear, prices drop quickly and the books retain only their social interest value. This could well be the case with the genre's three current front-runners: *Dandy, Beano* and *Rupert.*

Happily, however, the author has never met anyone who has collected annuals solely for investment: all have gleaned enormous pleasure (albeit, understandably, with an eye to appreciating value) from what is obviously an enjoyable and rewarding interest.

Whatever the motive for collecting, the purpose of this book is to summarise the long and rich history of children's annuals and to provide some guidance for those readers who seek detailed information and wish to price some of the more collectable titles.

CHAPTER 1

Victorian Annuals

Annuals for children first began to appear in the early part of the nineteenth century. One of the earliest was *The Christmas Box*, first published in 1828 and edited by Thomas Crofton Croker, who was well known for his previously published collections of fairy stories. Annuals at this time were small, approximately 4½ × 7 in (11 × 17 cm), with plain, undecorated board covers and were modelled on those previously published for adults. However, *The Christmas Box* was one of the first children's annuals to appear with the stated intention of printing stories solely for young children. It was Thomas Croker's boast that he was able to offer his 'young friends' a '... fund of that remarkable combination, instruction blended with amusement – well calculated to neutralise the contagion of lowering skies, and convert the long hours of a winter's evening into a "midsummer night's dream".'

The contents of this book of over 200 pages featured tales of orphans, historical adventures and a good deal of verse, with a half-dozen or more plates. But Croker's success was limited: *The Christmas Box* saw only a few editions, the final volume believed to be dated 1832.

'Disturbed By The Night-Mare', an illustration which accompanied a poem by Bernard Barton, Esq. *The Christmas Box* (1832).

Another early annual was a sturdy volume containing over 400 pages of text and entitled *The Excitement*. Published just before Christmas in 1829 and dated the following year, 1830, it was edited by Adam Keys, a Scottish schoolmaster. *The Excitement* differed considerably from its Victorian counterparts in that it made no concessions to religious dogma. Adam Keys's editorial policy was to print adventure stories founded on fact and to produce books that would be read 'by boys particularly, with the greatest attention; and also narratives of such striking incidents as are fitted to rouse the most slothful mind – incidents in which the reader cannot fail to imagine himself identified, as it were, with the parties concerned, and to enter with the deepest interest into all their various feelings...' Keys was ahead of his time. He had hit upon the concept of 'role models' for the young, something that would not come into vogue until many decades later.

The Keys approach was not popular and he was criticised by members of the Church. This caused him to reply, in the volume of 1837, 'that it had been hinted that it might be well to mingle more of pious sentiment with the details presented in *The Excitement* ... But it does not appear to us essential that *every* work put into the hands of the young should necessarily contain something of a religious nature...'

Puritanical pressure, however, proved too great and Adam Keys lost his editorship soon after, in 1838. The new editor of *The Excitement* was a man of the cloth, the Reverend Robert Jamieson, and over the next few years, not unexpectedly, the stories took on a more religious tone. Determined to stick to his guns, Adam Keys immediately started, with publisher William Innes, *The New Excitement*, which continued on much the same lines as before. Keys's new venture proved successful and the two annuals ran side by side for several years.

Several other children's annuals were published in the 1830s, notably the *Child's Own Annual* (Child's Own Magazine Publishing: 1832), *The Child's Own Book* (Murray and Medes: 1836) and *Fisher's Juvenile Scrapbook* (Fisher and Son: 1836). It is also worth mentioning *The Comic Annual*, edited by Thomas Hood. This was a series of annuals published between 1830 and 1842 which, although aimed at the adult market, was very popular with the young. The editor's son, Tom Hood, was also responsible for *Tom Hood's Comic Annual*, which included many older children among its readers and was published from 1867 until the late 1890s.

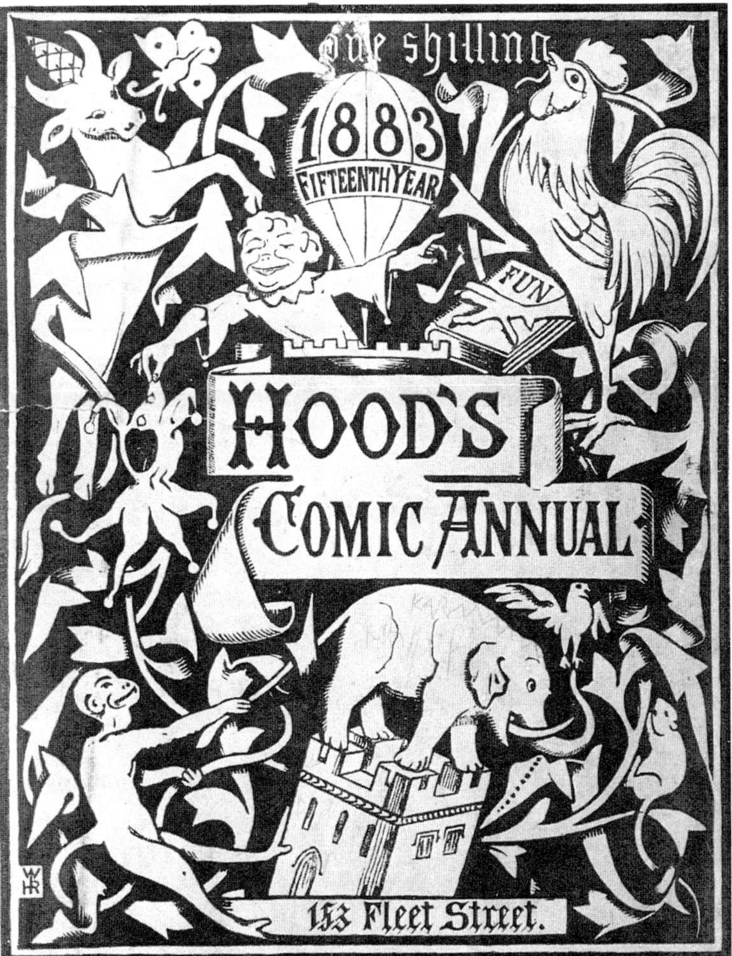

Tom Hood's Comic Annual was first published for 1869. Later, the title was shortened to simply *Hood's Comic Annual*.

The celebrated 'Peter Parley'

Possibly the best known annual of the Victorian era was *Peter Parley's Annual*, published by Simkin, Marshall & Co., London, and, later, by Ben George Ltd., which had the incredibly long run of fifty-two years. The name 'Peter Parley' is credited to countless works throughout the nineteenth century, and a casual observer could be forgiven for thinking that this author must have been the most prodigious of his time. But this is not so. 'Peter Parley' was the pseudonym of the prolific American writer, Samuel Goodrich (1793–1860), whose first book under that name, *Peter Parley's Tales of America*, was published

PETER PARLEY'S

ANNUAL:

A Christmas and New Year's Present

FOR YOUNG PEOPLE.

LONDON:
SIMPKIN, MARSHALL, AND CO.,
AND ALL BOOKSELLERS

MDCCCXL.

The title page from the first *Peter Parley's Annual* (1840).

in Boston in 1827. *Tales of America* contained adventure stories set against a thoroughly researched geographical and historical background, and was immediately popular with the children of the United States. Goodrich wrote several other stories in the same vein to satisfy the demand. By the mid-1830s Peter Parley was a household name in that country and it was not long before this fame spread abroad, although not in a manner of which Goodrich approved.

The first collection of his work, *Tales about Europe*, was published by Thomas Tegg and Son in London in 1835. The book was an unauthorised version of four stories that had previously been published separately in Boston. In the next few years Tegg and Son republished (still without seeking permission) all the Peter Parley tales they could find, and other London publishers quickly caught on to what was obviously a profitable business. Soon the plagiarism took a new twist: Charles Tilt and Edward Lacey began to issue volumes that used the name 'Peter Parley' but did not contain text written by Goodrich. Tegg responded by commissioning a hack writer, George Mogridge, actually to write a series of tales in the style of Goodrich and then published them under the Peter Parley pseudonym.

Samuel Goodrich was understandably furious over what he regarded as criminal activity and sought compensation. As a result, Tegg was eventually forced to make him an ex-gratia payment of £400. But the demand for 'Parley' books was so great that this did not stop other publishers using the name. Scores of titles appeared in the late 1830s and in 1839 a monthly magazine, published by Simkin, Marshall, was collated to form the first *Peter Parley's Annual: A Christmas and New Year's Present for Young People*, which was forward-dated to 1840.

Throughout its long life, the annual was always of a high standard. Usually bound in red cloth, with letters in gold block, the books were profusely illustrated. There were magnificent steel engravings by the best illustrators of the day and the text contained many woodcuts superior to those appearing in other publications of the time. The 1846 *Peter Parley's Annual* is viewed as a milestone in the field of book production for children. Previously, colour illustrations had been done by hand, a time-consuming but, in those days, inexpensive process. The 1846 annual contained a machine-printed colour frontispiece and title-page by the artist Harrison Weir (1824–1906). The quality of the work was immediately apparent, and from that time on each edition of the annual contained some colour printing. The high standards set by the publishers are directly attributable to its well-deserved long run, and the last edition did not appear until 1892.

Morality in the home

Another initially over-pious publication that was bound into annual form was *Chatterbox*, a half-penny weekly first published on 1 December 1866. It was founded by the Rev. J. Erskine Clarke and, although the tone in the earlier issues was religious, it was never 'grim'; and succeeding generations were to look back on it with affection. At first issued in plain boards, by the turn of the century the *Chatterbox* annual came in two editions: the first 'handsomely bound in extra cloth, bevelled boards with gilt edges', at five shillings, the other, in illustrated boards, at three shillings. Both were good value with over 400 pages and twelve coloured plates and literally hundreds of engravings, containing work by talented, but invariably anonymous, artists. The decorated covers were some of the brightest and most cheerful of the time. The first *Chatterbox* annual was published before Christmas 1867 by William Mackintosh, and the last in 1956 (although the weekly publication had been discontinued many years previously) by Dean & Son, a record run of ninety volumes.

The Children's Friend was typical of many of the annuals that appeared in the mid-to-late 1800s. It was a penny magazine first published in 1860 by Seeley, Jackson & Halliday with S.W. Partridge, the twelve monthly parts being bound and issued in book form before Christmas each year. No expressed aim was given either in an editorial or a preface, but it was self evident: the didactic tone was sternly moral and religious, extolling the virtues of hard work and toil. Many of the quality engravings featured inside were highly decorated quotations from the Bible, such as 'Lying Lips Are Abomination To The Lord' and 'Cease To Do Evil'. The general feeling was that the reader would be subject to eternal damnation were he or she to fail to follow the prescribed path through life that was advocated by the magazine. To some children this must have proved worrying, to say the least. Other illustrations, thankfully less severe, were by Harrison Weir and William Hunt. In time *The Children's Friend*, in keeping with other publications of the same type, largely abandoned its earlier pious approach and tone, and consequently had a long run which lasted beyond the turn of the century.

In May 1866, Mrs Alfred Gatty, a writer of children's stories, founded *Aunt Judy's Magazine*. This monthly publication was collected together at mid-year and Christmas, the latter usually being a massive tome of over 700 pages, complete with illustrations, entitled *Aunt Judy's Christmas Volume*. The annual had some distinguished contributors who included Lewis Carroll, Hans Andersen and Mrs Juliana Ewing. In fact, Mrs Ewing was the daughter of Mrs Gatty, and it was her Christian name which had been shortened to 'Judy' in order to give the magazine its title. There were also stories by the Rev. Alfred Gatty and by Mrs Gatty herself, writing as Margaret Gatty. The contents of *Aunt Judy's* catered to an eclectic taste: there were features on everything from 'The Snake Charmers of India' to historical stories and fairy tales; and there was a genuine warmth about this annual which distinguished it from its sanctimonious contemporaries.

Adventure for boys and girls

In the late nineteenth century almost every publisher issued an annual of some description. To mention some of the better known: Dean & Son had *The Prize* (1863); Raphael Tuck: *Our Darlings* (formerly *The Children's Treasury*:

Nister's Holiday Annual (1888–1916) was published by the German firm of Ernest Nister. This cover of the 1894 edition is typical of the delightful work which graced so many of his publications (artist unknown).

1868); Cassell & Company: *Little Folks* (1863); Routledge: *Every Boy's Annual* (1878) and *Every Girl's Annual* (1879); Ward Lock: *The Children's Picture Annual* (1888).

Two other major publishers at this time were the firm of Nister, which issued the first *Nister's Holiday Annual* in 1888, and the Religious Tract Society, which was responsible for two of the best known annuals ever published: *The Boy's Own Annual* and *The Girl's Own Annual.*

Nister's Holiday Annual (1888–1916) was an utterly charming blend of stories, rhymes, black-and-white illustrations and colour plates. Ernest Nister, the German printer and publisher, obviously took pride in his work and actively participated in all of the many volumes he published. The *Holiday Annual* differed from the majority of annuals being issued at the time because it did not comprise bound copies of a weekly or monthly paper. Instead, it included both original material and choice items reprinted from earlier books that Nister had published. There was a total absence of religion and the books portrayed Victorian children as they had not been seen before. Previously they had appeared as miniature adults, with overly large heads, dark eyes and solemn expressions. Within the pages of *Nister's Holiday Annual* they were blue-eyed, flaxen-haired, happy, normal youngsters whose faces shone with the innocence and joy of childhood. What made Nister's books and the *Holiday Annual* so immediately enchanting were the delightful paintings used to decorate the board covers. Executed in agreeable pastels by talented, although usually anonymous, artists, they were printed by Ernest Nister's own fine Bavarian printers. As a result, the annual stood out from its competitors.

The Boy's Own Annual was 'an illustrated volume of pure and entertaining reading' published by the Religious Tract Society (RTS), 56 Paternoster Row, London. The Society had been formed in 1799 by the Rev. George Burder of Coventry, with the intention of publishing tracts (short treaties on religion), sermons, books, commentaries and periodicals; and it was, eighty years later, a long-established success. By 1879, when the *Boy's Own Paper* (or the *BOP* as it was affectionately known), was first issued, the Society had several thousand titles in their catalogue.

The RTS had very little experience in publications for the young, the most notable and successful being *The Child's Companion* (1824). Nevertheless, the Society, worried by the effect the notorious 'Penny Dreadfuls' were having on the youth of the nation, embarked on what was an ambitious publication.

James Macauley was chosen as the supervising editor and the experienced George Hutchinson was appointed as sub-editor. It was Hutchinson who was the driving force behind the *BOP* and its annual.

The list of respected contributors throughout the formative years of the *BOP* was impressive and included Jules Verne, Arthur Conan Doyle, G. A. Henty, George Manville Fenn and R. M. Ballantyne, to name but a few. Typical of the annual throughout its life, the first volume, comprising the January to September weekly issues (thereafter October to October), contained features such as a first-hand account by Captain Webb entitled 'How I Swam the Channel' (he was the first man to do so), an article on keeping pets, a contribution on outdoor sports, 'Skating and Scuttling', and another on

No. 1.—Vol. I. SATURDAY, JANUARY 18, 1879. Price One Penny. [ALL RIGHTS RESERVED.

MY FIRST FOOTBALL MATCH.

BY AN OLD BOY.

IT was a proud moment in my existence when Wright, captain of our football club, came up to me in school one Friday and said, "Adams, your name is down to play in the match against Craven to-morrow."

I could have knighted him on the spot. To be one of the picked "fifteen," whose glory it was to fight the battles of their school in the Great Close, had been the leading ambition of my life—I suppose I ought to be ashamed to confess it—ever since, as a little chap of ten, I entered Parkhurst six years ago. Not a winter Saturday but had seen me either looking on at some big match, or oftener still scrimmaging about with a score or so of other juniors in a scratch game. But for a long time, do what I would, I always seemed as far as ever from the coveted goal, and was half despairing of ever rising to win my "first fifteen cap." Latterly, however, I had noticed Wright and a few others of our best players more than once lounging about in the Little Close where we juniors used to play, evidently taking observations with an eye to business. Under the awful gaze of these heroes, need I say I exerted myself as I had never done before? What cared I for hacks or bruises, so only that I could distinguish myself in their eyes? And never was music sweeter

The most famous annual of the Victorian era was *The Boy's Own Annual*. Bound in green cloth with titles in gilt, the first 588 page volume consisted of weekly issues of *The Boy's Own Paper* for January to September, 1879.

Opposite top 'Ally Sloper's Christmas Dinner': gratis plate from *Ally Sloper's Christmas Holidays* (1892)

Opposite below *Ally Sloper's Christmas Holidays* (1884–1913) drawn by W. F. Thomas.

'Evenings at Home: Pleasant Hours with the Magic Lantern'.

But it was for adventure stories that the *BOP* was best known and the editor was not one to ask his authors to pull their punches. The stories were vigorous and racy – an intoxicating blend of excitement and thrills. There were sea stories, jungle adventures, dangerous enterprises, pioneering in Indian country, tales of gallant soldiers facing fearful odds, and excitement in the sky (Jules Verne's 'The Clipper of the Clouds' appeared in the annual for 1886–7).

Hutchinson encouraged new authors, too, and the best of these was Talbot Baines Reed. His school stories, 'The Adventures of a Three-Guinea Watch', 'The Fifth Form at St Dominics', 'Willoughby Captains' and others, always featured prominently in the heyday of *The Boy's Own Annual*, and his works are still hailed today as classics of the genre.

The Boy's Own Annual was discontinued in 1940 due to wartime paper shortages. It re-emerged in a summer-holiday guise as *The Boy's Own Companion*, which lasted for five editions, and it was revived yet again as *The Boy's Own Annual* for Christmas 1964. In that form it lived on for another thirteen years. The *Boy's Own Paper* itself ended publication with the February 1967 issue.

A half-century of 'Chums'

Cassell and Company, having observed the success of the *Boy's Own Paper*, started their own periodical on 14 September 1892, aimed essentially at the same market. They called it *Chums*, and the editor, Max Pemberton, ensured that his young readers were provided with a lively and robust diet of sport and adventure stories. If anything, the tone of this weekly paper was a shade less formal than that of the *BOP*, although it certainly published the same type of full-blooded stories, full of danger and excitement.

The first *Chums* annual appeared in 1893 and contained several hundred pages, comprising the weekly issues of the paper to date; it was bound in what was to become traditional red cloth. For many years the picture of a cowboy swinging a lasso and seated on the back of a galloping horse appeared on the front. The illustration became a virtual trademark of the annual.

The second volume of *Chums* contained the serialisation of *Treasure Island* by Robert Louis Stevenson. Although this was not a first (the story had previously appeared in *Young Folks*, a James Henderson publication), it was very popular and resulted in a marked increase in circulation. Word of Stevenson's death, in Samoa, reached England as the last episode was published. Other well known authors who contributed on a regular basis included G. A. Henty, James Fenimore Cooper, Sax Rohmer (of Fu Manchu fame), Gundby Hadath (who bore the distinction of contributing to the *BOP* throughout seventy-five years of its publication), Major Charles Gilson and Percy Westerman.

Another frequent and regular contributor was Capt. Frank R. Shaw, whose real-life adventures were as thrilling as any boys' fiction. He had started as an apprentice on a windjammer at sea in the 1890s and eventually rose to the gold-braided rank of captain in the Royal Navy. Naturally, many of Shaw's stories were written about the sea, but he also wrote scientific and futuristic tales: 'The Secret of the Sargasso Sea', 'First at the Pole', 'The Terror from the East' and 'When the Sea Rose Up' were just some of the exciting stories recounted by him in the *Chums* annuals of the early 1900s.

Science fiction featured more prominently in *Chums* than in the annuals of its immediate rivals. The volume for 1922 contains a

splendid story, illustrated by Robert Strange and entitled 'The Lost Planet', which would not have been out of place in the better science-fiction 'pulp' magazines that were so popular a decade later. There was more than a hint of the pulp in *Chums*, something one could never quite bring oneself to say about the *BOP*.

In the mid-1920s, both *Chums* and its accompanying annual were taken over from Cassells by the Amalgamated Press. Cassells published thirty-three volumes and AP fifteen, the last to appear being dated 1941.

Ally Sloper and Father Tuck

George Newnes, another renowned publisher of the Victorian era, also issued a periodical in the same vein as *Chums* and *The Boy's Own Annual*. In April 1899 he had started a monthly 'Magazine for Boys and Old Boys' entitled *The Captain*. The 'Old Boys' was a frank admission that the readers of these robust journals were often beyond school age. The

A GAY CHRISTMAS EVE.

collected magazines issued as bound volumes, however, were not annuals, as they appeared at six-monthly intervals instead of the required twelve.

Annuals were not always hard-bound books. Perhaps the most popular character of the late 1800s was 'Ally Sloper' (so called because he was said to 'slope off' up alleys when the rent collector was about!) who had been created by Charles Henry Ross and his wife Marie Duval for the magazine *Judy* (naturally a follow-up to the famous *Punch*).

Sloper was a Micawber-like rogue who bears the distinction of being Britain's first regular comic character. In almost no time at all Ally Sloper was a national institution. This was mainly due to the efforts of publisher Gilbert Dalziell who had purchased rights to the character from Ross. He entrusted the task of drawing Ally Sloper to William Baxter (1856–88) an accomplished cartoonist who depicted the character as a gin-swilling, bottle-nosed good-for-nothing who exaggerated the prejudices of the working classes. Dalziell started a new publication, *Ally Sloper's Half Holiday*, which was an adult comic, tabloid in size with 16 pages and issued in May 1884.

The character was popular enough to be awarded a supplementary issue at Christmas entitled *Ally Sloper's Christmas Holidays*. It was unnumbered and had twice as many pages as the weekly *Half Holiday*. Usually, a 'Presentation Plate' was included as a gift and often, as well, there would be music for Sloper aficionados to sing at their Christmas parties. The first of these 'specials' was published in December 1884 and the last in 1913. Baxter's art appeared in the first three issues and then, in 1887, W. F. Thomas, another extremely talented artist, replaced Baxter when he left to join Charles Ross in another venture. There was also a similar 'summer number' of *Ally Sloper* too (1880–1887). Both this and *Ally Sloper's Christmas Holidays* were lively, if vulgar, additions to the annuals then on sale.

Raphael Tuck's *Our Darlings* (1882–1936) was one of the better known and 'acceptable' annuals purchased by the book-buying public for over half a century. But it was not the most famous of the titles issued by this prolific publishing house. That distinction belongs to *Father Tuck's Annual for Little People* (later simply *Tuck's Annual*) which appeared in bookshops before Christmas 1898, dated forward to 1899.

'Father Tuck' was an avuncular personage whom the readers never saw but who was likened to Father Christmas ('you know what good friends the two fathers are') by editor Capt. Edric Vredenburg. The yearly offering was aimed at the very young and contained stories, verses and music by A. L. Harris, Grace C. Floyd, E. M. Stanhope and Christine Bradley. Illustrations were of elves, fairies and animals, and included the work of G. H. Thomson (whose splendid cross-hatched line drawings of anthropomorphic zoo animals were a joy), R. C. Pethrick, J. A. Labrousse, Gordon Robinson, Beatrice Mallet and Louis Wain (and in what turn-of-the-century publications did Wain's cats *not* appear?).

In later years *Father Tuck's Annual* was to bear the coveted royal imprint 'Publishers to Their Majesties the King and Queen and to HRH the Prince of Wales' alongside their famous 'easel and pallet' trademark. And, as an innovation, the annual was given 'Come to Life Pictures' in the 1930s: full-colour 'stand-up' panoramas which appeared in three-dimensional relief within the book.

In the main, *Father Tuck's Annual* was aimed at parents, uncles, aunts and other book-buying relatives who wanted to give their 'little people' something bright and cheerful for Christmas.

The longevity of the annual (the last edition was for 1935), which had no weekly or monthly publication to kindle interest, must be attributable to its charmingly decorated board covers, the good name of Raphael Tuck and the type of adult market for which it was aimed.

As the nineteenth century drew to a close, publishers began to issue annuals containing never-before-published material. They had to, in order to meet the demand from a public hungry for new reading matter. The firm of Raphael Tuck had already pointed the way in this direction with *Father Tuck's Annual*, and so did the Amalgamated Press when it published, simultaneously, *Tiny Tots* (1899). But there were soon to be other publishers, Blackie, Collins, Cassell et al, ready to introduce new titles for the rapidly expanding market.

Father Tuck's Annual, first published in 1899, had a long run. All had delightfully decorated covers. This edition was issued in 1933.

CHAPTER 2

From Budgets to Band Waggon – A Golden Era . . .

The post-Edwardian era saw publication of a new type of annual which was to be exceedingly popular until well into the 1920s and 1930s. These books were of approximately the same size and shape: almost square, around two inches thick, and with less pages than might have been expected for their bulk. This was because the pages were of heavy, rough stock – almost stiff, more like thin card than paper. The reason for this counterfeit amplitude was to enable them to compete with the massive tomes issued by *Chums*, *The Boy's Own Paper, Young England* and other collected weeklies, all of which contained many hundreds of pages and were splendid value.

The best known of these post-Edwardian Christmas offerings were (for the boys): *The Empire Annual for Boys* (1909–33); *The British Boy's Annual* (1911–29) and *Herbert Strang's Annual* (1911–27), and (for the girls): *The Empire Annual for Girls* (1909–33); *The British Girl's Annual* (1911–29) and *Mrs Strang's Annual for Girls* (1919–26).

In this high noon of Empire, publishers were not slow to mine the rich vein of pride that the average Briton felt for his country and its achievements. The publishing house of Andrew Melrose had been one of the first, with the *Girl's Empire Annual* (1902), and this opening volley was quickly answered by the big guns of the Religious Tract Society (publishers of the *BOP* and *GOP*) with *The Empire Annual for Boys* and, similarly, *The Empire Annual for Girls* (both 1909). Naturally, the RTS had become well aware of the selling power of the Empire: the majority of stories in the *BOP* were based upon it.

The word 'British' had a good, strong, powerful appeal, too. Cassell's used it for *The British Boy's Annual* and *The British Girl's Annual* (both 1911); and the contents laid great stress on the same imperial themes. For the boys it was stories of jungle adventure, tales of flying around the world, motor racing, sport and practicalities such as 'How to Fix a Wireless Mast'. The girls were given a steady diet of school and historical stories, with tips on 'How to Make Homemade Presents' adding what was seen in those days as an especially feminine form of practical knowledge.

Both *The British Boy's Annual* and *The British Girl's Annual* had a high standard of illustration, as did so many of their counterparts. Included within the former was the work of Thomas Henry, who was later to become well known for his drawings of 'William' in the much-loved stories by Richmal Crompton. Henry's pen and ink drawings were familiar in many annuals of the period, notably *Chums*; his work was also familiar to readers of *The Captain*.

Splendid full-page pictures, some in full colour, by D. C. (Derek) Eyles were used to illustrate numerous stories. Eyles, like many of his contemporaries who supplied work for the annuals, was a craftsman. Particularly good at depicting horses, he could turn his hand to almost any subject. His penmanship brought not only quality but also zest and vitality to the stories he illustrated.

Serge Drigin, a Russian artist, was a gifted illustrator of action yarns. His work had appeared in *Chums* and was used to good effect in *The British Boy's Annual*. Drigin's principal talent was in the depiction of transport: steam locomotives, racing cars, speedway bikes, ocean liners, airships. His work came into its own in the books and annuals of the 1930s, when a major interest of youth was the power and speed of transport. He also illustrated science-fiction stories, and his beautiful paintings and drawings of spaceships and scenes in space are now much sought after by collectors. Despite the high quality of his drawing, he once admitted he had never received an art lesson.

The authors of the exciting tales from *The British Boy's Annual* that these illustrators pictured so vividly were A. G. Roper, Gundby Hadath, Major Charles Gilson, Percy Westerman and many more. Most, if not all, would have been familiar to the readers of the *BOP* and *Chums*. Westerman, in particular, was a writer of some repute and had published numerous adventure books for boys. His popular titles (*Under the White Ensign, Shanghai Adventure, Standish Gets His Man*, etc.) were converted into many languages and during the 1930s he was voted the 'most popular boys' author' at public libraries up and down Britain in a nationwide contest.

Good, solid reading entertainment for boys could be found in *The British Boy's Annual* (1911–1933). Cover art by Stanley L. Wood.

Illustration within *The British Girl's Annual* was of equally high quality and included the work of Noel Harrold, Charles Morrell, George Soper and A. Webb. Soper was particularly celebrated. He was an etcher, wood-engraver and watercolour painter who had exhibited at the Royal Academy. Renowned as an illustrator of adventure stories for both girls' and boys' annuals, his work was also regularly published in the *Strand* magazine.

The drawings that George Soper and his fellow artists submitted were used to illustrate stories by authors with names that read like

A superb illustration by the artist C. E. Brock. From: 'A Schoolgirl Friendship', a story of 1685; *The British Girl's Annual* (1913).

"Pray, sir, may I not go with her? She is my friend!"

School stories and historical drama were highly popular in *The British Girl's Annual* (1911–1933).

a 'Who's Who' of classic schoolgirl literature: Dorothea Moore, Dorita M. Fairlie Bruce, Bessie Marchant and Angela Brazil. All four were extremely successful. Dorothea Moore authored *Terry, the Girl Guide* (1912); Dorita M. Fairlie Bruce wrote *Dimsie Moves Up* (1921), followed by several other 'Dimsie' books; Bessie Marchant's *A Princess of Servia* (1912) was but one of more than 150 titles published; and Angela Brazil's prolific output included *A Fourth Form Friendship* (1912), *A Patriotic Schoolgirl* (1918), *For the School Colours* (1919) and *The Luckiest Girl in the School* (1916). Brazil was the queen of schoolgirl fiction and was one of the most popular writers of the day.

The 'Budgets'

In addition to the 'British' and 'Empire' annuals, there were also the various 'Budgets' that were offered for sale at the same time and which were very similar. The 'Budget' was so called primarily because it was a cheap edition (having paper-covered boards with a matt finish, rather than being cloth-bound), and thus within the price range of a larger number of would-be buyers.

Thomas Nelson and Sons were one of the first publishers to issue an annual with the word 'Budget' in its title (although the term has been in common use during the 1890s for various comic papers, C. Arthur Pearson's *Big Budget* (1897) being a prime example). This annual was entitled *The Girl's Budget* (1911) and was followed by similar titles from a number of publishers. The most notable of these was the firm of Blackie and Son, London, who made the '*Budget*' very much its own with titles such as *Girl's Budget* (1924); *Lucky Girl's Budget* and *Lucky Boy's Budget* (both 1926); *The Golden Budget for Boys* and *The Golden Budget for Girls* (both 1928); *The Big Budget for Boys* and *The Big Budget for*

Girls (both 1929); *The Big Budget for Children* (1931) and *Blackie's Children's Budget* (1936). Despite their cheaper format, authors and illustrators for all of these volumes were among the most reputable and popular of the day – a fact appreciated by the loyal readers who purchased the books in their thousands year after year.

Two illustrators whose work shared the pages of *The British Girl's Annual* and *The British Boy's Annual* were Charles Edmund Brock and his brother, Henry Matthew Brock. Charles and Henry were the most famous members of a large, illustrious and artistic family.

Both C.E. and H.M. (as they signed themselves) specialised in 'period' illustrations, revelling in Cavaliers, Roundheads, delicate Jacobean ladies and dashing young rakes of the Regency period. The style of the two brothers was remarkably similar and both contributed heavily to Victorian and Edwardian books and periodicals. C.E. Brock (1870–1938) was the illustrator of *Gulliver's Travels* (1894), *Tom Brown's Schooldays* and Thackeray's and Jane Austen's complete prose works; he became an R.I. in 1908. H. M. Brock (1875–1960) illustrated a large number of school stories, including many that appeared in *The Captain*; his drawings also appeared in *Punch* and *The Strand* as well as *The Boy's Own Paper*.

It was due to the calibre of artists such as the Brocks, Thomas Henry, Serge Drigin and D. C. Eyles, and writers with the skills of Percy Westerman, Gundby Hadath, Dorita Fairlie Bruce and Angela Brazil that *The British Girl's* and *The British Boy's* annuals, *The Empire* annuals, the *Strang* annuals and similar titles achieved such an excellent reputation.

The *Strang* annuals were *Herbert Strang's Annual* (1911) and *Mrs Strang's Annual* (1919). Readers could be forgiven for thinking that here was a busy husband and wife team diligently compiling and editing stories for teenage consumption, but this was not, in fact, the case. 'Herbert Strang' was the pseudonym of the partnership of two male writers: George Herbert Ely and James L'Estrange, both of whom had good credentials. They were the authors of many books, starting

The Big Budget for Boys (1930–1943) was only one of many 'Budget' titles published by the firm of Blackie & Son. This edition, 1930.

with *Tom Burnaby* in 1904 and following with titles such as *The Cruise of the Gyro-Car* (1911), *The Air Patrol* (1913) and many more; they also contributed several serials to *The Captain*.

Neither of the two men wrote a complete book or serial on his own, both contributing equally to the plots, although Ely did most of the actual writing while L'Estrange (who had travelled extensively) supplied much of the indigenous information. Most of the books were published by their employer, the Oxford University Press, whom they joined in the early 1900s and for which firm they both worked for more than thirty years.

After the considerable success of the *Herbert Strang's Annual*, the two authors were asked to compile a corresponding volume for girls: thus they became 'Mrs Strang'. There was also another annual for an even younger member of the family – *Mrs Strang's Annual for Baby* (1915–26). Both *Herbert Strang's* and *Mrs Strang's* had respectable runs, eventually, in 1927, changing their titles to the *Oxford Annual for Boys* and the *Oxford Annual for Girls*, which continued publication until 1941, when they were brought to an end by the paper shortages of the Second World War.

Louis Wain and his cats

Cat drawings were extraordinarily popular during the late Victorian era and remained so throughout the Edwardian years. Louis Wain (1860–1939), the man whose name became synonymous with cats, was the undisputed master of the feline form. The first annual to contain his work was *The Rosebud Annual*, issued in 1889 for 1890 by James Clarke & Co. The annual was rich in cat illustration, so much so that it was virtually a fetish: there were cats of every description, indulging in the wildest of activities – from sailing in boats to masquerading as policemen, butchers and other tradesmen – as well as appearing in their normal domestic role. Of all the various artists commissioned to supply cat illustrations, Louis Wain's drawings were always the most prominent and popular.

Wain's famous cat drawings began to appear in print in the 1880s: his first positively identified drawing (although uncharacteristically unsigned) was for the *Illustrated Sporting and Dramatic News* of 10 December 1881, and showed two bullfinches perched on some laurel bushes. This, incidentally, caused him some embarrassment as, due to a printer's error, the picture was entitled 'The Robin's Breakfast'. Soon the *Illustrated London News* was accepting his work and in 1886 the first book to be illustrated by him, *Madame Tabby's Establishment*, was published by Macmillan. In 1901 Anthony Treherne published *Louis Wain's Annual*, which was edited by Stanhope Sprigg and contained a collection of stories by well-known people (friends of Wain). The seventy or so drawings that appeared throughout had no connection with the text but were well received and further increased Wain's popularity.

The *Annual* proceeded on a fairly regular basis until 1913 (missing 1904 and 1911) and was issued by several publishers: Hutchinson (1902–03); King (1905); Shaw (1906 and 1912–13); Bemrose (1907–09) and Allen (1910). Two of these publishers also issued *Louis Wain's Summer Book*, which was obviously intended to be a summer annual; this was published in 1903 (Hutchinson) and 1906 (King), but clearly did not develop into a successful run. A final issue of *Louis Wain's Annual* was published by Hutchinson in 1921.

In 1914, Wain's career was briefly interrupted when he fell from a London omnibus and struck his head, causing him to be admitted to hospital suffering from concussion. This accident was said by some to be responsible for his later mental illness and subsequent committal to an asylum in 1924. But experts believe that there is evidence to indicate that his illness would have occurred in any event.

Louis Wain died in 1939. If some apt words of remembrance had been placed upon his tombstone, they would have read

'Louis Wain – the man who drew cats'. Yet cats were not the only animals his pen depicted. He was just as adroit at drawing dogs, as he was their natural enemy. He portrayed elephants in fine style, his careful eye accurately depicting their immense bulk and physical characteristics while, at the same time, cleverly endowing them with humour and a sense of fun. Throughout his life, Louis Wain's drawings appeared in hundreds of publications, bringing pleasure to young and old alike. Besides the *Rosebud Annual*, his drawings also featured in *Father Tuck's Annual* and in some volumes of the *Boy's Own Annual*; his popular work also abounds in many other turn-of-the-century annuals.

Two other artistic personalities who were sufficiently well known to have annuals published in their names were Harry Furniss and Harry Rountree.

Harry Furniss (1854–1925) was a talented penman who once worked for *Punch* and *The Illustrated London News*. Known as a brilliant caricaturist of parliamentary figures, he never drew for children's annuals; *Harry Furniss's Christmas Annual* (1905) was directed at an adult market.

Harry Rountree (1878–1950), however, had a great deal to do with publications for children. He was born in New Zealand and, after arriving in this country in 1901, was soon having his drawings published in *Little Folks*, usually in black and white, but also with occasional paintings for inside colour plates. He contributed to adult publications such as *Punch, The Sketch* and *The Graphic* but his metier proved to be the depicting of comic animals, and he would often spend hours at the London Zoo sketching their real-life counterparts. The reputation he quickly earned in England won him the accolade of the eponymous publication, by Anthony Treherne, of *Harry Rountree's Annual*, dated 1907.

Described as a 'witty, mercurial, bubbling character', Rountree drew countless 'one-off' pictures and illustrations for stories in children's annuals (all signed very distinctively) and for many years was a regular artist for the coloured comic paper *Playtime* (1919–29), for which an annual appeared in the early 1930s.

The interwar boom

The 1920s and 1930s were the eras of the big 'adventure annuals'. Typical of its type was the *Collins' Adventure Annual*. Some of the titles from a 'contents' page are indicative of the type of stories each contained: 'Under Arctic Skies', 'Deep Sea Vengeance', 'Captured on the Spanish Main', 'On Safari', etc. These stories were accompanied by fine illustrations

Collins' Adventure Annual: this edition published in 1932.

either in black-and-white or in full colour. As so often in the adventure annuals of the period, the leading artist invariably was Derek Eyles and, it has to be said, there weren't many who did it better. *Collins' Adventure Annual* was good value for money (192 pages for two shillings and sixpence) but, as the 1930s wore on, there was stiff competition, not only from the Amalgamated Press (with *Champion, Triumph* et al) but also from the firm of D. C. Thomson whose weekly story papers *Adventure, Rover, Skipper, Hotspur* and *Wizard* soon began to be issued with annuals. The last edition of *Collins' Adventure Annual* was for 1935.

Annual publishing boomed in the 1930s with most publishers offering at least one or more titles. Some of these publications came from surprising sources: the British Legion, together with Alexander Ouseley (London), issued for 1933 *The British Legion Annual*, which contained stories and verses by Jerrold Vassall Adams and which was 'published by arrangement with the British Legion to whose benevolent work part of the proceeds will be devoted'. This has a short dedication from HRH the Duchess of York to Princess Elizabeth, who was presented with the first copy. Today, the annual is of interest only as a curiosity, its value being negligible.

The phenomenal success of 'Band Waggon' on the wireless in the late 1930s resulted in the publication of *Arthur Askey's Annual* (Oxford University Press: 1940). This unique edition with illustrations by Fred Bennett featured all the characters that had become so familiar to millions of listeners: in addition to 'Big-Hearted' Arthur there were Richard 'Stinker' Murdoch, Nausea and Mrs Bagwash, Ernie Bagwash and Lewis the Goat. Written by Arthur Askey, Richard Murdoch and Hylton Cleaver, the annual is today quite rare but not particularly valuable. The Second World War put paid to further editions and it was left to the Amalgamated Press to recognise the attractions of publishing the 'adventures' of the diminutive comedian, which it did so very well and for so many years in the weekly and annual *Radio Fun* publications. But then, AP did everything well. . . .

Below left Sales of the *British Legion Annual* helped to provide worthwhile support to the organisation in the 1930s.

Below right *Arthur Askey's Annual* (1939): the only edition to be issued.

CHAPTER 3

The Annuals of the Amalgamated Press

In the 1890s the Amalgamated Press was a new and major force in publishing. The firm had been established by Alfred Harmsworth (later Lord Northcliffe) and had its origins in a weekly paper called *Answers to Correspondents* which the young Alfred had started on 12 June 1888. The success of *Answers* (as it became affectionately known) enabled Harmsworth to publish other papers: *Comic Cuts* (1890), *Illustrated Chips* (1890), *The Wonder* (1892) and many more, all of which were hugely successful.

Despite the popularity of his early comic papers, Harmsworth was apparently never tempted to place them in board-covers and offer them for sale as an annual at the end of each year. One reason for this was undoubtedly the excessively cheap quality of the paper on which he printed them; it is highly unlikely that they would have survived the process. Periodicals such as the *Boy's Own Paper* (published by the RTS) used far better quality newsprint and this is one of the main reasons why it is not uncommon to find issues of the *BOP* today, while Harmsworth papers of the same age, despite having had large circulations at the time, are very rare indeed. Harmsworth's publishing business grew rapidly and soon his attentions turned to newspapers. He acquired the Sunday *Observer* and the *Weekly Dispatch*, launched the *Daily Mail* in 1896, the *Daily Mirror* in 1903 and realised one of his greatest ambitions when he purchased *The Times* in 1907.

With such rapid expansion it was perhaps inevitable that the Amalgamated Press's move into book publishing was a slow one. But just before the turn of the century, in 1899, the firm issued its first annual for children, entitled *Tiny Tots*.

Tiny Tots' appeal was to the very young or, more correctly, to those who bought for the very young. This was a previously under-developed market which the aggressive and expanding AP had been quick to exploit. Bearing the legend 'A Picture Story Book for Little People' the *Tiny Tots* title lasted for an incredible sixty-one years and, in 1927, bore the remarkable distinction of spawning a comic of the same name: a quite singular case of a 'child' begetting a 'parent'. This large (the page size was four times that of the annual) bright and colourful weekly emulated its successful AP companion *Chicks' Own*, which had been published since 1920, by purporting to aid the young with their reading: a claim that held some credence as the print was large and clear, with long words split up in order to be more 'eas-i-ly read.' 'Buy *Tiny Tots* ev-er-y Thurs-day,' said 'Uncle Jack' the editor, in an advertisement on the back of the annual, 'and you will nev-er know what it is to feel dull or lone-ly.'

'Uncle Jack' was in reality Langton Townley, a long-serving and important editor at AP. Townley played a major part in *Tiny Tots'* success, soliciting work from some of the best illustrators and writers then working for the firm. These included artists E. Dorothy Rees, Frank Jennens, F. J. Noble and F. L. (Fred) Crompton, with stories by Dorothy Parkin, Helen Davidson, Edith Clifford and Margaret Huggins.

The first comic annual

For 1909 the Amalgamated Press, pleased with the response to *Tiny Tots* (1899), launched a new annual for children, one that for the first time had a starring character – Tiger Tim. They called it the *Playbox Annual* and it became the forerunner of a new type of book publication – the 'comic annual'.

Tiger Tim was allegedly the creation of an Irish illustrator, J. Louis Smythe, and the story of that creation (although possibly apocryphal), according to the

Tiger Tim and his chums: an illustration by Julius Stafford Baker; from the *Playbox Annual* (1909).

Who's Who of Children's Literature, is as follows:

> 'Smythe was called upon to picture an incident from a story. The passage chosen was one in which the heroine stepped from her carriage and entered a house ... "followed by her tiger, Tim." And Smythe, unaware of the fact that in this instance a "tiger" signified a page-boy or youthful attendant, drew instead a small striped tiger promenading serenely upright upon his hind legs! The editor who had commissioned Smythe's drawings gasped, laughed and mentally noted for future use a new and attractive character ... a character named "Tiger Tim".'

However, when that time arrived it was not Smythe but another artist, Julius Stafford Baker, who was called upon to draw the character for a 'one-off' three-picture strip in the *Daily Mirror* dated 16 April 1904. It was entitled 'Mrs Hippo's Kindergarten' and, although notable for the fact that it was the first-ever British newspaper strip, it cannot be said to have made a major impact. Yet the character was memorable enough for someone to suggest that Tiger Tim be included, in full colour, in *The Playbox*, a children's supplement to the magazine *The World and His Wife* (Nov. 1904). J. S. Baker was invited to be the regular artist and he remained so until the magazine was discontinued in 1910. Tiger Tim and his chums were transferred to *The Playhour* (another supplement) which was subsequentiy renamed *The Playbox* and later *My Magazine*; the characters were a regular feature for the next two decades.

The Playbox was not a new title for the Amalgamated Press and neither, incidentally, was the idea of a comic supplement. An earlier *Playbox* had been given away with *Home Chat* (1898), another Harmsworth magazine. Baker's work had appeared there too; he drew for many of the Victorian and, later, comic papers and was said to have created, among other things, the classic 'Casey Court' feature in *Illustrated Chips*, which first appeared in 1902.

Tiger Tim's chums were an elephant (Jumbo), a parrot (Joey), a dog (Fido), a pig (Porkyboy), a Giraffe (Georgie), a monkey (Jacko), an Ostrich (Willie) and a Bear (Bobby). 'Mrs Hippo' was given a name change and, as a result, they attended 'Mrs Bruin's Boarding School', earning them an additional epithet in the process: 'The Bruin Boys'. It was an establishment from which they were never absent, to judge by their Christmas and summer holidays adventures. It was also a school that appeared to be run by Mrs Bruin exclusively, for no other members of staff (or even a Mr Bruin!) were ever seen.

The idea of making Tiger Tim the 'star' of the *Playbox Annual* was a good one: it gave the book an identity, a continuing feature

Illustration by A. E. Jackson which accompanied the story 'The Runaway Kite': *Playbox Annual* (1909)

which helped bind it together. Tim and the Bruin Boys appeared occasionally on the cover of the book, regularly in colour plates inside and, in addition, there were several black and white strips of their adventures (usually six pictures over three pages). There were also full-page single pictures showing the Boys sledding. 'In the Bathtub' or 'Dressing Up'; and the 'Editor's Chat' ('My Letter to You ...') was subject to invasion by this odd but cheery group, who made the word 'naughty' synonymous with lively good humour and mischief. Julius Stafford Baker remained the 'Tiger Tim artist' until 1914 when he was replaced by one of the most talented illustrators to work for children's annuals: Herbert Sydney Foxwell.

The Amalgamated Press certainly had a winning formula on its hands when it issued the *Playbox Annual.* There were few 'good quality' nursery annuals and the *Playbox* admirably fell into this category. Stories, usually fairy tales, were utterly charming, although mostly anonymous, and they were profusely illustrated by artists such as A. E. Jackson, H. L. Sinder, Louis Jacobs, S. J. Cash and William Heath Robinson.

W. Heath Robinson became very famous in later years for his drawings that depicted crazy, scatterbrained mechanical inventions and also for his work in various books including *Don Quixote*, *Arabian Nights* and *The Water Babies.* His work for the *Playbox Annual* (actually reprints from the *Strand* magazine) was in the style of that great illustrator and caricaturist of the Victorian age, Aubrey Beardsley, and complemented the fairy stories.

A. E. Jackson was also an artist of some repute who later illustrated editions of classic children's books (*Alice in Wonderland:* 1913, etc.). Jackson's drawings for the *Playbox Annual* were of tiny elves and fairies with gossamer wings; for the young child, very real trips into fairyland.

Full-page black and white drawings of a group of cats, collectively named 'The Furry Fluffikins', were also common in the *Playbox* and, for once, they were not by Louis Wain, although his work did appear in the annual from time to time. The illustrators were either L. Church or S. J. Cash, two extremely competent artists who contributed a great deal to the publications of Amalgamated Press. S. J. Cash, in particular, is today a much underrated artist. Besides 'The Furry Fluffikins' he turned his hand to a wide range of comic drawings, and his paintings, used for colour frontispieces and interior plates, set a very high standard indeed.

Although *Tiny Tots* and *Playbox* annuals sold well, AP made no attempt to consolidate its success until the 1920s. There were two evident reasons for this: the first was that the company was still intent upon building up its empire of weekly periodicals; the second, and far more cataclysmic, was the First World War.

By the time the Amalgamated Press had firmly established itself and had, in 1912, moved into Fleetway House, a splendid new headquarters in London's Farringdon Street, the unrest in Europe had begun and any plans for expansion in publishing or any other business were soon brought to an abrupt halt by the declaration of war.

'The Holiday Annual'

The first annual to be published by AP after the war was destined to be one of the most popular and best known of all its publications – *The Holiday Annual for Boys and Girls*, subsequent editions being entitled *The Greyfriars Holiday Annual for Boys and Girls.*

Issued in 1919 for 1920, this annual was remarkable for the fact that it was mainly the work of one man, Charles Hamilton (1876–1961). But then Hamilton himself was a remarkable man –

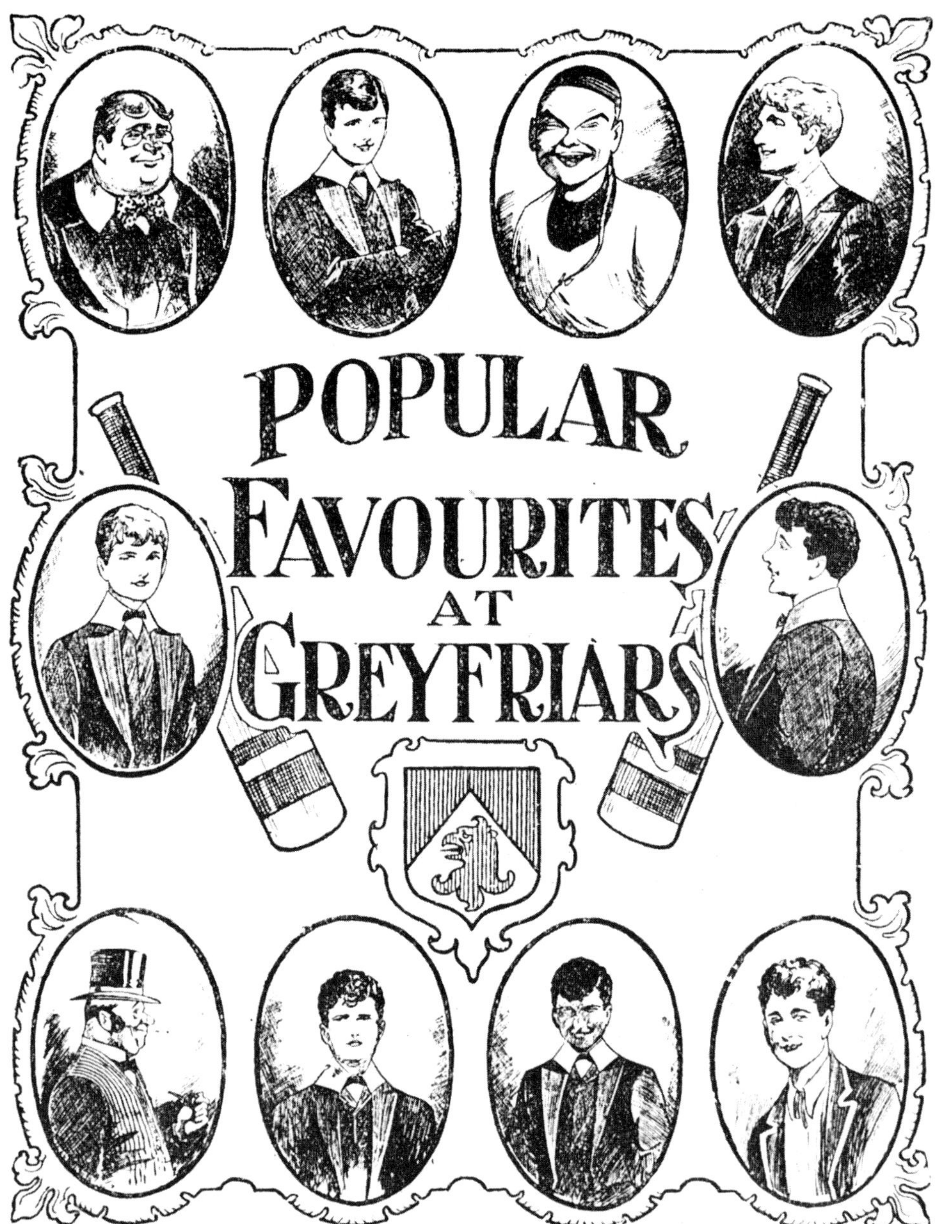

Reading from left to right: Billy Bunter, Mark Linley, Wun Lung, Bob Cherry, Frank Nugent John Bull, Mr. Gosling (porter), Harry Wharton, Hurree Singh, Robert Ogilvy.

Early portraits of the Greyfriars characters: *The Holiday Annual for Boys and Girls* (1920).

one of the most prolific and talented writers for juveniles that the world has ever seen. His first story saw print in 1894 and was followed by scores of others mainly, at first, for the firm of Trapps, Holmes and Co. and, later, almost exclusively for the Amalgamated Press. Hamilton used a large number of pseudonyms: Eric Stanhope, Ridley Redway, Owen Conquest, Frank Drake, Cecil Herbert, Robert Stanley and Clifford Owen were just a few of these appended to his enormous output; it is estimated that in his lifetime he wrote over 5,000 stories. In these he devised at least 100 fictional schools, some of which passed into national folklore and were even assumed by many readers to be real.

In 1906 he created 'St Jim's' (a public school, as were almost all his institutions) for the Amalgamated Press publication *Pluck* and, the following year, the characters of Tom Merry and his chums for *The Gem*. But it was on 15 February 1908, for another new story paper, *The Magnet*, that Charles Hamilton, writing under the name of Frank Richards, created not only the most famous school of them all but some of the best known characters in fiction – Harry Wharton and Co. of Greyfriars School.

The success of this long-running series (*The Magnet* ceased publication in 1940, but books and reprint volumes have continued into the 1980s) was based, however, upon a stroke of genius: the stories were centred not so much around Wharton and his chums Bob Cherry, Harry Nugent, John Bull and Hurree Singh, but a leviathan-sized, blimp-shaped lad named William George Bunter. Billy Bunter had none of the attractions of traditional fictional schoolboys. He was greedy, selfish, snobbish and seldom truthful; he was not good at cricket, 'rugger', football or any other form of sport, and his academic qualifications were almost nil. In short, Bunter had no redeeming features whatsoever. Nevertheless he gave the stories an interest – a vitality – that had not been present in any other school fiction up to this time: millions of readers roared at his escapades and chuckled at the antics of this anti-hero, while simultaneously enjoying the adventures of Wharton and the 'Chums of the Remove' among whom Bunter was, all too often, a parasitic and unwanted companion.

The Holiday Annual (as it was affectionately known throughout the term of its publication) contained stories and features about Charles Hamilton's most popular schools: Rookwood (stories of Jimmy Silver & Co. by Owen Conquest, and which appeared weekly in the *Boys' Friend*), St Jim's (Tom Merry and his chums, by Martin Clifford) and Greyfriars (Bunter, Wharton and Co., by Frank Richards). The first edition contained 360 pages, of which around 300 were written by Hamilton, a proportion of the book that he continued to fill until the paper shortages of the Second World War brought its long run to an untimely end, the last one being published for 1941.

Readers of the stories could be forgiven for assuming that these fictional public schools were real: maps of the establishment were provided, showing the school buildings and the surrounding districts, and descriptions of the pupils were given in considerable detail (very often in verse). *The Holiday Annual* was also profusely illustrated with scenes from the stories and pictures of the schoolboys. Two popular artists of the early editions were Warwick Reynolds Jnr and George William Wakefield. Reynolds, whose father had also been an artist for boys' journals, was well known and respected for his work in papers such as *Pluck*, *Popular* and *Dreadnought* and was already established as the main artist of the St Jim's stories appearing in *The Gem*. His strong style of illustration was well suited to Hamilton's school stories.

G. W. Wakefield was the principal artist of the Rockwood stories in *Boys' Friend*. He was an extremely prolific illustrator and his work appeared in many weekly publications, including *Surprise* and *Bullseye*; but it was for his later work, drawing 'Laurel and Hardy' on the front page of *Film Fun*, that he is best remembered.

Charles Hamilton also wrote several school stories for girls under the nom-de-plume of 'Hilda Richards'. The implication, of course, was that 'she' was the sister of 'Frank Richards', the author of the Greyfriars stories; it was a neat tie-in with the fact that the girls' stories were of 'Bessie' Bunter, a pupil of Cliff House School and the sister of Billy Bunter. Also bespectacled and of similar immense girth to her brother, she was, in the early stories, a perfect 'twin', and her adventures a mirror-image of those of her brother at Greyfriars.

Hamilton's school stories have lived on in some excellent editions produced by the publishing house

The first edition of *The Champion Annual*, edited by Francis Addington Symonds; cover art by John Harris Valda.

of Howard Baker which, in the 1970s, issued *Holiday Annuals*, containing reprints from the original versions. Purchasers of these new editions included not only the older generation, renewing their fond memories, but a new and younger audience reading them enthusiastically for the first time.

Rockfist Rogan and the 'Champion'

Shortly after D.C. Thomson had launched the *Adventure* in September 1921 (the first in its 'Big Five' series of story papers), AP issued on 28 January 1922, the *Champion*, a boys' paper in a similar mould. The *Champion Annual*, a 'Monster Adventure Story Book for Readers of All Ages', was published in 1923, dated 1924. The editor was Francis Addington Symonds, who was inspired by his boyhood favourite reading, the *Big Budget*.

'It offers me great pleasure to present to you this, the first issue of the *Champion Annual*', said F.A. Symonds proudly in the introduction to the 1924 edition (grandly entitled 'The Editor's Overture'), 'and it gives me still greater pleasure to be able to say that this Annual has been issued in response to the universal desire, often expressed in their letters, of the many hundreds of thousands of readers of the *Champion*. ...'

The stories and characters in the *Champion* were never quite as outlandish and eccentric as those appearing in Thomson's 'Big Five', but there were similarities in style. The *Adventure* might have had Dixon Hawke, 'the renowned detective', but the *Champion* had no less than Panther Grayle, the criminologist, otherwise known as 'The Modern Methods Detective'. It was written by Howard Steele (in reality, editor Symonds) and illustrated by Arthur Jones. The story in the 1924 annual was accompanied by a full-page colour plate of Grayle, who sat smoking a cigarette, looking into the distance, with a brooding expression on his face. It must have riveted the attention of every boy who saw it.

The *Champion Annual* also had some rollicking adventure stories. In the first edition was 'The Land of the Shadow Men', a tale of action and thrills in the Chinese Desert; 'The Lake of Death: an astounding tale of breathless adventure'; 'Moreton Stowe's Triumph', a hair-raising adventure in New Guinea (Chapter I: 'The Map on Human Skin'; Chapter II: 'Attacked by Blood-Sucking Bats'). There was also some exciting science fiction, 'The Last of the Martians' by Reid Whitley. The rest of the contents were more traditional with stories about cycling, boxing, the circus and Robin Hood.

Although comparatively small in size, 8½ × 7in (22 × 18 cm), the 1924 annual, priced at six shillings, had 360 pages and was good value. Soon it became standard sized, and was printed on better-quality paper. There were also six colour plates from paintings by E.E. Briscoe, D.C. Eyles and J.H. Valda.

John Harris Valda was a regular contributor to the pages of the *Champion* and its annual who appeared to specialise in the more eerie subjects, such as vampire bats and monsters. During the 1920s he was also the regular cover artist for the annual, and there were many who say it was never the same again, after others took over.

F.A. Symonds, the first editor of the *Champion*, left the publication in 1924. His post was taken by Reginald Eves, under whose expert editorship the weekly story paper and the annual went from strength to strength. The annual

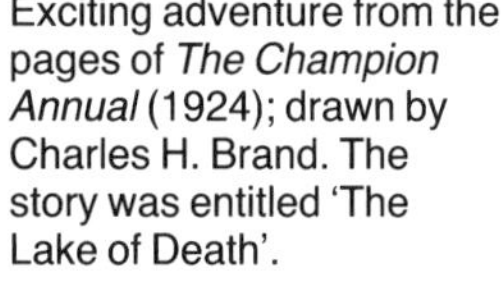
Exciting adventure from the pages of *The Champion Annual* (1924); drawn by Charles H. Brand. The story was entitled 'The Lake of Death'.

A gripping scene from 'The Land of the Shadow Men': *The Champion Annual* (1924); drawn by J. H. Valda.

was soon declared firmly for members of the male sex when it became the *Champion Annual for Boys*, almost certainly an 'Eves' touch; he was a man who liked to define his market between the sexes (*The School Friend*, AP's first story paper for girls, was his brainchild).

There was no *Champion Annual* for the years 1943–6, but publication recommenced in 1947 when wartime paper restrictions had eased. There had been many changes since the early years, not least the advent of new heroes, nearly all of whom had a sporting emphasis. From the late 1940s the annual also adopted its own regular colours: red lettering bordered in white against a yellow background, which was to be continued until the end of its run.

The most famous of all the heroes appearing in the *Champion* was Rockfist Rogan, created by Hal Wilton. Wilton was the pen name of Frank S. Pepper, a freelance writer for the Amalgamated Press, who once estimated that he had written over 1,000 Rockfist Rogan stories. Rogan was an RAF pilot who was also a boxing enthusiast ('He Fought Germans in the Air and Boxers in the Ring'). The excitement of the Rockfist Rogan stories was tinged with realism, a lot of it stemming from Frank Pepper's personal experiences in the Forces (many were written while sitting on the barrack room floor when he was still enlisted). Other writers who were allowed to use the name Hal Wilton were Edward R. Home-Gall and Edward Cowan, who had been a tail-gunner before being invalided out of the RAF. Story illustrations (which were never signed) were mostly by R. Simmonds.

Frank Pepper was also the author – using the pseudonym John Marshall – of another *Champion* favourite, 'Danny of the Dazzlers'. Danny was a precursor of 'Roy of the Rovers' in *Tiger*, in that his presentation was more realistic than that of previous fictional footballers.

In later years the *Champion* had a new detective: his name was Colwyn Dane, a character created by Edward R. Home-Gall, using the pseudonym 'Mark Grimshaw'. Home-Gall wrote many stories for the *Champion* and other AP publications, using either his own or an assumed name. After Charles Hamilton, Edward R. Home-Gall was probably the most prolific writer of boys' stories for the Amalgamated Press.

In the final 1950s editions of the *Champion Annual*, picture strips were introduced, still with a sporting theme: 'Kalgan, the Jungle Boxer', 'Some Footer Boots Are Lucky', etc., but it wasn't enough. The last annual was dated 1956; it was an early victim of the shrinking market for children's publications which were not entirely in picture strip form.

Title page from the first *Schoolgirl's Own Annual* (1923).

For girls only

Annuals specifically for girls were late in getting started at AP. The first annual for girls was the *Girl's Own Paper* published in 1880 by the Religious Tract Society; the RTS and several other publishers had not been slow to develop the market. Some of the best-known titles were: *The Empire Annual for Girls* (RTS: 1909), *The British Girl's Annual* (Cassell: 1911), *Mrs Strang's Annual* (Oxford University Press: 1919) and the many 'Budgets' issued by both Blackie and Thomas Nelson.

The reason for AP's reticence could be attributed to its previous lack of success in the female market. The firm had issued weeklies, *Girls' Home* (1910), *Girls' Reader* (1911) and *Our Girls'* (1915), but none had been very successful, with circulations which could only be described as limp.

It was Reginald Eves, who was on the staff of *The Magnet* and *The Gem*, two important boys' papers published by AP, who realised that a large number of readers were female, and it was he who decided that a girls' paper could be successful. Eves created *School Friend*, a schoolgirl companion to *The Magnet*. Instead of Greyfriars, the school was Cliff House; and it wasn't Billy Bunter who was the fat anti-hero, but Bessie Bunter, his sister. The writer of the stories, as already mentioned, was 'Hilda Richards' who, like 'Frank Richards', was a pen name of Charles Hamilton, author of the stories in *The Magnet*.

School Friend fared much better than its predecessors. It was issued on 17 May 1919 and ran (in two series) until 27 July 1929. Even more successful was *Schoolgirl's Own*, issued on 5 February 1921, and published weekly until 23 May 1936. AP decided at first to issue only one annual for the two titles: it was the *Schoolgirl's Own Annual*, the first dated 1923.

'My Dear Girls, I place before you the first volume of the *Schoolgirl's Own Annual* with the feeling that it will satisfy a long-felt wait. From the day the *School Friend* made its appearance, in May, 1919, I have received thousands of letters from schoolgirls, requesting me to issue an annual publication,' said the editor, in an introduction written from his Fleetway House address.

The lead story was 'Mystery Mansion: A Tale of the Girls at Cliff House', by Hilda Richards. By this time, Charles Hamilton had, in fact, given up writing these stories in the *School Friend*; his successor was Horace Phillips, who was the experienced editor of a succession of AP story papers. Tired of writing about the Cliff House girls, who were in most instances simply feminine counterparts of the boys at Greyfriars, Phillips created his own school, Morcove, with its own resident cast of individual characters.

Stories of Morcove School began in the first issue of the weekly *Schoolgirl's Own* story paper. Using the name Marjorie Stanton, Horace Phillips created a range of splendid characters centred around Betty Barton and her chums. The stories (which were often serialised) appeared in all 798 issues of the paper, before it folded in 1936. With very few exceptions, all were written by Phillips who was a master of characterisation and had the ability to inject strong emotions into his tales. Morcove School stories appeared in all the *Schoolgirl's Own Annuals*, except for the 1940–3 editions (the last to be issued).

Today, there is a small group of collectors who eagerly seek out the *Schoolgirl's Own Annual* for its Morcove stories. Another group which competes with them comprises those who collect the work of Alfred Bestall (1892–1986). The popularity of Bestall's artwork stems from the large following of his best known work, the writing and drawing of Rupert Bear in the *Daily Express* newspaper for thirty years (see Chapter 7). He supplied the cover paintings for the *Schoolgirl's Own Annual* for several years and he also did pen-and-ink illustrations, usually for historical stories. A *Punch*, *Strand* and *Tatler* artist, Bestall was a talented draughtsman whose work contributed a great deal to the quality of the annual.

Finally, a *School Friend Annual* was issued, the first dated 1927. *School Friend* was produced by an almost totally male team; the only female contributors (in later years) were two of the artists who supplied illustrations for the stories: V. Gaskell and Evelyn Flinders. The stories, by writers such as Gail Western (C. Eaton Fern, the editor), 'Hazel Armitage'

A result of the success of *The Schoolgirl's Own Annual* was *The School Friend Annual* (1927).

(John Wheway) and 'Enid Boyten' (Horace Boyten) featured 'daring escapades' and 'madcap mistresses', and the themes were of mystery, sport and adventure. The girls were middle-class, and invariably attended non-coeducational public schools which could have been on another planet as far as the majority of readers were concerned. But it was appealing to a large readership, and not only to girls. In an amusing reversal of roles, although they would not actually purchase such a paper for themselves, many boys read and enjoyed *School Friend* as much as their sisters did.

In 1950, *School Friend* was reissued as a weekly picture story paper, becoming AP's first comic for girls. The lead feature, in full colour pictures, was 'The Silent Three at St Kitts', written by Stewart Pride, the editor, and drawn by Evelyn Flinders. Flinders's attractive drawings also appeared as illustrations to the text stories in the annuals. The *School Friend Annual* had, in fact, never ceased publication, apart from an occasional missing year or two during the war; it was still being published in the 1980s, long after the *School Friend* comic had been discontinued.

The Golden Annual For Girls: first edition (1925).

The *Golden Annual for Girls* was first published for 1925 and ran continuously until 1939. Unlike the other AP girls' annuals, this was not associated with a weekly publication, which was something quite new for the company. However, it was widely advertised in story papers where it was known that a likely readership could be found.

There was a preponderance of schools in the pages of the *Golden Annual.* St Naomi's, Cliffley, Bessborough, Heatherleigh, St Jennifer's and many more. Stories were credited to Joan Inglesant, Iris Holt, Ellen Draycol, Mildred Gordon and others; almost certainly all were pseudonyms for male writers.

The team that produced the *Girls' Crystal Annual* was also a predominantly male bastion. It began long after *School Friend* and *Schoolgirls' Own*: the weekly story paper was launched as *The Crystal* on 26 October 1935, and was retitled from No. 10 to *The Girls' Crystal Weekly*. Its market was the girl fast approaching school-leaving age and, although school stories were featured, others were about people with exciting and colourful jobs. The first edition of the *Girls' Crystal Annual* was dated 1940.

'Tony, the Speed Girl' was a racing car driver; there were also 'Nurse Rosemary', 'Film Struck Fay' and 'Noel Raymond', described as 'the world's most fascinating detective'. The Noel Raymond series were the only stories ever credited to a male writer, 'Peter Langley' (the nom de plume of Raymond's creator, Ronald Fleming), for AP firmly believed that stories about girls should only be written by women. Noel Raymond (always called 'Mr Raymond' by the girls who were involved with his cases) was a popular character and ran for many years before eventually giving way to female sleuths such as Vicky Dare, 'the famous girl detective', and Rex, 'her clever Alsatian partner'.

One of the best known series of stories featured in the *Girls' Crystal* and which appeared in the annuals throughout the 1940s and 1950s was 'The Cruising Merrymakers'. The author was C. Gravely (writing as 'Daphne Grayson'). The Merrymakers – Sally Warner, Fay Manners, Johnny Briggs and Don Weston – spent their free time (which they seemed to have in abundance!) travelling the world from South America to Switzerland, from the pyramids to the Festival of Britain; all illustrated by V. Gaskell.

A well-used theme in the *Girls' Crystal* and its annuals was the Secret Society. The concept was a popular one with its romantic atmosphere, clandestine meetings, ancient crypts flickering with candlelight, and righting of injustices. The *Girls' Crystal Annual* for 1945 contained the story 'Hilary and the Phantom Three' by Gail Western (C. Eaton Fern); the girls wore long, grey robes, cowl-like hoods and black eyemasks. It was dress common to all such groups and the theme reached its apex in 1950 when the *School Friend* comic introduced 'The Silent Three'.

After 908 issues the weekly *Girls' Crystal* was converted into a comic, a virtual copy of the *School Friend* comic. Picture strips were then introduced in the *Girls' Crystal Annual*, although for many years it contained many written stories as well. The last edition was in 1976.

Wartime issue of *Girls' Crystal Annual*. Cover art by V. Gaskell.

Title page from *Girls' Crystal Annual* (1934) depicting a typically innocent boy-girl relationship.

The first *Puck Annual* (1921). Cover art by J. Louis Smyth.

The success of 'Puck'

Next to follow the *Greyfriars Holiday Annual* was *Puck* (1921), a sumptuous amalgam of pictures and stories and very similar in format to the *Playbox Annual*. *Puck* was a penny weekly comic, first issued on 30 July 1904. Published every Thursday, it had twelve pages, the front, back and centre of which were printed in full colour with the remainder in black. It was first intended for the adult market, as many of the Victorian papers had been, but it was quickly realised that the ever growing numbers of literate Edwardians were eager to buy quality reading matter for their children.

The first *Puck Annual* was issued in the autumn of 1920, two years after the war in Europe had ended. This did not, however, preclude the battlefield from entering its pages. One of the lead stories was 'Peggy of the Trenches', a tale of a cat caught up in the war against the Boche. Billed as 'an exciting nature story' it had a grim beginning:

> 'She sat on the Tommy's knee and purred sweet nothings into the Tommy's ear, and Tommy stroked her round smooth head till it was the feel of satin. Once he kissed her.
>
> Then Peggy hopped down and ran off into the night. The Tommy said: "There now! Little cat!" as a rifle bullet drilled a hole in the earth just one inch away from the Tommy's ear, with a noise like "Phtt!"
>
> Tommy got to his feet, but yet another bullet came, and this one laid Tommy low.'

The story had all the hallmarks of being written by a soldier recently having joined the ranks of civilians; the mood of the story was well caught in the powerful illustrations by the artist, Warwick Reynolds.

Although the annual did occasionally borrow from its stable of *Playbox* artists, such as S.J. Cash and J. Louis Smyth (whose paintings adorned both the cover and frontispiece of the first edition), other new hands were commissioned to illustrate what was to become a formula of adventure and nature stories, fairy tales and picture strips. Albert Lock was the principal illustrator of the adventure tales (mainly about Robin Hood and Cowboys and Indians) and, in later years, it was Ruth Cobb, Sydney Stanley and C.E.B. Bernard who provided charming pictorial accompaniment to fairy stories.

Other well-known artists made 'guest appearances': Leonard Shields, a favourite illustrator among readers of the story paper *Pluck* (1904–16) and, later, of the Billy Bunter stories in *The*

Magnet; A. B. Payne (taking time off from *Pip & Squeak*); and Harry Rountree with some splendid humorous animal paintings. The work of Molly Brett was also featured, her cosy, delightful drawings of woodland creatures having an instant appeal for children.

'A Few Words From The Editor', an open letter to readers, was located in the back of the book and an important regular feature of the annual. 'The Editor' was Walter Purchase, a long-standing member of the AP staff and a writer of many of the serials and stories in *Puck* and its companion papers; he made a proud statement in his first letter:

> 'Before you lies my first *Puck Annual* and I hope you will like it. Something tells me that you will. Anyhow, I have done my best to provide you with a volume that, from cover to cover, is packed full of pictures and reading matter that will afford interest, amusement and excitement. You will find that I have given you over three hundred pictures – not including the coloured plates – and nearly fifty stories. Then there are lots of verses and many pages of games, tricks etc.'

Several editions later, when the annual had proved successful, Purchase made the following boast about *Puck*:

> 'It has earned as cordial a welcome in the mansion as it receives in the humble cottage. Schoolmasters, schoolmistresses, parents and guardians of children, rich and poor alike, have written to express approval of its pictures and stories and general healthy tone. Can more be said?'

Undoubtedly not! Although the price of six shillings was out of reach of children who only received a few pence weekly as pocket money, parents would certainly have been impressed by its value for money; this was essential, as the book would be expected to provide entertainment throughout the year in an age when there was no television and even the wireless had yet to establish its hold on the public.

Title page from *Puck Annual* (1921).

Illustration from the Editor's Letter, *Puck Annual* (1921). The artist is A. B. Payne who became well-known for his work on 'Pip, Squeak and Wilfred'.

Tiger Tim and the Bruin Boys

'For ever such a long time I have wanted to have an annual of my very own, and now here it is before you!' began the letter 'To My Readers' in the first edition of *Tiger Tim's Annual* (1922).

Tiger Tim and his chums had first been seen as far back as 1904 in a picture strip in the *Daily Mirror* and had gained considerable popularity in *The Playbox*, the children's supplement to the magazine *The World and His Wife*; the 'Bruin Boys', as they were also known, had also appeared regularly since 1909 in *The Playbox Annual.*

On 14 February 1914, a new coloured weekly comic had been issued by the Amalgamated Press from its offices at Fleetway House. It was entitled *The Rainbow*, and its stars, appearing on the prestigious front page (a place they were to continue to occupy until the comic's demise in 1956), were Tiger Tim and the Bruin Boys. Initially the boys were drawn by Julius Baker but, later in 1914, a new artist took over, Herbert Sidney Foxwell. Foxwell was to emerge as one of the great talents of British comics and comic annuals; Tiger Tim's popularity in the Twenties and Thirties was very much attributable to his genius.

Born in London in 1890, Foxwell had previously worked for Fleetway House as a staff artist, and his work had appeared in the weekly comic papers such as the *Favorite Comic* and *Comic Cuts* before he embarked full time on drawing Tiger Tim and his friends. His stylish art enhanced the look and feel of all the publications for which he worked. Recognising his talents, AP allowed him the rare privilege of signing either his name or initials on each of his drawings.

On 1 June 1919, another comic appeared on the news-stands: *Tiger Tim's Tales*. Printed in red and black, it contained artwork by Foxwell and another artist named Fred Crompton, who was also to play an important part when *Tiger Tim's Annual* was published. Soon, this nursery comic was renamed *Tiger Tim's Weekly* and, after a first series lasting two years, a second series was published which featured Tiger Tim and his chums in full colour on the front page.

When *Tiger Tim's Annual* was launched in 1921 for 1922, Tim and the Bruin Boys were already appearing in *The Rainbow, Tiger Tim's Weekly* and *The Playbox Annual*, all of which contained art by Foxwell, although in the last he shared Tim with other artists. The annual itself had a colour cover, complete with dust-wrapper, that had been reproduced from a painting by Herbert Foxwell (as they all were for more than a decade). It showed Tim, hands on hips, quill pen thrust at a jaunty angle behind one ear; to his right, a single picture showing the Bruin Boys misbehaving in the classroom. Inside the weighty volume (it was printed on heavy-quality paper stock with sturdy board covers), the 160 pages were printed in a variety of coloured inks: blue and red inks were used on their own and, very often, there were full colour adventures of Tiger Tim or the 'Brownie Boys'.

The Brownie Boys, drawn by Fred L. Crompton, a long-term staff member of the Fleetway House, were four young lads dressed in one-piece suits, three in red and one in black, with matching hats. Their names were Peter Pippin (the one in black), Archie Artichoke, Dicky Dandelion and Billie Buttercup, and they were a mainstay of the Tiger Tim publications throughout their long runs.

Foxwell's Tiger Tim was an immediate improvement on the versions depicted by Julius Baker for the *Playbox Annual*, and by S.J. Cash, who had contributed some of the front-page art for the weekly *Rainbow*. Although

Title page of the first *Tiger Tim's Annual* (1922). Under Foxwell's hand Tiger Tim became one of the most popular and famous of all children's characters.

Baker's version (which Cash had duplicated) had its charm, his Tim was a diminutive, rather 'weedy' character; Foxwell's Tim was larger, more 'fleshed-out', more stylish and far more sophisticated; under his hand, Tiger Tim evolved into one of the most popular and best-loved comic characters of the twentieth century.

It is no exaggeration to say that under Foxwell's influence the front pages of *Tiger Tim's Weekly* and *The Rainbow*, and the many pages he did within the annual, ranked as genuine works of art. Particularly good were the Tiger Tim text stories (as opposed to Tim's appearance in comic-strip form) that he illustrated within the annuals: pages were bordered with glorious designs comprised of fruit, leaves, florid graphics and (as the annual appeared just before Christmas) holly, crackers, plum puddings and other festive

First edition of *The Rainbow* (1924). Artist: H. S. Foxwell.

Opposite 'The Two Pickles': *The Rainbow* (1924). The characters were popular enough to inspire a series of films released in the Twenties.

paraphernalia. His art work became an integral part of the text and although the techniques he used were also practised by some of his contemporaries, none accomplished them to equally good effect.

Other story contributors to *Tiger Tim's Annual* were often anonymous, although many were presumably the work of staff writers. Artists were mainly those who had worked previously for the *Playbox Annual*, such as A.E. Jackson and S.J. Cash; again, Cash's beautiful frontispieces were of special note. In addition, S.B. Pearse, C.E.B. Bernard, 'Locke' and Margaret Banks added their considerable talents to the book's contents.

The success of *Tiger Tim's Annual* resulted, in 1924, in the issue of *The Rainbow Annual*. The hero, of course, was Tiger Tim, and to all intents and purposes this annual was *Tiger Tim's Annual* under another title. Both were identical in format, contained many pages of the Bruin Boys' adventures, and had art and stories indistinguishable from those in its counterpart. Fred Crompton was there, too; not with his famous 'Brownie Boys' but with his equally endearing 'The Wee Woolly Boys'. The Woolly Boys were a band of cheerful youngsters, all of whom wore coloured woolly suits that covered them completely, but for their faces. The merry mayhem resulting from their antics was depicted in full-page, full-colour drawings. Other popular features from the weekly *Rainbow* comic were to appear in the annual year after year: one of the best known was 'The Two Pickles', drawn by H. O'Neill. Indeed, so popular were these two characters that they even starred in films; a series of twelve 'shorts' was made, starting in 1922, and shown in cinemas around the country.

The Hippo Girls

Incredibly, in 1926 and 1927, two other 'spin-off' annuals were published by the Amalgamated Press: *Mrs Hippo's Annual* and *The Bruin Boys' Annual*. With the relaunch of *Playbox* in 1925 as a weekly comic (in a format similar to that of *Rainbow* and *Tiger Tim's Weekly*), Tiger Tim and his friends were featured in three weekly comics and no less than five annuals, an unprecedented event in the history of publications for juveniles and a tribute to the strength of their popularity.

To be strictly accurate, *Mrs Hippo's Annual* featured as its

THE TWO PICKLES.

1. "Oh, look!" whispered Peter. "Mary is making a pudding for dinner." "I hope she is putting some bones in it," said Fluff. "It would be a nice surprise." "Don't be silly!" said Pauline. "I hope she is putting in lots of currants. I love currants!" "Let's creep in and see," said Peter. "Mary is so busy stirring she won't see us. Come along, Pauline."

2. On their hands and knees the Pickles crept in, without Mary seeing them. "I believe I can smell it," said Fluff. "I think it must be an almond pudding." "With little bits of nut in," added Pauline. "Hush, be quiet!" whispered Peter. "Mary will hear you." And, ever so quietly, they crawled along until they were all sitting under the table.

3. They sat there very quietly until they saw Mary walk away to the kitchen cupboard. "Now is our chance for a peep," whispered Peter. "We can tell whether it is almond pudding." "Hold me up, Peter," said Fluff. "I can't see." It was a huge basin that was standing on the table. "If that is full, it will be a fine large pudding!" said Pauline.

Title page from the first *Mrs. Hippo's Annual* (1926): Herbert Foxwell in typically ebullient mood.

stars not Tiger Tim & Co. but Tiger Tilly and the Hippo Girls! The association was obvious. Tilly and her chums were mere carbon copies of Tim and his friends. Mrs Hippo, of course, was the name given to the proprietor of the kindergarten in the very first *Daily Mirror* picture strip which had later been dropped in favour of Mrs Bruin. However, Mrs Hippo had returned as the front-page star, together with the female counterparts of Tiger Tim and his chums, when *Playbox* was reissued as a weekly comic.

The Hippo Girls, drawn by Foxwell from the first issue, were never as popular as their brothers, the Bruin Boys, and by the early 1930s had been relegated to the back page. Later they were allocated only a few small pictures in the middle of the comic; the annual, however, retained its popularity for fourteen years.

'I feel so excited about this first number of my new annual and I should just love to watch your faces when you receive your copies and begin to enjoy all the pictures and stories,' wrote Mrs Hippo from 'the offices of *The Playbox*' at Fleetway House. It would indeed have been interesting to witness those small faces: the title page bore a quite stunning piece of Foxwell Art Deco – a peacock in full, glorious display, the tips of its enormous feathers showing the faces of the Hippo Girls. Other contributing artists were Fred Crompton ('The Bumpty Boys'), Louise Jacobs (fairy stories), 'Locke' (usually historical pieces of knights in armour and Robin Hood) and Muriel Jackson (a daughter of the celebrated A.E. Jackson) who did much of her work in silhouette, a popular style in the Twenties and Thirties. The last edition of *Mrs Hippo's Annual* was published in 1939 for 1940.

The Bruin Boys' Annual (1926–40) bore the description 'Tales to Read to Little People' and, like *Mrs Hippo's Annual*, used the same formula as *Tiger Tim's Annual* and *The Rainbow Annual*; the last two were for 'Boys and Girls of All Ages', *Mrs Hippo's Annual* had a girl readership in mind, and *The Bruin Boys'* aimed to capture an audience of little boys. The participating role of the parent was taken for granted. 'This year I have filled our annual with jollier pictures and stories than ever,' wrote the editor in the traditional letter to readers. 'I know you will love listening to the exciting stories and many of you, I dare say, will be old enough to read some of them by yourselves.' The Editor's Letter in *The Bruin Boys' Annual* was charmingly entitled 'Good Night' and ended, as they all did in each of the annuals, with a plug for a weekly comic featuring Tiger Tim; in this case, *The Rainbow*.

Unlike other annuals which contained a letter in the front of the book, the Tiger Tim group of annuals always had the traditional letter to readers on the very last page. Tiger Tim himself was the writer in his own annual, Mrs Bruin in *The Rainbow Annual*, Mrs Hippo in *Mrs Hippo's Annual* and, simply, 'The Editor' in *The Bruin Boys' Annual*. The writer of all these letters, for many years, was the man in charge of the enormously successful Tiger Tim group: William Fisher, a senior editor at AP. Fisher, who had risen to the post from office boy, and suffered from deafness caused by an incident during war service, was a professional who maintained the highest standards in all the publications under his control. It was this quality of production which enabled Fisher and AP to include the children of the Royal Family among their readers. A letter of congratulation from the Queen, written in the 1930s, hung proudly on the board room wall of Fleetway House for many years.

The final edition of *The Bruin Boy's Annual* (1940).

One of the biggest upsets to the Tiger Tim publications came in 1933 when Herbert Foxwell was offered considerable financial inducement to work for the *Daily Mail*, inviting him to take over its popular and long-running 'Teddy Tail'. The paper planned to publish a comic supplement, *The Boys & Girls Daily Mail*, and, in addition, to start an annual.

Originated by Charles Folkard in 1915, 'Teddy Tail' had been taken up by his brother Harry when Charles left the strip in order to spend more time on book illustration. Harry Folkard was not in the same artistic class as his brother, and thus the *Daily Mail* recruited Herbert Foxwell. *The Boys & Girls Daily Mail* ran from 1933 until 1937, Foxwell drawing the entire front page in his exuberant, sophisticated style.

Consternation at the Fleetway House offices eventually subsided when Bill Fisher found that he had a suitable replacement in Bert Wymer, who rendered a good duplication of Foxwell's style. Even so, Herbert Foxwell was very much missed, and this major coup by the *Daily Mail* is thought to be one reason why, from then on, Amalgamated Press actively discouraged artists from signing their work. If Foxwell had not been so easily identifiable by his signature, the *Mail* might never have found him in order to make an offer; in the future it was only by the rarest concession that an artist could sign his work, and not for over forty years did it become common practise. It was Bert Wymer's work that predominated in the *Tiger Tim Annuals* from 1933, although in later years several different artists were known to have been employed.

The heyday of the Tiger Tim group was in the Twenties and Thirties (during this time there was some merchandising of goods using Tiger Tim and the Bruin Boys: the firm of Britains issued a set of lead model figures and another company sold jigsaw puzzles featuring the characters); but their appeal extends well into the Eighties when they were appearing regularly in the nursery comic

Endpaper illustration by H. S. Foxwell from the first *Bubbles Annual* (1924). The annual remained in print until the 1943 edition.

Jack & Jill. As a result, a *Tiger Tim's Annual* was published in the Seventies, the then regular artist being Peter Woolcock.

This odd and humorous group of comic animals has clearly made an important contribution to children's literature. Through them, Fleetway House tapped the secret of the ages: given that the characters were sufficiently appealing, children would *want* to read about them, rather than be pressed to do so, like their less fortunate Victorian counterparts. The Tiger Tim publications are a significant part of annual publishing history, and the remarkable fact that four books were published simultaneously, based essentially on the same characters, has never been equalled.

Blowing bubbles

The Tiger Tim group of annuals and comics were not the only Amalgamated Press publications to use Herbert Foxwell's art. *Bubbles Annual* (1924), 'A story and picture book for boys and girls' also contained much of his work. This volume was the annual for a nursery comic paper entitled *Bubbles & The Children's Fairy*, which was first published on 16 April 1921, and aimed, essentially, at the same readership as *The Rainbow* and others. This was a standard AP marketing technique: the issuing of nearly identical publications which 'overlapped'. If a child didn't like Tiger Tim – fair enough! But why buy a comic from a rival publisher? Here was *Tiger Tim's Weekly* without Tiger Tim! It was a practice which proved successful, stifled the competition and gave Fleetway House a virtual monopoly.

The front page stars of this coloured twopenny weekly were 'The Bunty Boys', six young lads from half a dozen different countries. The boys were stereotypes of their national images: a fat little Eskimo named Snowball, Hans the Dutchboy, Ching from China, Redwing (an American Indian), a black boy named Pompey, and Jackie who was British. Inside, 'The Merry Boys at Mister Croc's School', with their naughty antics, were the bane of Mr Croc's existence. A familiar formula indeed! The contents of the first *Bubbles Annual* was typical of those for subsequent years: as well as 'The Bunty Boys' and 'Mister Croc's School', there were 'Peeps into Fairyland' (full-page coloured pictures), tales of Robin Hood, stories of knights in armour and, illustrated by 'Locke', 'The White Redskin', described as 'A Thrilling Complete Story of the Prairies'. In later volumes there was the popular 'Dick True, the Boy Inventor', beautifully drawn by an unknown artist. Other illustrators would have been familiar to *Playbox Annual* readers: Helen Jacobs, with some truly astonishing pen-and-ink line illustrations, S. J. Cash, at his best with some splendidly executed 'one-off' humorous pictures, and Louis Wain with (what else?) some 'cat' drawings.

The earliest editions of *Bubbles Annual* were an unusual size: tall and thin, they measured approximately 12 × 9 inches (30 × 23 cm) as opposed to the more standard 11 × 8 inches (28 × 20 cm), and each edition, up to the last in 1941, contained exactly 100 pages (by comparison, *Tiger Tim's Annual* for the same year, 1924, had 160 pages). This did, naturally, result in a difference in price: *Tiger Tim's Annual* cost six shillings; *Bubbles Annual* was almost half that at three shillings and sixpence.

Bubbles were put to good use as a theme: the picture on the cover of the annual (pasted down on to the boards) always used them as an integral part of the illustration. The 1924 edition had a splendid example of what would be the style of all the following volumes: from a painting by Herbert Foxwell, it showed a large bubble, blown from an elf's pipe. Enclosed in the bubble were Mrs Bunty and

First edition of *The Chicks' Own Annual* (1924). An outsize annual which featured Rupert the Chick and hyphenated words.

her boys, all of whom were using pipes to blow yet more bubbles. In addition, each letter of the annual's title and date appeared within bubbles. The effect was both cheerful and attractive.

During the 1930s *Bubbles Annual* became a little less tall (although the book was always larger than its contemporaries) and had the appearance of being thicker; this was due to the heavier quality paper stock on which it was printed. 'I send you my best wishes for a very jolly Christmas and a happy New Year, and shall look forward to meeting you again in next year's *Bubbles Annual*,' wrote 'Your Loving Friend, The Editor' in the 1941 edition. But it was not to be. The bubble finally burst for this popular nursery annual as the battle against Nazi Germany began to bite deeply into the nation's paper supplies.

'Chicks' Own'

The *Chicks' Own Annual*, issued in 1924 by Fleetway House, was a testimony to the success of the weekly *Chicks' Own* comic issued in 1920. The weekly boldly declared as part of its masthead, 'Teaches Young Children To Read', a boast supported by large easy-to-read text containing hyphenated words.

'My dear Chums,' usually began the word of introduction on page one of the annual, 'I know you will all like this fine new book. And I know, too, you will all want to know more of all the jol-ly folk you will meet in-side. There is a ve-ry eas-y way to do this! Buy the *Chicks' Own* ev-e-ry week. Don't for-get, *Chicks' Own*, price Two-pence ev-e-ry Tuesday!' It was signed 'Lots of Love from Rupert'.

Rupert was a bright yellow chick who wore a beret on his head; his choice of best friend – a black chick – would today be hailed by equal opportunity and minority groups, although the choice of name certainly wouldn't. It was (hyphenated, naturally) 'Nig-ger'; but, of course, in the Twenties and Thirties this was seen as apt and in no sense derogatory. The adventures of the pair, which often included the very large 'Stri-pey Tiger', who walked on his hind legs, and fairy tale and pantomime characters such as Aladdin, Robinson Crusoe and Dick Whittington, were in the form of large picture strips printed in full colour. The artist was Arthur White, who also drew for the weekly *Chicks' Own* comic.

Art tended to be simplistic, but this well-known children's annual did occasionally attract an artist of merit – George Catcombe for one, who couldn't resist embellishing his pictures with a good deal of

Playbox Annual: first edition 1909.

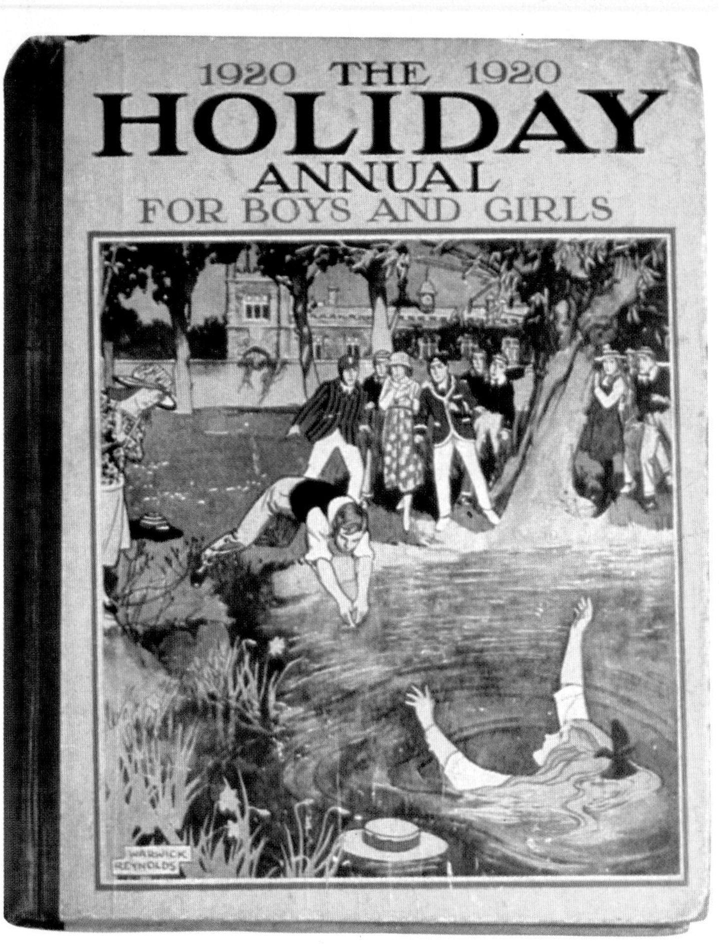

The Holiday Annual for Boys and Girls: first edition 1920

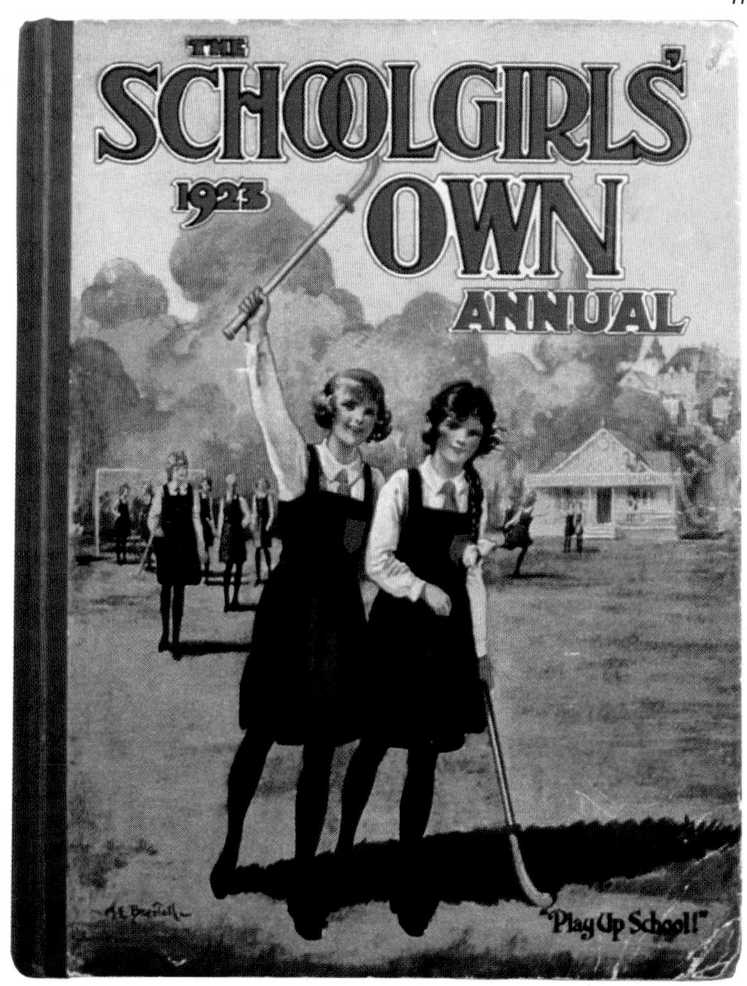

The Schoolgirl's Own Annual: first edition 1923.

Tiger Tim's Annual: first edition 1922.

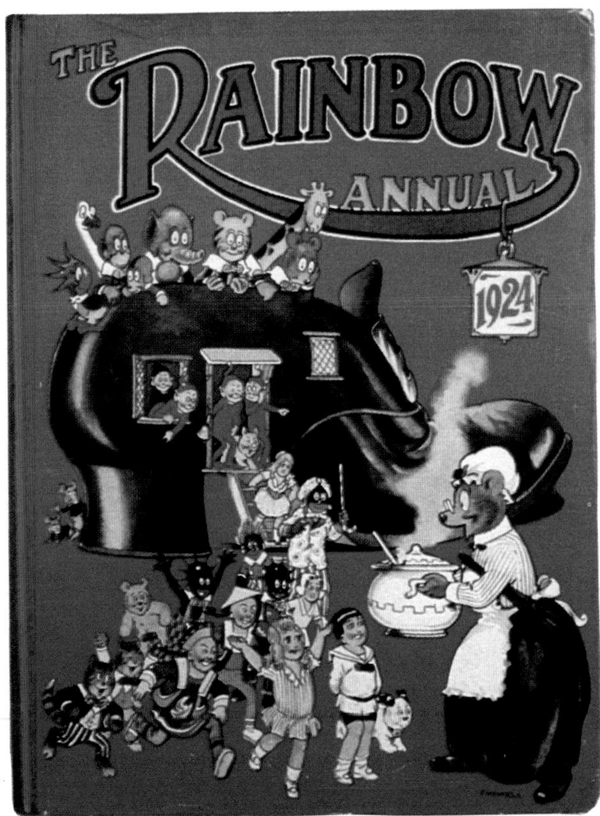

The Rainbow Annual: first edition 1924.

Mrs. Hippo's Annual: first edition 1926.

Bubbles Annual: first edition 1924.

detail and did it with considerable style; Arthur Mansbridge, a popular illustrator for *Punch*, was another.

In the 1920s and 1930s it was the sheer size – or perhaps 'outsize' would be a better word – of the annual that demanded attention in bookshops. It measured a huge 18 × 14 in (46 × 36 cm), compared with the more standard 10 × 8 in (25 × 20 cm) for other annuals, and contained 100 pages printed on stiff paper. During the 1940s, however, when it was one of the few annuals that continued to be published by the Amalgamated Press throughout the war, it reverted to standard size and for a time was subject to wartime economy measures, which meant softer board for the cover and poorer-quality paper.

The last edition was dated 1957, the year in which the weekly comic was also to end. Rupert and his chums were gone for-ever....

Wonders and hobbies

The *Wonderland Annual* was 'issued from the offices of *Playtime*, The Fleetway House, Farringdon Street' in 1920 for 1921. It, too, was in the *Playbox Annual* style and used work by many of the same artists. One was J. Louis Smythe. His contributions included not only splendid colour plates and pen-and-ink pictures to accompany fantasy stories, but also comic animal pictures of the kind that only he could draw (although there was a touch of Edward Lear's 'nonsense' humour in many of his illustrations).

Other artists were Arthur White, Ruth Cobb, Leonard Shields, Arthur Mansbridge, L. Church and H. O'Neil. O'Neil, a prolific artist of comic drawings, was the illustrator of one feature that would raise many an amused eyebrow in later years: 'Mickey Mouse and His Jungle Friends'. In all innocence, he had given the star of his comic strip the name of the character who, in 1928, would become the world's best-known cartoon and comic-strip star. It was something that Walt Disney could not possibly have known, of course, but it is amusing to see a British 'Mickey' years before the creation of his American counterpart.

This British Mickey Mouse (appearing several years before Walt Disney had introduced his animated film star) appeared in *The Wonderland Annual* (1922).

The *Wonderland Annual* was incorporated with the *Playtime Annual* (the yearly issue for a weekly comic of the same name) in the 1927 volume which was entitled, for the one issue, *Playtime & Wonderland*; then the name *Wonderland* was dropped. The *Playtime Annual* was continued for some years, with several of the *Wonderland Annual* features, until the last of the *Playtime* series was published in 1933 for 1934.

A new entrant to the annual's market appeared for 1927: *Everyboy's Hobby Annual*, issued by the

Amalgamated Press. The *Hobby Annual* (as its readers came to know it) was published every year until 1938 (when it was renamed *The Modern Boy's Book of Hobbies*). The 208-page book contained information designed to keep any boy busy during the long evenings, rainy afternoons, weekends and school holidays in the years before television. There were scores of articles which gave him instructions on things to make and which told him how things work. Subjects included aeroplanes, engineering, railways, photography, wireless, woodwork, stamps and ships. He could discover how to make a kite, a knife-box, a wireless cabinet, or build a catamaran; and he could even take lessons in orange-peel art (cutting the peel of the fruit into elaborate, exotic shapes).

It was a book aimed at the practical boy who was at home with a carpentry or metalworking set; a youth set for a future in industry and with a keen interest in the world about him. The tone was 'chummy', that of an older schoolboy writing to those a little younger than himself. Articles began, 'Any fellow who likes making things...' or 'There are quite a number of fellows who...' and the narrative style was that of an editor and his staff filled with wonder at the modern world and its achievements. The theme was a popular one and weekly papers and annuals soon followed. The most popular of the weeklies were *Modern Boy* (AP), *Modern Wonder* and *Modern World* (both Odhams), but only *Modern Boy* had its own annual, which was issued for the years 1931–40, although the *Hobby Annual* was also generally regarded as a 'companion annual' to the weekly *Modern Boy* paper. There were many 'spin-offs', too, which included *Modern Boy's Book of Motors, Ships & Engines* (1933) ... *Engineering* (1934) ... *Adventure Stories* (1936) ... *True Adventure* (1938) ... *Racing Cars* (1939) ... *Pirates* (1940) ... *Firefighters* (1940).

During the 1930s the most popular children's comics were those published by the Amalgamated Press. Competition was almost non-existent; if it did pose a threat AP would purchase its rival, whose titles would quickly be merged with its own comic publications. This happened in 1939 to Target Publications of Bath. Tolerated throughout the preceding years by AP, Target's comics, *Dazzler, Bouncer, Merry Midget, Rocket, Target, Rattler* and others, were taken over and within weeks were naught but a memory; not even the characters or strips were carried over. This, however, was no surprise. Although Target comics had circula-

Title page from the first edition of *Every Boy's Hobby Annual* (1927). In the days before television publications such as this were immensely popular.

This *Modern Boy's Annual* (1940) was published in the Autumn of 1939 when Britain had just declared war on Germany. The nation's mood of militarism was captured perfectly by this marvellously evocative cover.

tions which obviously affected the sales of AP titles, the standard of artwork and the quality of material being offered was exceedingly low – far too low for the very high standards of Fleetway House.

Throughout the 1920s AP had concentrated on a rapid expansion of the 'Tiger Tim' group, to supply the annual market. By the end of the decade the 'Tiger Tim family' appeared in no less than five different books: *Playbox, Tiger Tim, Rainbow, The Bruin Boys' Annual* and *Mrs Hippo's Annual*. Clearly, if there was going to be further development of a lucrative market, other comics had to have annuals as well.

Into the Thirties

The first annuals to be issued by the Amalgamated Press in the 1930s were *My Favourite Annual* (1933) and *Crackers* (1933). *My Favourite* was a weekly comic which began publication on 28 June 1928, cost twopence and was printed in full colour on the front page (which featured a strip called 'Round the World in the Jolly Rover', drawn by George Wakefield who later was respon-

Title page from the first edition of *My Favourite Annual* (1933).

First edition of *My Favourite Annual* (1933).

sible for 'Laurel and Hardy' in *Film Fun*). Although the weekly comic was attractive, the annual was dull, with too many text stories and stiffly drawn, uninteresting picture strips aimed at an audience slightly older than the comic's readership. In fact, the book was barely recognisable as one affiliated to the weekly comic, using almost none of the regular features or artists. The only redeeming features were some pleasant paintings by Frank Insall and good pen-and-ink illustrations by Molly Brett. There were only three editions, the last dated 1935.

Crackers Annual was a new departure for Amalgamated Press annuals. Standard-sized, 11 × 8 in (28 × 20 cm), it had stout board covers and contents which, for the most part, were printed on thick, rough and, by modern standards, poor quality paper. Certainly it lacked the evident care and attention paid, say, to *Tiger Tim's Annual* or *The Rainbow*. There was far less in it, and it included reprints of features that had appeared in weekly comics. Some strips even had their names changed in the process: 'Pitch and Toss', two comical sailors from the back page of the weekly *Funny Wonder* comic, were reprinted in *Crackers Annual* as 'Jack and Andy, Our Merry Mariners'; and, seeking a slightly up-market approach (and losing a great deal in the process), another strip, 'Marmy and His Ma', was retitled 'Marmy and His Mother'.

Pasted on to the board cover was a full-colour picture from a watercolour painting by one of AP's leading artists. The 1933 *Crackers Annual* had both cover and frontispiece by Alex Akerbladh, a specialist in this kind of cheerful single-picture scene.

Cover and frontispiece were not the only illustrations to appear in full colour. In addition, there were two or three colour sections printed on better quality paper. These sections were usually text

First edition of *Crackers Annual* (1933). The illustrator was Alex Akerbladh.

stories, highly illustrated by one of the best AP artists of the day, and the result was a perfect blend of the comic strip and the written story: pictures with word-balloons mingling with the text in a manner which was not obtrusive upon either medium. Other artists, besides Alex Akerbladh, whose work appeared in *Crackers Annual* were Reg Parlett, Roy Wilson, Don Newhouse (well known for his depiction of 'Crackers the Pup', a regular comic strip feature in the weekly *Crackers*) and George Parlett (brother of Reg), although Akerbladh was responsible for almost all the cover paintings.

My Favourite may not have been successful (the comic itself was discontinued in 1934) but *Crackers* certainly was, and AP continued to increase its range of new titles, keeping them in the same mould. The next new annual to be published was *The Funny Wonder Annual* in the autumn of 1934 and dated 1935.

The Funny Wonder was another successful weekly comic issued by Fleetway House, with origins that extended back to the previous century. In the 1930s the front-page stars of the comic were 'Pitch & Toss' ('Jack and Andy' to *Crackers* readers) and so, naturally, they were used as subjects for the cover pictures. Six of the seven *Funny Wonder Annuals* published (dated 1935–41) featured the two sailors; the other (1937) showed another favourite of the weekly comic, Charlie Chaplin. All of the cover paintings were by Roy Wilson (1900–65), without doubt the finest and most prolific comic artist ever to work for the Amalgamated Press and, indeed, one of the best graphic artists Britain has ever produced. Unknown and unrecognised throughout his lifetime, he now has a substantial following and deservedly so. Wilson played a major role in shaping the traditional British comic art style and there are those who believe he created it. Roy Wilson's work for the *Funny Wonder Annuals* was some of his best. His watercolour paintings were a delight, and his pen-and-ink drawings were small masterpieces of draughtsmanship.

Funny Wonder Annual: first edition 1935.

In the following year, 1936, AP launched three more annuals for its more successful weeklies: *Jester, Jingles* and *Sparkler*. The first *Jester Annual* and the first *Jingles Annual* had cover pictures by R.E. (Reg) Parlett; the *Sparkler Annual* by Roy Wilson. All had the same thick, rough paper and format as the *Crackers Annual. Jester & Sparkler* ceased publication with the editions dated 1940; the last *Jingles Annual* was issued dated 1941.

Other annuals based on weekly comics followed: *My Tip Top Book* in 1937 (for *Tip Top* comic) and *Chips, Golden* and *Butterfly* in 1939. *Chips Annual* (dated 1939–41) was that for the famous and long-lived comic, *Illustrated Chips*, which had been first published in 1890 and which, from the first issue, boasted as front page stars, Weary Willie and Tired Tim. Willie and Tim were two tramps who, through their popularity and longevity, became nationally famous. Their names were used as pseudonyms for the work-shy and even in the course of

Jester Annual: first edition 1936.

Jingles Annual: first edition 1936.

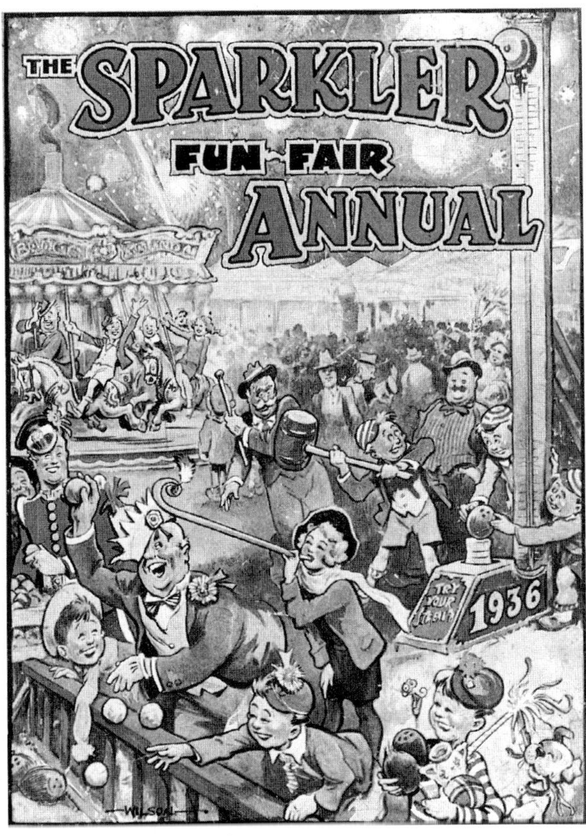

Sparkler Annual: first edition 1936.

Tip Top Annual: 1938.

Golden Fun and Story Book: first edition 1939.

debates in the House of Commons. Naturally, the two endearing vagabonds were featured on the front of all three *Chips Annuals* though, sadly, never drawn by their regular artist, Percy Cocking. Cocking had drawn the strip regularly since around 1910 without missing an issue, having taken it up from the well-known Victorian painter and illustrator Tom Browne, who had created them. Percy Cocking continued to draw the strip until 1953 when the comic itself was discontinued after a record run of sixty-three years.

'All Aboard for the *Golden!*' was the introduction to *Golden Fun and Story Book* of 1939. This was the annual for the weekly comic of the same name; not one of the long-established publications of the firm, but a bright and cheery newcomer, the first weekly issue of which was dated 23 October 1937. This was the start of a common practice among publishing companies: the publication of an annual immediately a comic had established a readership.

'As I present to you the first of the *Golden Fun & Story Books*, I am a proud and happy man,' the letter went on to say, as the writer proceeded to extol the virtues of the annual's weekly counterpart. It was signed 'Your cheery friend and Editor, Sam Smiles' – not the celebrated professional moralist of the Victorian era, but a tubby, cheerful little man whose compendium aimed simply to entertain. Stories were anonymous, as they were in all annuals of the type, but among the artists (although comic strips were unsigned, styles were immediately recognisable) were Roy Wilson, Percy Cocking, and the very accomplished adventure strip artist, Reg Perrott. Perrott was one of the foremost comic-strip artists of the Thirties, who soon turned his hand to book illustration (*East India Adventure:* Collins 1945; *King Harold's Son:* Nelson 1946) but who regrettably died of cancer at the young age of thirty-two in 1947.

The Butterfly Annual (1939) was identical to its companions but managed somehow to maintain its own identity, mostly by ensuring that it stuck to its own characters. The marvellous cover pictures benefited considerably from the talents of Walter Bell (1939 edition) and Roy Wilson (1940 edition). Interestingly, not all of the stories within this annual were anonymous. Although unsigned, the 'Roy Keene, Detective' stories, one of the most popular features, were written by G. M. Wilson, wife of Roy Wilson. Mrs Wilson was a regular contributor for some twenty years to the same comics and annuals (see *Radio Fun Annual* and *TV Fun Annual*) to which her husband contributed.

Sadly, 1940 and 1941 spelt the end for this successful series of

Butterfly Annual: first edition 1939.

annuals published by Fleetway House. Wartime paper shortages led to the discontinuation in 1940 of *Jester, Butterfly, Golden* and *Sparkler* and, in 1941, of *Funny Wonder, Jingles, Chips* and *Crackers*. Only *Tip Top* survived, continuing throughout the war and after; the last edition was dated 1955.

Fun with the film stars

One annual which got off to a particularly late start for a comic title that commenced publication as far back as 17 January 1920, was the *Film Fun Annual*, first issued for 1938. *Film Fun* featured stars of the early cinema: Harold Lloyd, Buster Keaton, Jackie

Coogan, Joe E. Brown, Lupino Lane and many more.

Much of the comic paper's success was due to its editor, Fred Cordwell. Cordwell had begun his career at Amalgamated Press around 1910 and was an important and respected figure at Fleetway House. He edited several comic papers, among them *Fun & Fiction, Merry & Bright, My Favourite, Surprise* and *Bullseye*; but he was identified most particularly with *Film Fun.*

From the beginning, Fred Cordwell had chosen as his chief artist George William (Bill) Wakefield, an illustrator he'd already used, prior to *Film Fun*, on some of the other titles he edited. Cordwell felt that Wakefield's style was so appropriate for *Film Fun* that he insisted all his other artists conform to it. Bill Wakefield's first work for *Film Fun* was to draw the adventures of Ben Turpin and Chester Conklin and those of Babe Marie Osborne; but in 1930 he found his metier when he was asked to draw the famous comedy team, Laurel and Hardy, in a new feature within the comic. Immediately popular, it was promptly promoted to both the front and back pages where it was to remain for the next quarter of a century.

Bill Wakefield was asked to illustrate the cover of the 1938 *Film Fun Annual*. It showed Laurel and Hardy, Shirley Temple (who didn't actually appear inside!), Wheeler and Woolsey, Jimmy Durante, Sidney Howard and Harold Lloyd. Printed on good quality paper stock (immediately noticeable by the weight of the annual), it had 160 pages, divided roughly half and half between picture strips and text stories. The picture strips were as they appeared in the weekly comic (often literally so, as some were straight reprints): rectangular in shape, they were always drawn from a flat perspective, as though the reader were viewing the action on a cinema screen, which was, of course, the idea. Interestingly the first Laurel and Hardy picture strip to appear in the 1938 annual, *The Ghosts of Mildew Manor*, was not a reprint, being especially drawn for this first edition. The originals for these now reside in the author's collection. The text stories were adaptations of popular films and were written by AP writers.

The next two editions (1939 and 1940) had the same format. But in 1941, as wartime paper shortages began to bite, the high-quality paper was replaced by some of a poorer standard; in addition, the number of pages was reduced by 48 to 112. Ironically, because of the sub-standard paper, which was thicker, the annual now appeared to have increased rather than decreased in size.

Fred Cordwell was an ebullient character who took great delight in some of his editorial responsibilities. In 1938 he wanted to feature *Film Fun's* resident detective, Jack Keen, in an exciting story in the 1939 annual. Cordwell commissioned a story from an AP writer and, requiring illustrations, decided to have photographs taken which would depict scenes from the story. He gave himself

Photographic title heading from *Film Fun Annual* (1939). 'Lewdroc' is editor Fred Cordwell's surname spelled backwards, minus an 'l'. Cordwell, a relation and staff took starring roles in this story.

LAUREL AND HARDY BRING TO YOU THE TRUE CHRISTMAS SPIRIT!

1. 'Twas Christmas Eve and the day before Christmas and nothing but the workhouse stared L. & H. in the whiskers. They were hard-up, fed-up, cold and unhappy, and it is needless to add that they felt very down in the dumps. Although they had roofs to their mouths they had not a roof to go above their heads.

2. Then Oliver Hardy, Esq., stopped, looked and listened, and he overheard the words spoken by the estate agent. "Hark! I hear what I hear, see?" cried Olly. "Unless my eyes mistake me, my ears are not playing me tricks. This is our tuni-opperty. Mildew Manor is the place for us." But Stanley had heard all, too.

3. The snow was coming down in bucketfuls, without the buckets luckily, and L. & H. were feeling very ker-old, especially Stan. Then Mildew Manor came into view and little Stanley suggested giving it the cold shoulder. "It looks gug-gug-ghostly!" cried Stan. "When I see a ghost I always think I'm seeing things."

4. But Olly would not back out then, although he wasn't in yet. "Follow me, I'll lead the way!" he cried. So through the front door waltzed our pair of prize lads, first opening it, of course. 'Twas indeed a dark and ghostly place and Stan began to shiver. "I hope we don't see any ghosts, Olly!" he cried.

5. "You've nothing to worry about, silly," replied Olly. "Be like me, brave and unafraid. Ooer! W-w-w-what w-w-w-was th-th-th-that?" As he spoke there sounded ghostly footprints from farther along the passage and Olly's usually cheery face turned from a pale pink to a paler pink. Stan was just as frightened.

6. Nearer and nearer came the footsteps. Then, out of the darkness came a wraith-like figure. It shimmered in the moonlight, whilst our pair shivered in the darkness. Slowly the phantom-form paced down the corrdor, and Stan and Olly were hard-pressed to stop their teeth chattering and knees ker-nocking.

A Laurel and Hardy Christmas adventure drawn by G. W. Wakefield especially for the first *Film Fun Annual* (1938). The addition of holly-bordered comic panels was a traditional feature at Christmas.

the principal role, assigned the part of Jack Keen to his brother-in-law and that of Jack Keen's assistant, Bob Trotter, to his Fleetway House assistant, Jack Le Grande (who eventually became an important Managing Editor at IPC). The story told how 'Jack Keen, the famous Baker Street 'tec, pits his wits against the cunning of Professor Lewdroc, an unscrupulous and merciless rogue'; it was entitled 'The Singular Case of Professor Lewdroc'. Few outside Fleetway House realised that Lewdroc (Cordwell spelled backwards and minus an 'l') was the editor of *Film Fun.*

Bill Wakefield died in 1942. In 1945, his son, Terry, demobbed after the war, who had worked at Fleetway House from 1927 until called up in 1940, began to work as a freelance artist for *Film Fun.*

Terry Wakefield's first opportunity to draw 'Laurel and Hardy' had been in 1937 for the *Laurel & Hardy Book of Wisecracks*, a free gift booklet which was given away in a bumper weekly issue. Fred Cordwell had been pleased to find that the younger Wakefield's drawings of the comedy duo were nearly indistinguishable from others done by his father, George. Not surprising, as the elder Wakefield had taught his son all he knew. After the elder Wakefield's death, 'Laurel and Hardy' had been drawn by at least two other artists: Norman Ward and Walter Bell. Both were good, but neither had the distinctive 'Wakefield' touch that Cordwell believed to be so essential. He therefore had no hesitation in offering his front page feature to Terry as soon as it was apparent that he was available.

Fred Cordwell's appearance as 'Professor Lewdroc' was not the only occasion he appeared in the pages of *Film Fun*. Terry Wakefield would often picture him in the 'Laurel and Hardy' sets as 'Eddie, the Happy Editor', who purportedly wrote the libretto which appeared beneath the pictures; on more than one occasion he would be giving 'our pals' a helping hand or sitting down to a hefty Christmas dinner with them. And dinners of the type that only appeared in *Film Fun*: Christmas puddings half covered with icing, with a piece of holly on top; glazed hams, 20 lb turkeys and mince pies accompanied by crackers and bottles of pop. The meals took place either at the 'Hotel Haveitonme' or the famous (to *Film Fun* readers) 'Hotel de Posh'.

Fred Cordwell died in 1948. The man and his personality were sorely missed. Jack Le Grande once talked of some of Cordwell's eccentricities, readily familiar to his artists: 'He would never allow an artist to include an octopus in any of the drawings, nor a man with a wooden leg, which were supposed to bring bad luck. And of course there was no alcohol and no cleavage. If an artist forgot and there was the slightest hint of cleavage, it was whitened out in the office.' A somewhat coarse character whose language could turn the air blue if things weren't to his liking, Cordwell also sported, incongruously, a longish cigarette holder which he would use with some sophistication as he was sitting at his desk in Fleetway House. Fred Cordwell was succeeded as editor by Phil Davis, one of his sub-editors; in later years it was Jack Le Grande. But neither had the editorial control exercised by Cordwell.

Film Fun Annual had been reduced to 96 pages in 1944 and remained in this size until 1956

Title illustration for 'Jane X'. Stories told by this 'Famous International Radio Scout' appeared in *Radio Fun* in the 1950s. The writer was actually G. M. Wilson, wife of artist Roy Wilson whose work appeared in many annuals.

Title illustration for 'Inspector Stanley' who, with the help of G. M. Wilson, wrote 'exclusively for *Radio Fun*' in the 1950s.

when the page count gradually began to increase. From year to year, different stars were introduced: Lancashire funny man George Formby (superbly drawn on different occasions by both Wakefields), the cowboy favourite Buck Jones, American comedians Abbott and Costello, Old Mother Riley and a host of others.

But by the late 1950s *Film Fun* was beginning to look very dated. Improvements were introduced: comic sections were printed in full colour and there were more 'action' stories and strips. In addition, the older generation of artists, among them Terry Wakefield, were replaced by European artists or by others deemed capable of drawing in a more modern style. Reg Parlett and Roy Wilson, leading artists on other comics, were commissioned to do important features.

The death of Oliver Hardy prompted the discontinuance of the 'Laurel and Hardy' feature, and stars like Terry-Thomas, Tony Hancock and Frankie Howard were used to replace them. But it was to no avail. The annual, which in its prime was a Christmas treat for tens of thousands, had had its day. The last edition was dated 1961.

Radio takes a bow

The Dandy Comic issued by D.C. Thomson on 4 December 1937, was the inspiration not only for *The Beano Comic* published the following year, on 15 October 1938, but also for two comics published by the Amalgamated Press: *Radio Fun* and the *Knock-Out*. Both comics had a long-running series of annuals, starting in 1940 and 1941 respectively.

As soon as AP management saw the immediate success of the *Dandy*, their plans to create some worthy opposition went into high gear. Aware of the impressive circulation of *Film Fun*, which used the stars of the cinema, it was inevitable that someone should think of *Radio Fun*, a comic that featured the big names of wireless. Acknowledging that the format of the *Dandy* had played a part in its success, AP similarly decided that it, too, should be half-tabloid size, and that it also should be published with a front page in full colour.

But something went amiss with this splendid idea. Rumour has it that, in the latter stages of development, it was decided to turn the idea into two comics, the other hopefully entitled *The Knock-Out Comic*, reserving for it half of the best features produced for *Radio Fun*. As a result, the first issue of *Radio Fun* had on page one 'George the Jolly Gee-Gee' (certainly never a radio star, and the character had been used a few years previously in *The Pilot*, a story paper for boys); and *Knock-Out*, when launched on 4 March 1939, had 'Our Crazy Broadcasters', an odd juxtaposition of features which was a result of the rush to get two new comics issued in a short time.

One of the stars of the *Knockout Annual* (1941–1961) was Billy Bunter, here drawn by artist Frank Minnitt.

All was resolved within a few months when 'Big-Hearted Arthur' (Arthur Askey) was moved from the back page to page one of *Radio Fun* and the *Knock-Out's* 'Crazy Broadcasters' were dropped in favour of 'Deed-a-Day-Danny', a young Boy Scout whose 'good deed' never turned out quite right in the end.

Radio Fun was edited by Stanley Gooch, and it was he who was also responsible for the first annual issued in the autumn of 1939. 'Hello, Folks,' began his cheerful introduction to the 128-page book, 'This is your Editor calling, and I am calling you to something that is going to give you hundreds of laughs and thrills.' The laughs were provided by Arthur Askey, later accompanied by Richard 'Stinker' Murdoch, Sandy Powell (catch phrase 'Well now you can see me!'), commediennes Ethel Revnell and Gracie West, the 'Lancashire Laughter King' Duggie Wakefield, and Tommy Trinder. The thrills were supplied by picture strips of James Cagney and cowboy Tom Keene; there were also written stories of 'action and adventure'.

Stanley Gooch's stable of humour artists included some of the best then working for the Amalgamated Press: Reg Parlett (who drew 'Big-Hearted Arthur' and 'Revnell and West'), George Parlett, 'Bertie' Brown and Roy Wilson. Wilson drew for Gooch 'Stymie and His Magic Wishbone'; the character was based on the black American radio favourite, Stymie Beard, who had been one of the original 'Our Gang' – the famous Hal Roach comedy film series. Stymie attempted to right wrongs with his Magic Wishbone. The trouble was that the Wishbone invariably misunderstood what was wanted, sometimes with happy results and sometimes with comically disastrous ones. This beautifully drawn and very funny comic strip appeared regularly in the *Radio Fun* annual throughout its twenty-one year run.

Tommy Handley, the star of one of the most popular radio programmes of the 1940s, *It's That Man Again (ITMA)*, was for many years very popular in comic strip form as well. When Handley died in 1949, Bertie Brown had completed the cover painting for the 1950 annual, which showed a caricature of Handley standing in front of a large wireless. This had to be hastily redone, replacing Handley with 'Have-a-Go!' star Wilfred Pickles. Although no Handley editions of the 1950 annual were printed, one 'dummy' copy (bound around a girls' annual) was found by a collector in a bookshop many years later. Almost certainly the only copy in existence, its unique nature makes it one of the most collectable items.

During the 1950s, some of *Radio Fun's* most popular features were the stories. 'Inspector Stanley' of Scotland Yard ('The Man With a Thousand Secrets') was mostly written by G. M. Wilson (wife of Roy Wilson) who also contributed many of the adventures of 'Jane X', a 'Famous International Radio Scout'; 'The Happy

Hauntings of Goofy the Ghost' ('You'll Shiver and Shake With Laughter') was written in the main by Sid Rositter, who served for a time as the editor of *Radio Fun* after Stanley Gooch had died in 1958. Other stories were written by freelance contributors.

The last *Radio Fun* annual was the 1960 edition; inside were Benny Hill, Cardew ('The Cad') Robinson, Norman Wisdom, Lonnie Donegan, Stan Stennett, Hylda Baker, Issy Bonn and the Beverley Sisters. The last issue of the weekly *Radio Fun* was dated 18 February 1961, but long beforehand it had been decided that due to poor circulation, it was to be 'joining *Buster* comic', the usual euphemism for a comic facing the axe. As a result there were no more *Radio Fun* annuals.

'Knockout' and 'Whizzbang'

One reason for the fall in readership was undoubtedly the archrival of radio – television. If *Radio Fun* was a logical follow-on to *Film Fun*, then *TV Fun* was a natural successor to both. The comic was published in 1953 and an annual followed in 1958, lasting for four editions. Although slightly smaller in size and containing more colour than *Radio Fun*, *TV Fun* was distinguishable only by its different stars: Max Bygraves, Sally Barnes, Jimmy Edwards, Shirley Eaton and Derek Roy.

No. 1 of *The Knock-Out Comic* was published on 4 March 1939, and was edited by Percy Montague Haydon. The annual followed in 1940, dated 1941, and was entitled the *Knock-Out Fun Book*. The cover painting was by Hugh McNeill, who was responsible for many of the annual's cover paintings during the following years. McNeill was also the artist of two of the best-known British comic strips to appear in the 1940s and 1950s: 'Our Ernie' and 'Deed-a-Day Danny'.

Hugh McNeill was a welcome addition to the team of artists being established by 'Monty' Haydon. The first comics publisher to use McNeill's work had been D. C. Thomson: his drawings appeared in *The Beano Comic* from the first issue and in the *Beano* annuals in the early 1940s. It was one of Haydon's sub-editors, Leonard Matthews, who was responsible for talking the artist into working for AP comics, although possibly he didn't need much persuading: AP payment rates were, and always have been, higher than those of the Scottish publisher.

In the first year of publication, Hugh McNeill worked on three popular comic strips, all prominently featured in the early annuals: 'Simon, the Simple Sleuth', 'Deed-a-Day Danny' and 'Our Ernie'. But it was 'Danny' and 'Ernie' who were to earn him a place in comic history. 'Deed-a-Day Danny' was a boy scout determined to do a good deed. It was a 'formula' strip which always ended in the deed misfiring and Danny being angrily pursued by the recipients of his 'favours'.

'Our Ernie' was a lad from Wigan who ended up in the most extraordinary situations: reading a book about life in the Stone Age would result in his being magically whisked back through time; a story about pirates would mean that Ernie would soon be found fighting alongside seventeenth-century buccaneers. The only formula for this comic strip was that Ernie should be home in his Wigan back-street in time for tea. His Dad's comment on Ernie's latest adventure is legend: 'Daft, I call it,' he'd say, puffing away at his pipe as he glanced over his newspaper.

The Knock-Out Comic's and therefore the *Knock-Out Fun Book's* other main humour artist was Frank Minnitt. Minnitt was responsible for several comic strips but his best known was 'Billy Bunter' ('The Fattest

This *Sexton Blake Annual* (a paperback) issued in the early 1940s shows Blake, his assistant Tinker and hound Pedro, as depicted by artist Eric Parker, doyen of all Blake illustrators.

Schoolboy on Earth'), a feature he drew continuously from 1939 until his death in 1958. Minnitt's art style perfectly suited Frank Richards's famous character who bore the distinction of appearing in every edition of the annual.

Sub-editor Leonard Matthews became editor of the *Knock-Out* publications in 1948. Matthews had a penchant for historical adventure strips and a preference for two artists in particular: Eric Parker and Derek Eyles. The annuals under his editorship are full of their work; Matthews also was responsible for commissioning work from artists not previously associated with the comic strip: Sep. E. Scott and H.M. Brock were two of his most notable successess; in addition, he used Geoff Campion, Patrick Nicolle, Reg Bunn and Ted Holmes.

Matthews' heroes were those of the classics: highwaymen, outlaws, cowboys, pirates, musketeers and detectives, and some of the stories published were scripted by him. But he liked his 'funnies' men, too (something of an artist himself, he'd drawn 'Daffy, the Cowboy 'Tec' for the *Knock-Out Fun Book* in the 1940s), and always ensured that there was an equal balance between action and laughter features.

'Sexton Blake and the High Speed Pirates' was the first adventure of the famous detective to appear as a comic strip in an annual. It was drawn by Jos. Walker (who drew the 'Buck Jones' picture strip in *Film Fun*), and appeared in the *Knock-Out Fun Book* for 1941. Blake, drawn by a succession of artists, was popular enough to appear in many of the *Knock-Out* annuals and, indeed, was still appearing in 1960s editions.

The *Knock-Out Fun Book*, always called the *Knockout Annual* by readers, was not officially given that title until 1957. In its twenty-one year run, there were few changes, the most significant being those brought about by Leonard Matthews. But it remained quite different from the other Amalgamated Press annuals on sale; more of a cousin than a sister publication to those edited by Stanley Gooch or Fred Cordwell. It always maintained its identity and used some excellent artists. As well as those already mentioned, there was Reg Wooton, whose work also appeared in the national Press, Eric Roberts, A.J. Kelly, Fred Robinson and Michael Hubbard.

Triumph was one of the first story papers to increase its comic strip content. The weekly began on 18 October, 1924 and contained all text stories until 1939, when strips were introduced. Interestingly, one of the first was 'Superman', which had just begun to be published in the USA in *Action*

Chips Annual: a complete set of three editions – 1939, 1940, 1941.

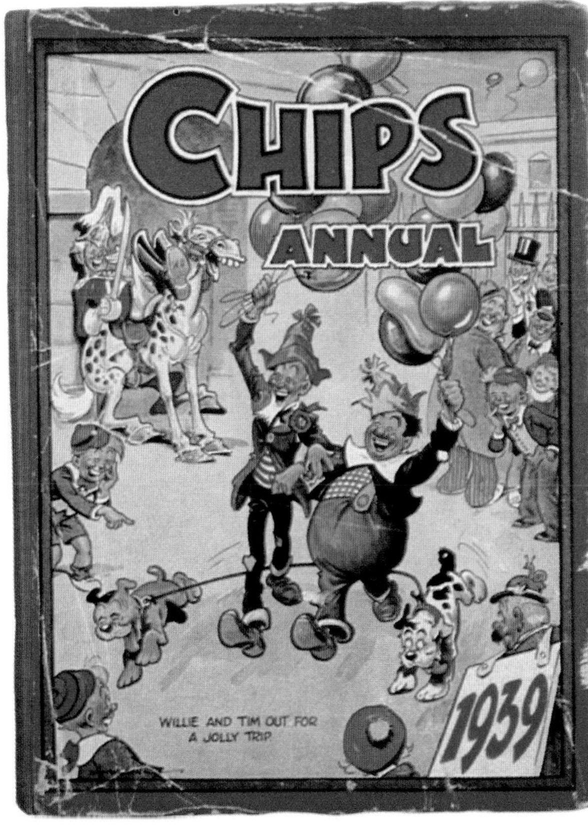

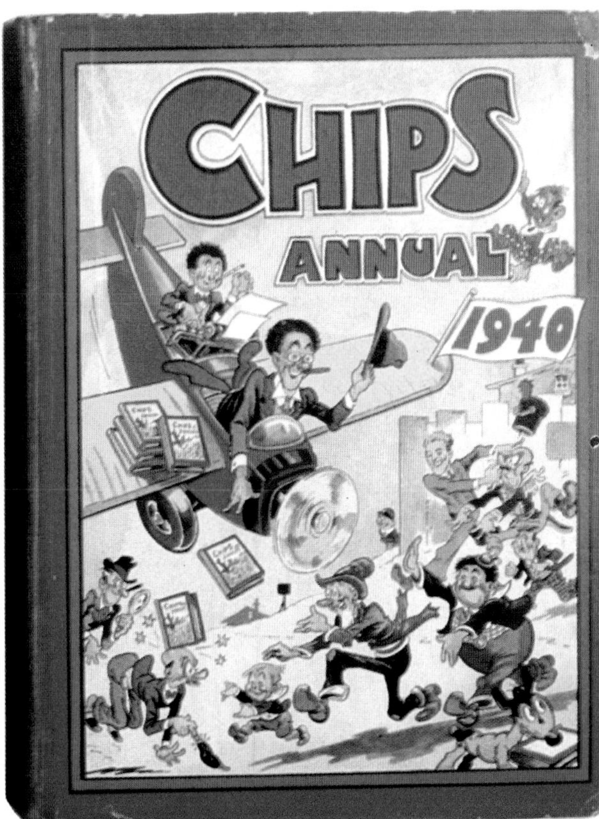

Triumph Annual: first edition 1937.

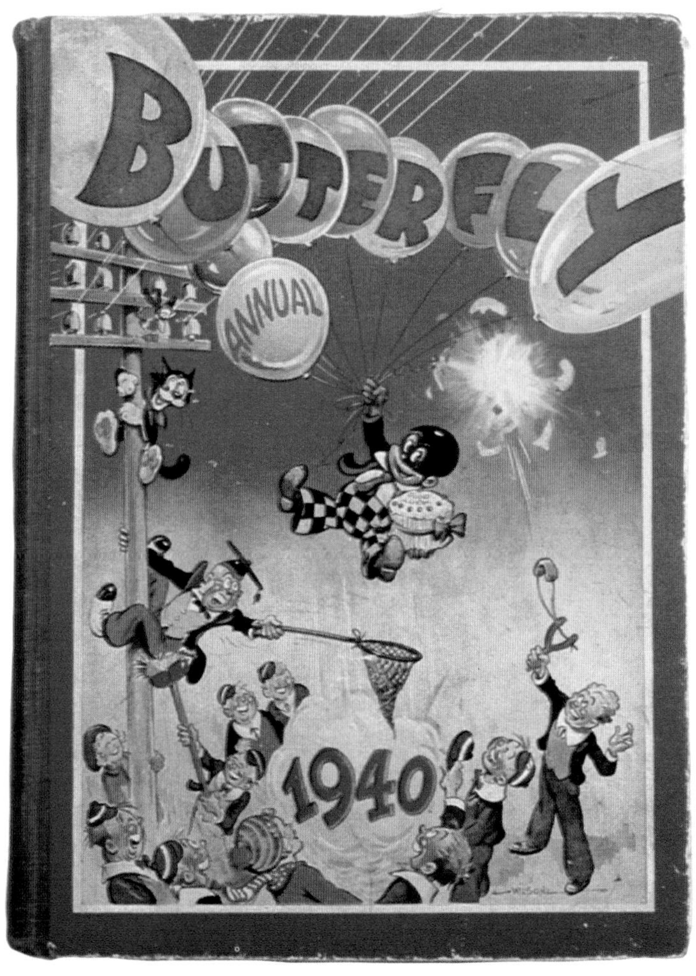

Butterfly Annual: 1940.

Film Fun Annual: first edition 1938.

Radio Fun Annual: first edition 1940.

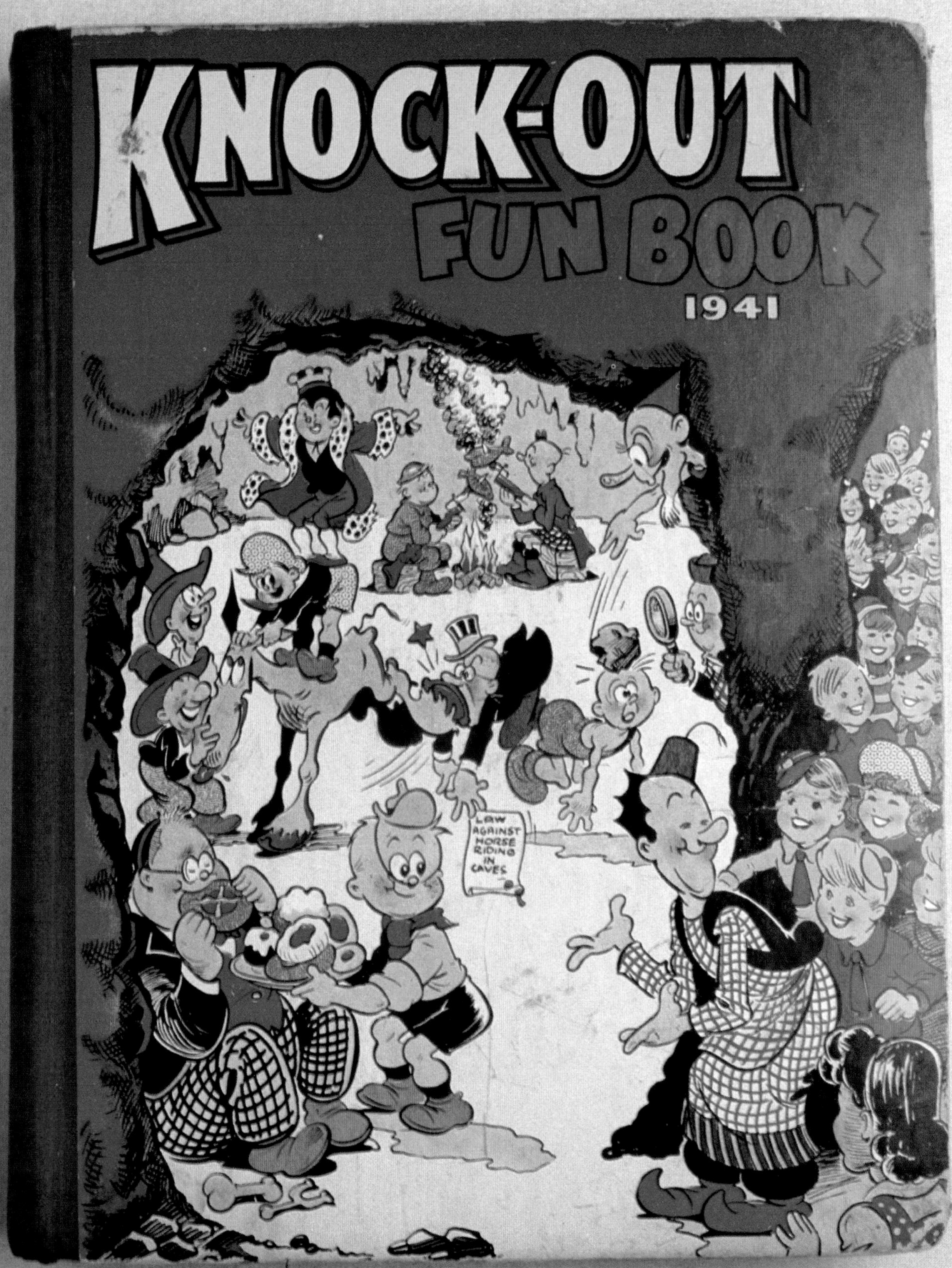

Knock-Out Fun Book: first edition 1941.

Comics, and which was reprinted in *Triumph* in black and white. Others were 'Derrickson Dene', drawn by Nat Brand, and 'John Irons', by Stanley White. *Triumph* bore similarities to *Champion* and perhaps this was understandable as they had the same editor: Reginald Eves. *Triumph* annuals were issued for the years 1937–1941 and are uncommon. The weekly was discontinued in May, 1940.

A now very rare annual published by Amalgamated Press was the jauntily titled *Whizzbang Comics*, which was issued for 1942 and 1943. This book was a departure for Fleetway House at a time when most annuals were being discontinued.

'Please take your seats for 104 pages of Fun and Thrills,' read the caption on page one. What was this new annual with no 'weekly' to support it? It looked as though AP had been planning more than the *Knockout* and *Radio Fun* as a suitable riposte to its Scottish rivals; or perhaps such a comic had been planned but, due to wartime restrictions, had subsequently been cancelled. On the other hand, *Whizzbang Comics* could have been a package of reprints under a new title, and simply a device for avoiding the then tightening rules governing the use of paper.

Certainly, *Whizzbang Comics* had more than its fair share of reprinted material. Almost all of the comic strips, drawn by Roy Wilson, Bertie Brown, Ray Bailey and Reg Perrott, had previously appeared in weekly issues of *Sparkler, Butterfly, Golden, Puck* and *Jolly*. But there was also an improvement: the thick, almost card-like paper used for other AP annuals in the 1930s was gone. In its place was a soft, coarse paper which gave the books a much better 'feel'.

The annual was a lively addition to a contracting market; it is a pity that so very few copies of either edition exist today. Possibly, because of the existing restrictions, each had a very low print run; the fact that most children's publications ended up in wartime paper drives doubtless contributed to the scarcity.

No other new annuals were published by AP in the 1940s. The main titles continued to be *Tiger Tim, Rainbow, Playbox, Radio Fun, Film Fun, Tip Top* and the *Knock-Out Fun Book*. The war and its restrictions curtailed the activities of all publishers (paper rationing was still in force long after 1945).

Lions and Tigers

In 1950, Hulton Press had astonished everyone with its new 'Strip Cartoon Weekly', *Eagle*, a high-quality photogravure comic which immediately received the

Whizzbang Comics (1943): the only edition traced of this rare wartime annual.

'The Jungle Robot' (*Lion Annual*: 1954) soon became familiarly known as 'Robot Archie'; his popularity has lasted well into the 1980s.

Lion Annual: first edition 1954.

support of the establishment, giving it a huge circulation; parents rushed to buy this exciting new publication for their children. At last the dark years of the 1940s could be forgotten; here was a new and brighter decade, with the hint of a rosier future to come in the adventures of 'Dan Dare, Pilot of the Future' (see Chapter 5), on the front page of *Eagle*.

AP quickly realised that the main attraction to readers of *Eagle* was 'Dan Dare', which was impeccably scripted and drawn by Frank Hampson and his team of artists. Fleetway House decided that it had to create not only its own version of *Eagle*, but also a rival to 'Dan Dare'.

Hulton had chosen the King of the Air as the symbol for its new comic; AP therefore had to come up with an equally strong title, and it did – *Lion*. It was launched as a weekly comic in 1952 and the first annual was dated 1954. The competition for Dan Dare turned out to be no competition at all; more of an alternative. He was 'Captain Condor', a young space pilot on the run from a dictator who ruled the solar system. The artist was Ron Forbes, and the drawing was crude in comparison with that of its rival. Most of the stories, told in pictures, were by Frank S. Pepper, an experienced freelance writer who did much work for Fleetway House either under his own name, one of many pseudonyms or anonymously. 'Captain Condor' lasted for several years and the character was pictured on the cover of the *Lion Annual* 1954–58.

Lion had two other very popular characters: 'Robot Archie', initially billed as 'The Jungle Robot', and 'Sandy Dean', a schoolboy. 'Robot Archie' was certainly the more enduring. His appeal has lasted well into the Eighties and his reprinted adventures have found a large market overseas. 'Sandy Dean' lasted for several years, disappearing only when the readership lost interest in stories about public schools.

The *Lion Annual* was in continuous publication until a few years ago, the later editions usually featuring Robot Archie on the cover. In the late Sixties, due to a take-over of Hulton by IPC (formerly Amalgamated Press), the weekly *Lion* comic absorbed *Eagle*, although the *Eagle Annual* continued to be published by IPC until the mid-Seventies.

Lion never achieved the huge circulation of *Eagle* – of which, reputedly, a million copies an issue were printed in the early Fifties – but it was successful, and it did beget a companion: *Tiger*, 'The Sport and Adventure Picture Story Weekly', issued as a weekly comic in 1954. The first annual was dated 1957.

Adventure in the *Tiger Annual* was partly supplied by borrowing old favourite Rockfist Rogan from another AP publication, *The Champion*. Again, Frank S. Pepper was the author of many of the stories used. Sport, which also included boxing, motor racing and swimming, was represented principally by Roy Race, star of Melchester Rovers and otherwise known as 'Roy of the Rovers'.

'Roy of the Rovers' has proved itself the most popular sporting picture strip in the history of comics. In the early days it was written by Stewart Colwyn (another pen name of Frank Pepper) and drawn by Joe Colquhoun. The feature was popular from the very beginning and, as

The stories in *Tiger Annual* placed emphasis on sport and the covers of each edition reflected this.

Rockfist Rogan, RAF, Flying Ace of *Champion* and later, *Tiger*. Written by Frank S. Pepper (using the pseudonym Hal Wilton); this title illustration by R. Simmons.

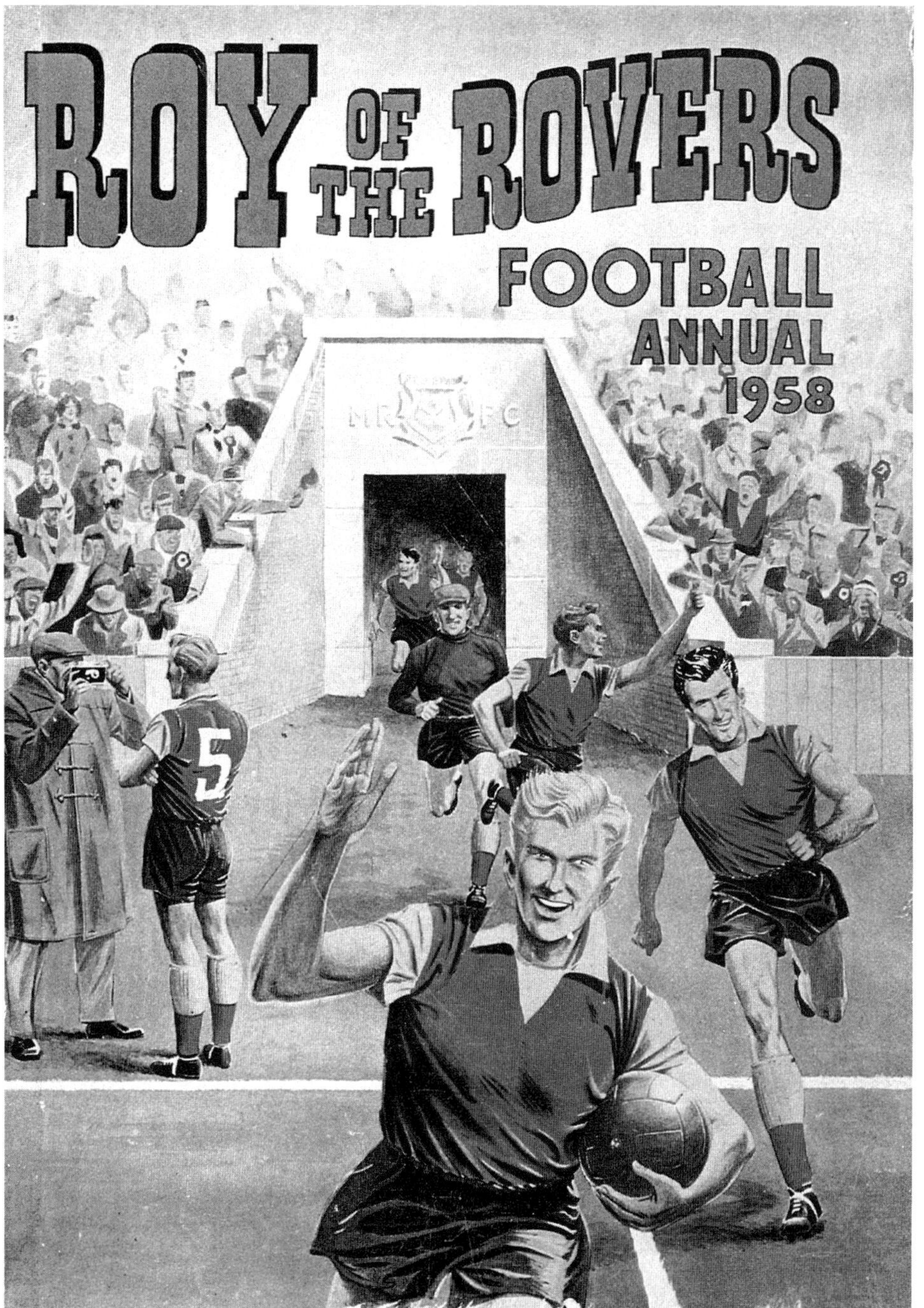

Roy of the Rovers Football Annual: first edition 1958.

well as appearing in the *Tiger Annual*, was in 1958 given an annual all to itself: the *Roy of the Rovers Football Annual*.

Thanks to enthusiastic editors, especially Barrie Tomlinson, 'Roy and the Rovers' has gone from strength to strength. The weekly *Tiger* comic has now been discontinued but another title, *Roy of the Rovers*, was launched some years ago and maintains a healthy circulation, looking set to do so for many years go come. The *Roy of the Rovers Annual* is still a best-seller every Christmas, sales boosted no doubt by many fathers who enjoyed Roy's adventures when they were young.

Both the *Lion* and *Tiger* annuals had 'companions'. In the case of *Lion*, these were usually 'one-off' publications such as *The Lion Book of Speed* (1963) and *The Lion Book of Motor Racing* (1970). But *Tiger* had the *Tiger Book of Soccer Stars* which was an annual issued 1970–4, and the *Tiger Book of Sport*, published for the years 1978–81.

CHAPTER 4

The Annuals of D.C. Thomson and John Leng

Amalgamated Press (AP) had the market for comics, story-papers and annuals virtually all to itself until 1921 when it began to face stiff competition from D.C. Thomson & Co., a Scottish firm which had offices in Dundee.

D.C. Thomson was established in 1905 and for many years its main publications were two newspapers, *The Courier* and *The Argus*; but as circulation grew, the company rapidly expanded its line of publications. The firm set its sights on the youth market; a series of highly successful boys' papers was launched and, by the late 1930s, at least a dozen different and popular children's annuals were being issued by D. C. Thomson.

The annuals published by D.C. Thomson are the most sought after of all, particularly the *Dandy* and *Beano*, which are two of the three 'most collected' annuals (the other is the Daily Express *Rupert* annual). Until 1965, it was Thomson's policy not to place a date on the cover of any of its book publications. Exactly why is unclear, but it was probably due to a sensible business practice of giving them a longer shelf-life. Annuals are traditionally dated the year following publication, issued in September, and marked down or returned to the publisher if they have not sold by January. An annual without a date could, theoretically, be kept on sale for much longer.

The undated pre-1965 editions led to much anxiety and confusion on the part of collectors. But in 1975 the writers and researchers W.O.G. Lofts and D.J. Adley compiled and published the 'Identification Guide to the D.C. Thomson & John Leng Children's Annuals 1921–1965' (reissued 1986 by Yesterday's Paper, 5 Cornhill, Wellington, Somerset). This useful booklet gives a description of each annual cover, preceded by the publication date, and is an invaluable guide for every serious collector and bookseller.

The first children's annual to be published by D.C. Thomson was the *Billy & Bunny Book* in 1921 for 1922. This was aimed at very young children and, although it never achieved the status of being a 'national favourite', it was regularly published every year until 1941 when it ceased due to the war. Subsequently, it appeared for at least another three editions, dated 1947–9.

Another annual for the young was the *Willie Waddle Book*. This was issued for the years 1928–1949, missing some years during the Forties. It was sometimes published in softcover as well as hardback.

'The Big Five'

On 17 September 1921, Thomson launched *Adventure*, a weekly story-paper for boys. Stories were of detectives (the most popular being Dixon Hawke, who would later appear in his own publication), sporting heroes and daring young men; yarns were set in far-flung corners of the globe. 'Adventure is the breath of life,' breezed the editor in the first issue, going on to promise 'stirring developments' in future weeks, as well as exciting up-to-date tales of 'Sid Osborne, the Wireless Kid' and 'Non-Stop Ned, the Daring Young Motorist'.

The *Adventure* was itself a stirring development considering what else was available at the time: *The Magnet, The Gem* (both AP) and several others contained little else but stories about public schools. Other publications which did feature adventure stories, *Chums, Boy's Own Paper, Union Jack* and many more, although very popular, lacked the down-to-earth, often sensationalist approach of the Thomson paper. Stories in *Adventure* were not necessarily about public schoolboys or about 'chaps doing their duty for King and Country' but were vigorous, imaginative tales about ordinary lads in extraordinary situations. It was a market previously untapped and the paper was an immediate success. Thomson followed it with four other long-running boys' papers, all in the same mould: *The Rover* (4 March 1922); *The Wizard* (23 September 1922); *The Skipper* (6 September 1930) and *The Hotspur* (2 September 1933). With the *Adventure*, all were known collectively as 'The Big Five'.

Title page of *Adventureland* (1924), the first D. C. Thomson story paper annual. © D. C. Thomson & Co. Ltd.

Although similar, each of the papers managed to maintain its own identity; a paper was readily identifiable by its resident heroes or the types of stories featured. The *Adventure* had the detective, Dixon Hawke; the *Wizard*, 'The Wolf of Kabul and his assistant, Chung', a native who was quick to leap into a fight to 'crack some skulls' with his 'clicky-ba' (cricket bat) which he would swing around his head and use ferociously as a weapon. It also had Wilson, an athlete who lived in the open on the Yorkshire Moors, whose diet was herbs and berries, whose appearance was youthful but who was in fact about 120 years old. The *Skipper* had a bent for 'scientific' stories and the *Hotspur* was best known for its 'school' stories, the most popular of which were the 'Red Circle' tales. Red Circle teachers and pupils became as familiar to schoolboys as any from Greyfriars or St Jim's, the schools of the Amalgamated Press. Indeed, in a survey of children's reading published in 1940 ('What Do Boys and Girls Read?: A.J. Jenkinson) the Thomson 'Big Five' head the list of favourite papers read by boys. The Thomson stories may have contained many 'gimmicks' but they certainly paid no homage to convention and were, above all, exciting. It is this that caused all of the five papers to sell by the million, week after week for several decades.

The *Adventure* had its own annual published in 1923. Undated, as were all of Thomson's book publications for some forty years, it was entitled *Adventure Land*. Priced at five shillings, it contained in its 188 pages more than a dozen stories, photo-picture features, the occasional comic strip and miscellaneous features such as puzzles and tricks and woodlore. Its format was 7½ × 10¼ in (19 × 26 cm) and it had thick board covers, on the front of which was pasted a coloured picture, its subject an outdoors adventure topic (a castaway on a desert island, hiking through the mountains, etc.). There were six coloured plates, all depicting exciting 'action' scenes and, in the early years, endpapers.

As in the weekly, each story in the annual was preceded by a 'block-heading' line drawing with several scenes from the story pictured on subsequent pages. One marked difference between the weekly publication and the annual was that the stories were credited with an author's name and illustrations were frequently signed. This did not happen in any periodical issued by Thomson, as the firm was notorious for its reticence in these matters. The writers' names have been seized upon by present-day collectors and devotees of story-papers, but it has been to no avail: well-used names like 'Arthur Radcliffe', 'Falconer Mackenzie', R.M. Fraser', 'Foster Wood' and others were pseudonyms for freelance writers, editorial teams, or both; it is widely known that many of Thomson's characters and stories were the result of story and staff conferences. Illustrators' names were no doubt real but the practice of allowing artists to sign their work

Title page of *Rover Book for Boys* (1942). © D. C. Thomson & Co. Ltd.

was soon dropped: to this day, artwork appearing throughout the Thomson publications is still uncredited. Fictional authors were obviously used to give the books a necessary appearance of quality which might help to persuade a parent or relative to purchase the volume.

The first *Rover* annual, *The Rover Book for Boys*, was for 1926. Quite different in size to its companions, the book was a dumpy 8¼ × 6¾ in (21 × 17 cm) with 188 thick, stiff pages. It was priced at two shillings and sixpence, half the cost of *Adventure Land*, and had but one colour plate, a frontispiece. The *Rover Book for Boys* was published every year until 1942, discontinued throughout the paper shortages of the 1940s, and then re-emerged after the war for several editions.

The *Skipper Book for Boys* was issued barely a year after the weekly comic had begun. It was identical in every way to the *Rover Book for Boys*. Also undated, the 1932 first edition had a typical 'wrap-around' colour picture on its covers, of two laughing sailors seated on turtles racing up a beach. The weekly *Skipper* was

Mr. Smugg and some of the pupils of Red Circle School, the cast and scene of a famous *Hotspur* series. © D. C. Thomson & Co. Ltd.

the only one of the 'Big Five' to fall victim to paper rationing (and possibly circulation problems too). Its last issue was dated 1 February 1941, although there were several editions of the annual after this; the last to be printed was in the late 1940s.

Both the *Rover* and *Skipper* annuals abandoned their earlier format after a few years to try a new over-sized approach, 8¼ × 12¼ in (21 × 31 cm). After the war, however, the books became the size of all other annuals on sale.

The Hotspur Book for Boys (there was never any doubt as to the sex of the readership of the Thomson 'Big Five') was first published in 1934 for 1935. The cover showed a schoolmaster, known as 'The Big Stiff', amid mountain scenery, teaching boys arithmetic with the aid of a blackboard. On the board was what appeared to be a sum, but a sum which didn't add up! It was typical of the Thomson style: the numbers were prominent enough for most would-be purchasers of the book to do a quick mental check on the addition and find it wrong. Naturally, the reason for the error could be found only by reading the story inside!

The Hotspur Book was in yet another size, 7½ × 10 in (19 × 25 cm). It had 126 pages, one colour plate (more in later editions), many full-page line illustrations and it cost two shillings and sixpence. The stories, like those in the weekly, were mainly about schools, with the Red Circle series being the most prominent. Illustrations were, by this period, unsigned but it is known that one contributor was James Walker, notable for his clean, robust style. Another great *Hotspur* favourite which appeared in the annual was 'The Iron Teacher', a robot in charge of a class of schoolboys.

The fifth annual of the 'Big Five', *The Wizard Book for Boys*, was first issued for 1936. The cover illustration was in 'comic strip' style, showing a party of fifty or so boys enjoying themselves amid the mayhem of a camping holiday. It was drawn by Chick Gordon, one of the first comic artists to draw for the Thomson boys' papers. He specialised in this type of large 'one-panel' scene showing lots of activity. As early as 1922 he was drawing 'The Cheery Chinks' for the *Rover* weekly before also starting 'Spadger's Isle' in the *Wizard* weekly in 1930. Interestingly, the *Wizard* annual contained a greater number of comic strips than any of its contemporaries, which reflected the developing interest in this area. The long-running favourite from the weekly, 'Spadger's Isle', was present (the setting was a South Sea Island inhabited by a sailor, Spadger, his young campanion and a tribe of natives). There was also 'Nero and Zero' (two ancient Romans), 'Softie Simpkins' and 'Our Artist at Work', all three of which were drawn by Allan Morley. Morley's work had begun regularly to appear in the Thomson story-papers from the mid-1920s onwards. He had supplied work for several Amalgamated Press weeklies (*Funny Wonder, Jester, Merry & Bright*) before becoming a Thomson staff artist. As well as his work for *The Wizard Book for Boys*, he drew 'Nosey Parker' for the *Rover Book* and had strips appearing in all of the 'Big Five' weeklies. His work was soon to be in even greater demand for the two new publications planned by the Dundee firm: *The Dandy Comic* and *The Beano Comic*.

The Wizard Book was identical in size and format to *The Hotspur Book*. The one colour plate, the frontispiece, showed an enthralling scene: it pictured a huge idol, behind which was a man with a machine-gun firing through its mouth into the jaws of a monstrous snake, curled and poised to strike; in the background stood a group of sinister looking Orientals. The scene was from the splendidly entitled story, 'Idol Talk', the heroes of which were 'Jock Pyke' (a Britisher who had

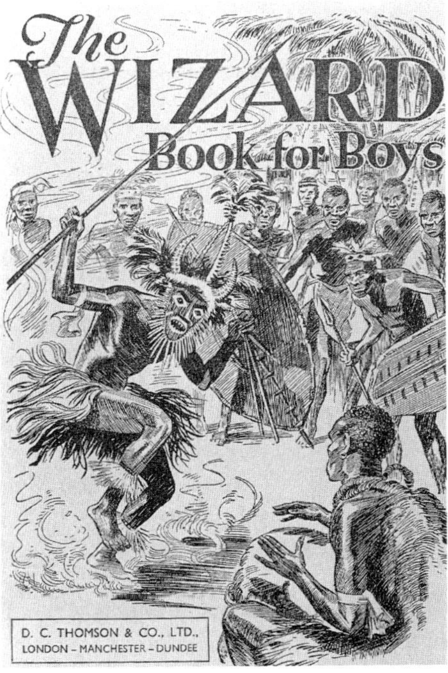

Title page of *The Wizard Book for Boys* (1936). © D. C. Thomson & Co. Ltd.

spent so many years under the tropical sun that his face was 'swarthy almost to the colour of mahogany') and his servant 'Ming' (a tough little Chinaman who 'with his inscrutable mask-like face, was a perfect fiend in a fight'). Pyke was a force to be reckoned with. 'At the slightest sign of danger' he 'would have brought his six feet of bull-necked manhood erect like a released spring'. It was a tale in the grand tradition of 'The Wolf of Kabul' stories, so popular in the weekly *Wizard* throughout the Thirties. Indeed, it seems strange, considering the huge following the 'Wolf' stories had, that a story was not included within this annual. The equally popular stories of 'Wilson' the super athlete were not present either, but this was because he had not yet made his debut; the first Wilson story appeared in the weekly *Wizard* in 1943.

Dandy Monster Comic (1940). © D. C. Thomson & Co. Ltd.

Thomson also published a *Wizard* 'Summer' annual in the Thirties. This was *The Wizard Holiday Book for Boys* (1938 and 1939); it had paper covers and cost one shilling. Publication of the *Wizard Book* was sporadic throughout the Forties, the last edition being issued for 1949.

Dandy Monster Comic (1941). © D. C. Thomson & Co. Ltd.

'Beano' and 'Dandy'

Amalgamated Press comics such as *Funny Wonder, Jester, Jingles*, etc. may have outsold all their rivals throughout the Thirties but then, there was no effective competition. Certainly, the 'Big Five' were the favourites of many a schoolboy, but they were catering to a different market. The Thomson story-papers were in competition with AP papers like the *Magnet* and the *Gem*. This must have been worrying for the editors of these papers but the comics had nothing to fear from north of the border. Or had they? On 4 December 1937, Thomson launched *The Dandy Comic* and, seven months later, on 30 July

Dandy Monster Comic (1942). © D. C. Thomson & Co. Ltd.

1938, *The Beano Comic*. Both were hugely successful and the Amalgamated Press no longer had the field to itself.

The *Beano* and the *Dandy* were as vigorous and brash as the 'Big Five'. Both were about half the size of their AP counterparts. Each had 28 pages, the front one in full colour. The *Beano*'s picture strip stars were 'Lord Snooty', 'Morgyn the Mighty' (who had previously appeared in the weekly *Rover*), 'Big Fat Joe' and 'Pansy Potter'. The *Dandy* had 'Korky the Cat', 'Desperate Dan', 'Keyhole Kate', 'Our Gang' (adapted from the film shorts produced by Hal Roach for MGM), 'Hungry Horace' and 'Invisible Dick' (who had also appeared in the weekly *Rover*; the writer credited, Frank Topham, was also the author of a book of the same name, published by Thomson in 1926).

The two comics, with their all-too-often crude drawings and sometimes vulgar humour were, in comparison with the Fleetway House comics, enticingly fresh and non-conventional to the children who bought them. All the more remarkable, then, that the *Beano* and *Dandy* and many of their characters have become national institutions. Neither paper has made any significant changes during the last half-century. Lord Snooty still appears, as does Desperate Dan; the comics have become more conventional than anything else sold at the local newsagents.

Encouraged by the success of the *Beano* and *Dandy*, Thomson issued *The Magic Comic* on 22 July 1939. This was aimed at a slightly younger age group but, although similar in format to its companions, it did not do well. The last issue was numbered 80, a rare failure for the successful Scottish firm although, in all fairness, it was undoubtedly due to the war-time paper shortages that killed off so many fine comics.

All three of the new comics had annuals issued: *The Dandy*

Dandy Monster Comic (1944). © D. C. Thomson & Co. Ltd.

Dandy Monster Comic (1945). © D. C. Thomson & Co. Ltd.

Dandy Monster Comic (1946). © D. C. Thomson & Co. Ltd.

Monster Comic (1939), *The Beano Book* (1940) and *The Magic Fun Book* (1941). The *Dandy* annual followed the contemporary vogue for titling any 'outsize' publication 'monster', and comic it certainly was, containing as it did 128 pages of 'Cartoons' and 'Picture Stories' and, in addition, the occasional written story. Artwork was unsigned but many illustrators were easily recognisable by their style of drawing: 'Korky the Cat' (James Crighton, who was to draw the strip for twenty-five years), 'Keyhole Kate', 'Hungry Horace' and 'Freddy the Fearless Fly' (Allan Morley), 'Jimmy and His Grockle' (James Clark), 'Bamboo Town' (Chic Young) and 'Boneless Bill' (Frank Minnitt).

There was one artist, however, who did manage occasionally (and, later, always) to sign his work. His name was Dudley Dexter Watkins. Watkins, like his contemporary, Roy Wilson (who worked exclusively for AP) was a comic artist of genius. He was a talented draughtsman who, it was said, 'could draw so fast it was like writing a letter'. But it wasn't just his drawing that made him special; it was his subjects too. He was able to combine the familiar and the bizarre in a way that approached surrealism. His 'Desperate Dan' (which he drew without a break for 1,454 issues of the weekly *Dandy* and in some thirty *Dandy* annuals) combined a Scottish town with the American Wild West of the 1880s. Tramcars, chimney sweeps, motor-cars and factory chimneys were cheek by jowl with horses, cacti, sheriffs and other Western attributes. Dan was also famous for his diet of 'cow pie': an enormous hunk of pastry and meat which always had a pair of horns on top and a tail appearing from its side.

Dudley Watkins was also one of the most prolific artists working for comics. He was responsible for other *Dandy* strips and drew as well for the *Magic* and the *Beano*. Nor was it only on the 'funny' side of the comics that he showed his genius; he was also adept at adventure picture strips, which, because of his personal interest in the Middle Ages, more often than not had a historical slant. In the 1940s two of his most popular *Dandy* features were 'Danny Longlegs', the adventures of a ten-foot schoolboy, and 'Peter Pye', a cook to the lord of a castle; both were set in medieval England. *The Dandy Monster Comic* was retitled *The Dandy Book* with the 1953 edition and it has carried this name since then. The annual has been published every year, without exception, since the first edition was issued in 1939.

The Beano Book was published in the autumn of 1939 for 1940. On the front cover it showed another character who has since become well known from John O'Groats to Land's End – Pansy Potter. The title of this comic strip betrays the Scottish origins of the comic: 'Pansy Potter, the Strong Man's Daughter', if read with anything other than a Scottish accent, has no 'ring' to it at all; but, if tried again in a suitable Gaelic brogue, with its missing 't's, 'Pansy Po-ur, the Strong Man's Do-ur', suddenly takes on an unexpected appeal. The annual's contents included several 'Lord Snooty' comic pages by Dudley Watkins, 'Big Eggo' (the front-page star of the weekly *Beano* for many years) by Reg Carter (a talented illustrator who was also well known as a postcard artist) and, naturally, Pansy Potter, sometimes drawn by Hugh McNeill, who later became renowned for his 'Our Ernie' and 'Deed-a-Day Danny' strips for AP's *Knockout* comic.

In later years Dudley Watkins was the illustrator of another picture strip with an historical angle which appeared in several editions of the *Beano* annual. 'Jimmy and His Magic Patch' was the tale of a schoolboy who had his torn trousers repaired with a piece of a Gypsy's Magic Carpet. A mere

Left *Dandy Monster Comic* (1947). © D. C. Thomson & Co. Ltd.

Right *Dandy Monster Comic* (1948). © D. C. Thomson & Co. Ltd.

Left *Dandy Monster Comic* (1949). © D. C. Thomson & Co. Ltd.

Right *Dandy Monster Comic* (1950). © D. C. Thomson & Co. Ltd.

Left *Dandy Monster Comic* (1951). © D. C. Thomson & Co. Ltd.

Right *Dandy Monster Comic* (1952). © D. C. Thomson & Co. Ltd.

The Beano Book (1941). © D. C. Thomson & Co. Ltd.

The Beano Book (1942) © D. C. Thomson & Co. Ltd.

wish from the lad was enough to cause the Magic Patch to whisk Jimmy back to the days of Robin Hood, Queen Elizabeth, the Battle of Hastings or any ancient time period. Watkins brought all his considerable knowledge of historical costume to this picture story and it would seem that he encouraged schoolboys to take interest in a subject that has always proved a challenge to teachers.

When the *Magic* comic was discontinued, the annual also ceased to be published. From the 1943 edition the *Magic Fun Book* was amalgamated with *The Beano Book*, the title changing to *The Magic-Beano Book*. *Magic* characters were also included within the annual and, from 1943–50, the cover picture showed both Big Eggo, the *Beano* star, and Koko the Pup, the *Magic* front page regular, taking equal parts in the action. From 1951 the annual was once again retitled *The Beano Book*, with *Magic* characters then being dropped.

From a collector's point of view, the *Dandy, Beano* and *Magic* annuals are among the most sought after and difficult to obtain of the D.C. Thomson annuals. Only one set of the *Dandy* annual is known to exist and there are no known sets of the *Beano* annual in private hands. In both cases the files of the British Museum are incomplete, the wing of the building in which they were kept having been hit by a bomb during the war. *Magic* annuals are especially rare and when one or other of the two editions has emerged for sale, each has fetched an exceedingly high price.

North of the Border

D.C. Thomson were also responsible for two other annuals issued around 1940; or, to be more precise, biennials, as each was – and still is – published every two years alternately. These are *Oor Wullie* and *The Broons*, two books of such a pronounced Scottish nature that

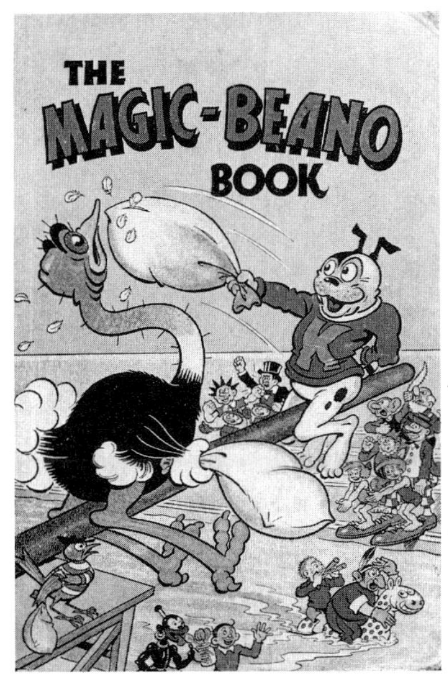

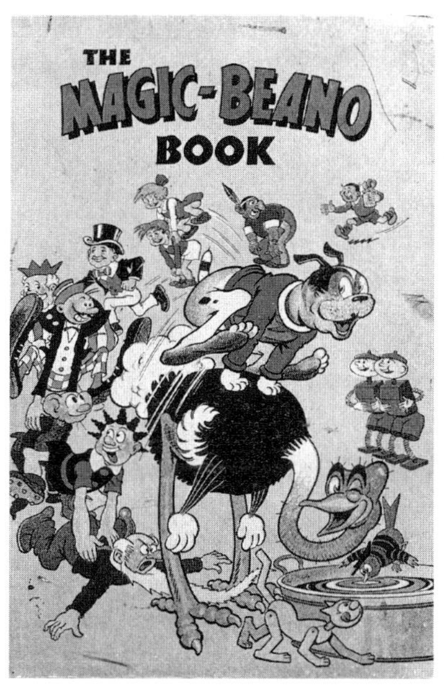

Left *The Magic-Beano Book* (1944). © D. C. Thomson & Co. Ltd.

Right *The Magic-Beano Book* (1945). © D. C. Thomson & Co. Ltd.

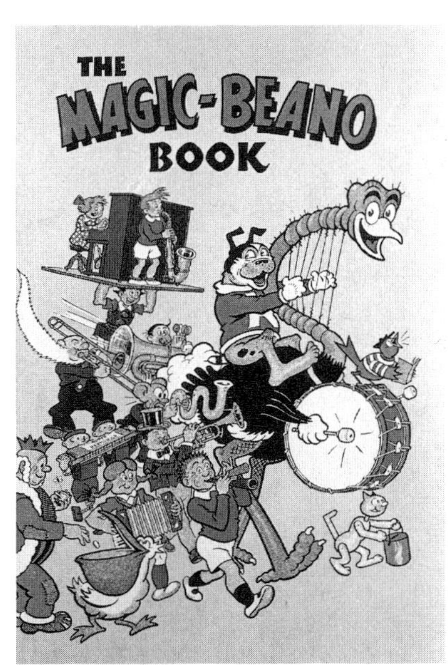

Left *The Magic-Beano Book* (1947). © D. C. Thomson & Co. Ltd.

Right *The Magic-Beano Book* (1948). © D. C. Thomson & Co. Ltd.

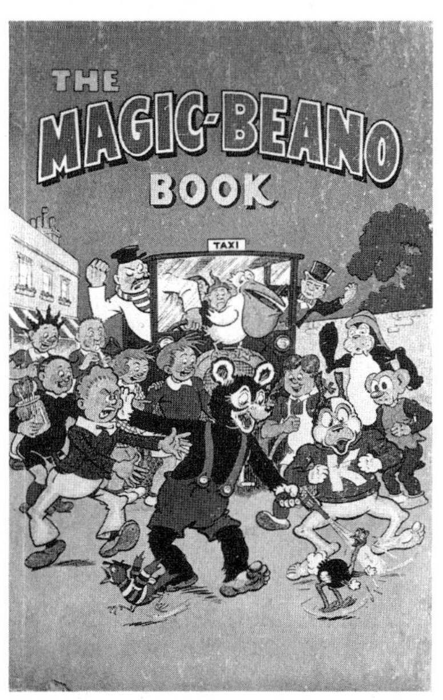

Left *The Magic-Beano Book* (1949). © D. C. Thomson & Co. Ltd.

Right *The Magic-Beano Book* (1950). © D. C. Thomson & Co. Ltd.

Title page of the first edition of *Oor Wullie* (1941). The signature 'Watty' is that of Dudley D. Watkins. © D. C. Thomson & Co. Ltd.

they are rarely sold south of the Border.

'Oor Wullie' (Our Willie) is a small Scottish boy with fair hair who, to judge by its 'hacked-off' appearance, has been the recipient of a home haircut. When not indulging in well-meaning actions – usually interpreted by his peers as mischief – the lad who is nobody's fool is to be found sitting on an upturned bucket, elbows on his knees and chin in his hands, ruefully contemplating life's idiosyncracies.

'The Broons' (The Browns) are a family living at No. 10, Glebe Street: Paw, Maw, Grandpaw, Joe, Maggie, Hen, Horace, two twins and a 'bairn'. Paw, Maw and their family holiday together, entertain themselves and huddle around open fires in a Fifties-style parlour in the depths of northern winters. They are a close-knit clan whose diet includes porridge, dumplings, haggis and black bun; and, on Hogmanay, they wait eagerly for their neighbours to come 'first-footing' so that they can celebrate the New Year together.

For years, the books were a triumph: an accurate reflection of Scottish values and family ties; a true depiction of the way in which many of their readers actually lived and, importantly, talked. But, since Dudley Watkins died in the mid-1960s, it has been sad not only to see the decline in the standard of artwork but also to witness the elimination of a good deal of the rich Gaelic brogue in which the characters spoke. Admittedly, it made their conversation almost incomprehensible to readers down south, but the dialect was an integral part of 'The Broons' and 'Oor Wullie' and the books have been all the poorer for its dilution. Happily, though, the traditional humour has been retained.

Both 'Oor Wullie' and 'The Broons' appear each week in the *Fun Section* of *The Sunday Post*, Thomson's own huge-circulation newspaper, and have always been enormously popular since the day both features were introduced with No.1 of the *Fun Section* on 8 March 1936. The *Fun Section* is a four-page supplement which can be removed from the newspaper, folded in half and cut along its edges to give an eight-page comic. It was the brainchild of R.D. Lowe, an influential Thomson editor, and he had Dudley Watkins draw both pages in a lively style with lots of pictures (around eighteen to a page); the scriptwriters (in the early days, reputedly Lowe himself) approached the humour with sophistication, bearing in mind the fact that the *Fun Section* would be read by adults as well as children (as were American newspaper comics, where Lowe may have got the idea). The *Fun Section* was an obvious precursor of

Adventure Land: first edition 1924.
© D. C. Thomson & Co. Ltd.

The Skipper Book for Boys: first edition 1932.
© D. C. Thomson & Co. Ltd.

The Rover Book for Boys: 1942.
© D. C. Thomson & Co. Ltd.

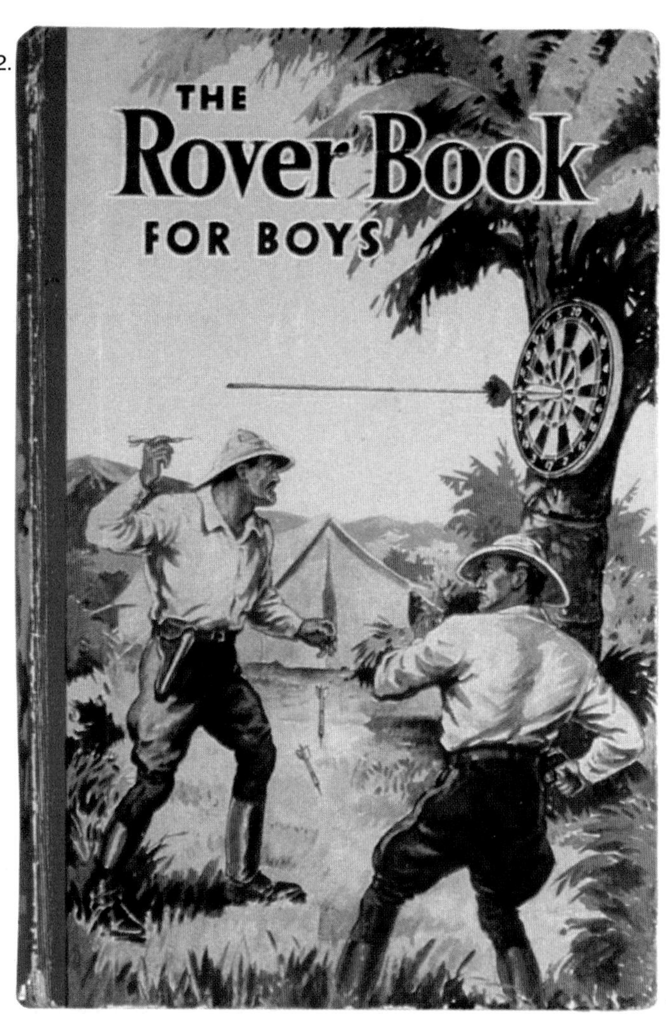

The Hotspur Book for Boys:
first edition 1935.
© D. C. Thomson & Co. Ltd.

The Wizard Book for Boys:
first edition 1936.
© D. C. Thomson & Co. Ltd.

Dandy Monster Comic: first edition 1939.
© D. C. Thomson & Co. Ltd.

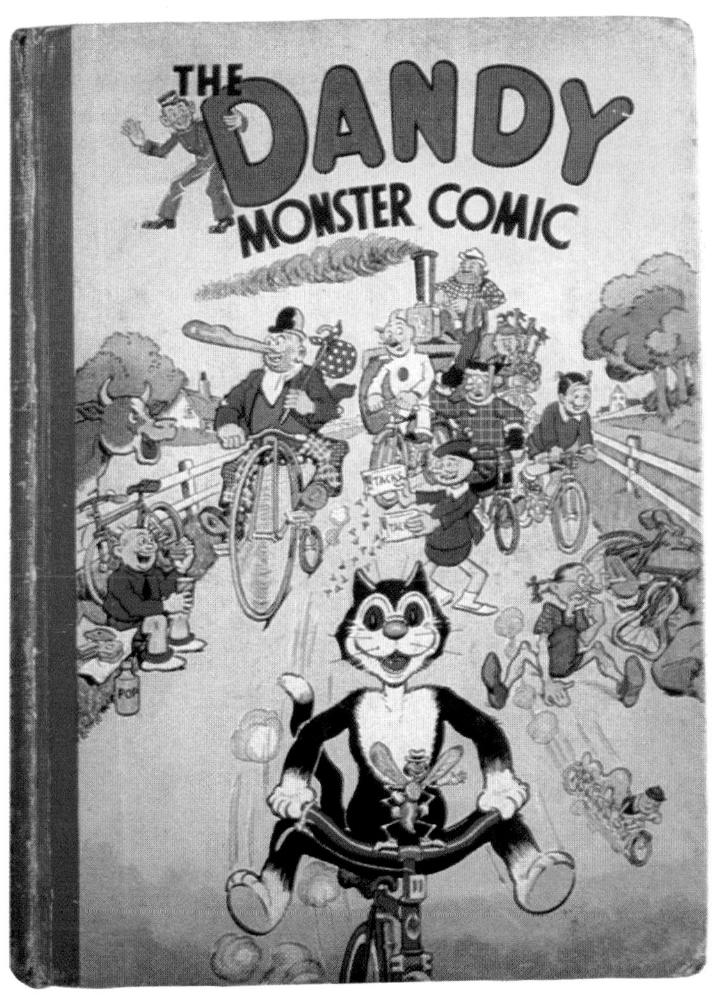

Dandy Monster Comic: 1943.
© D. C. Thomson & Co. Ltd.

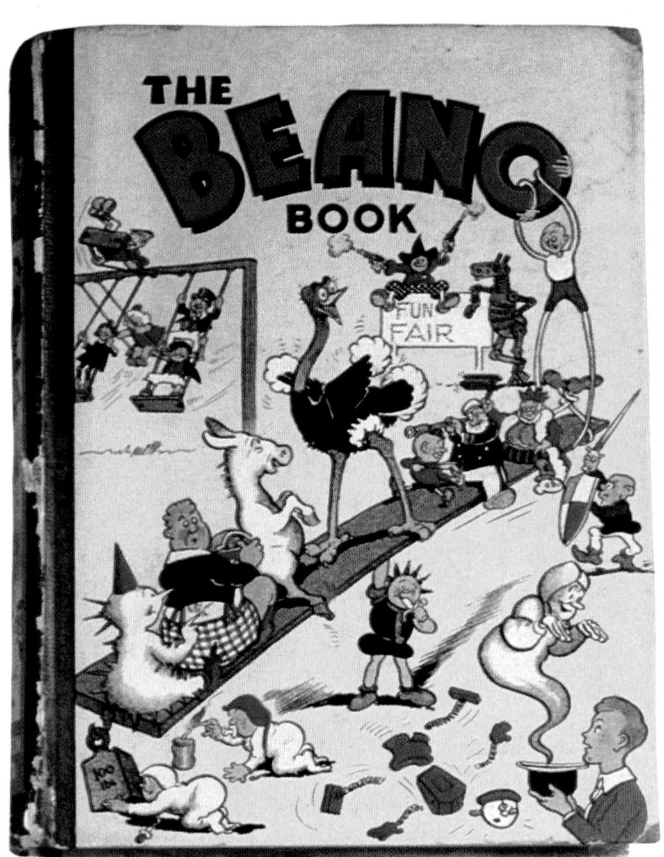

The Beano Book: first edition 1940.
© D. C. Thomson & Co. Ltd.

The Magic-Beano Book: first edition 1943.
© D. C. Thomson & Co. Ltd.

The first post-war annual to be published by D. C. Thomson was *Black Bob – The Dandy Wonder Dog* (1950). The artist was Jack Prout. © D. C. Thomson & Co. Ltd.

the *Beano* and the *Dandy* which were introduced in 1937 and 1938 respectively.

The first of the two annuals issued, *The Broons*, appeared before Christmas, 1939, for 1940; a year later *Oor Wullie* was published. This alternating publication schedule has been met ever since, apart from the years 1945 and 1947, when the biennials were affected by the then paper shortage. Both books have always reprinted material which appeared first in *The Sunday Post*.

In later years, Dudley Watkins signed each and every page he drew. But in the early *Oor Wullie* and *The Broons* books all work is unsigned but for the signature 'Wotty' on the frontispiece, one of the first occasions upon which he had been permitted to sign any of his work.

After the war, with paper restrictions lifted and artists and other staff demobbed and ready for work again, the company should have been set to expand its business. But it was a slow process. Periodicals like the *Beano* and the *Dandy* began a gradual climb back from fortnightly to weekly schedules and no new publications were issued in the immediate post-war period.

The first annual to be published by Thomson after the war was *Black Bob* (1950), subtitled 'The Dandy Wonder Dog'. Bob was a sheepdog, a black-and-white collie who lived and worked with his master, shepherd Andrew Glenn, in the Border country between Scotland and England. Black Bob had been introduced in *The Dandy Comic* in a series of written stories which began in November 1944, but the dog had also appeared in Thomson's tabloid newspaper *The Weekly News* in picture adventures from October 1946. Later, in the 1950s, these strips were reprinted in the weekly *Dandy*.

Black Bob's artist was an Englishman, Jack Prout, who drew

the Border country with the feel of a native. No word-balloons were used; each picture was a carefully drawn illustration serving the text which appeared beneath, and the life and times of pre-war Britain were beautifully evoked. Prout's handling of the feature (it was something more than a comic strip) never changed and when it ended its long run in the *Dandy* in 1982, the setting was still that of Britain in the 1920s and 1930s.

There were eight *Black Bob* annuals published between 1950 and 1965 (the book was issued in alternate years, missing 1963). All but two editions were an unusual oblong shape, approx. 7 × 10 in (18 × 25 cm) and included a mix of both picture and written stories. Of the eight, it is the 1961 and 1965 volumes that collectors find the hardest to track down, but it is the earlier books which cause the most confusion when an attempt is made to date them: the cover illustrations are very nondescript, merely showing a sideways view of the dog's head.

'Topper' and 'Beezer'

Thomson's next book publication was *The Topper Book* (1955), the annual for a new tabloid weekly comic, *The Topper*, launched on 7 February 1953.

The Topper Book was notable for two reasons: the first was its shape, which was oblong, 11 × 8 in (28 × 21 cm), and the second was the sumptuous colour used throughout. For the first time, a Thomson comic annual looked like a quality product and was to establish a lead over its competitors in superior colour printing that has continued to this day. The oblong editions of *The Topper Book* continued until the 1960 edition, when it reverted to the size and format of a standard Thomson annual, that is 10½ × 7½ in (27 × 19 cm), which it retains to this day.

Two of the established artists who supplied work for this new annual were the familiar *Beano* and *Dandy* artists Dudley Watkins and Allan Morley. But some splendid work also came from the pen of artist Paddy Brennan on comic strips like 'Wulf of the Arrows' and 'Flip McCoy, the Floating Boy'. Brennan, a talented newcomer to D.C. Thomson in the early 1950s, was destined to become for some years the leading adventure artist of all the firm's weekly and annual publications. Unusually for the Scottish firm, the annual also included reprinted foreign comic strips: there was 'Nancy' from the USA and 'Ferd-'nand' which had originated in Denmark.

One eye-catching and consistently funny comic strip was 'Beryl the Peril' drawn by the artist David Law (1907–71) who had also illustrated Dennis the Menace for the *Beano*. Both Beryl and Dennis were popular enough to be given their own annuals in subsequent years: the *Dennis the Menace* annual was first issued for 1956 and published in alternate years with *Beryl the Peril*, the first edition of which was dated 1959. Initially comprised mostly of reprints from weekly *Beano* and *Topper* comics that had appeared a few years earlier, these gave way in later editions to wholly original material.

Beryl and Dennis seem to be as popular as ever these days: Beryl still appears in the *Topper* weekly comic, each year in *The Topper Book*, and in the *Beryl the Peril* book which was last issued for 1988. Dennis has gone from strength to strength: his weekly comic strip has been moved to the front page of the weekly *Beano* and the *Dennis the Menace* book has continued to be published biennially. Dennis's popularity has been boosted by the introduction of a crudely drawn pet dog, Gnasher. Although Gnasher's appearance may not be a work of art, he is a genuinely funny creation and his permanence has been acknowledged by including his

Title page of *The Topper Book* (1955). © D. C. Thomson & Co. Ltd.

name on the cover of the *Dennis the Menace* annual.

The success of *The Topper* led to a companion, *The Beezer*, which was published as a tabloid weekly comic on 21 January 1956. The first annual, *The Beezer Book*, was dated 1958.

Like *The Topper Book, The Beezer Book* was printed in full colour throughout (but in standard size and format) and used the work of both established and new artists. The most important of the latter was Leo Baxendale who drew what was a popular and long-running comic strip called 'The Banana Bunch'. They were a group of young mischief-makers in the style of Bash Street Kids whom Baxendale had illustrated in 1954 for the *Beano*.

Initially, Baxendale drew the Banana Bunch in single or double page pictures; the endpapers of the first *Beezer* annual were a good example of what Baxendale could accomplish: this double-page picture showed the kids of Banana Crescent (where the Bunch lived) in full-scale war against the Establishment, in this case the local Police Force. They lit fireworks, walked tightropes, dismantled cars, derailed trains and indulged in a score of other activities. It was mayhem on a grand scale, drawn in a style reminiscent of a Carl Giles *Sunday Express* cartoon, but more anarchic and equally funny.

Besides 'The Bash Street Kids', Leo Baxendale was also the illustrator of 'Little Plum', 'Minnie the Minx' and 'The Three Bears' which appeared in *Beano* annuals in the 1950s. 'Minnie the Minx'

Title page of *Dennis the Menace* (1956). © D. C. Thomson & Co. Ltd.

and 'The Bash Street Kids' have remained in print and are still popular today, although drawn by other hands since Baxendale left D. C. Thomson to join Odhams in the early 1960s. Indeed, so successful were 'The Bash Street Kids' that they were given their own annual for 1980 which has since been published biennially.

Paddy Brennan also regularly drew for the *Beezer* annual adventure features such as 'Showboat Circus' and one-off historical comic strips. *The Beezer Book* additionally included many splendidly drawn factual historical picture features during the Fifties and Sixties, and both artwork and presentation improved with every issue. John Millar Watt, the creator of the character 'Pop' for the *Daily Sketch* newspaper, was likewise a frequent contributor.

Paddy Brennan and Leo Baxendale were but two of the important artists who represented a 'New Wave' of contributors to the Thomson publications in the 1950s. A third was Ken Reid (1919–87), a talented illustrator who had a truly unique style. Reid was new to comics, but not to comic strips: he had drawn the 'Fudge the Elf' feature for the *Manchester Evening News* since 1938. Ken Reid's work, like that of Paddy Brennan and Leo Baxendale, was used primarily for the pages of the *Beano* and *Dandy*. Well known comic strips by Reid were: 'Roger the Dodger', 'Bing Bang Benny', 'Angel Face', 'Grandpa' and 'Jonah'. All of these and more appear in the early Fifties and mid-Sixties *Beano* and *Dandy*, when Reid left Thomson to join Odhams in 1964.

Inevitably, giving popular leading characters their own annual has not always proved successful. The firm's most famous comic creation, Desperate Dan, was issued in book form as *The Dandy's Desperate Dan* (1954). This was a lovely book, made up of reprinted Desperate Dan adventures, which should have sold well, but puzzlingly and obviously didn't. No other 'Dan' books were issued for twenty-five years and then again the same thing happened: a splendid book, *The Desperate Dan Book* (1979), was produced but again with no more to follow. From a collector's point of view both books are interesting, reprinting as they do many of the best adventures drawn by Dudley Watkins. However, the 1954 edition is uncommon and, on the collector's market, in good condition, it sells for around £25. The 1979 annual is much easier to find and is worth about £3.50.

The one-off *Dandy-Beano Summer Special* (1963) successful enough to lead to the many Summer Specials published ever since. © D. C. Thomson & Co. Ltd.

Summer Specials

Desperate Dan, together with Dennis the Menace from the *Beano*, was also featured on the front page of the *Dandy-Beano Summer Special* issued in 1963. This 32-page paper-covered Bumper number included the work of leading Thomson artists (including Dudley Watkins) and it is the only occasion when the two titles have been combined. Today, it is extremely scarce. The following year, in 1964, both the *Dandy* and *Beano* were given their own separate Summer Specials and these have been published every year since. Later, Summer Specials were also issued for *Beezer* (1973), *Topper* (1983) and *Bananaman* (1984), and certain other selected publications. In effect, all these publications are annuals too, albeit in a different form to the hardcover Christmas annuals.

D.C. Thomson was the first company to issue Summer Specials, but 1963 did not mark the first occasion: a precursor was the *Rover Summer Fun Book* issued in June 1936 as a free pull-out supplement to the *Rover* story paper; also, a paperback entitled *The Wizard Holiday Book for Boys* had been published in the summers of 1938 and 1939. When the idea proved successful in the 1960s, initially with the *Dandy-Beano Summer Special* and subsequently with separate editions, competitors were quick to emulate this new and successful venture. The last twenty-five years has seen an ever-increasing number of these summer annuals published between April and August each year.

Another Summer Special was *Bunty*, which has been issued since 1969. *Bunty* was an all-picture comic for young girls, first published on 18 January 1958 with an annual, *The Bunty Book for Girls*, issued for 1960. 'Bunty', a teenager, was front-page star of the comic which for thirty years has followed the pattern of all such publications for girls: there were stories about schools, ghosts and orphans, and about career women – air hostesses, swimmers, gymnasts, ballerinas and so forth. This was hardly the kind of reading that a feminist would applaud but, like so much of D. C. Thomson's output, it was traditional and exceedingly popular.

Among the drawings in *Bunty*, some merited genuine admiration. These were usually by Paddy Brennan who had done such fine work for the *Dandy, Beano* and *Topper* comics and who, as the 1960s progressed, began to draw increasingly for the girls' comics; not only *Bunty* but also *Judy*, another weekly girls' comic in the same mould, published on 16 January 1960, with an annual, *The Judy Book for Girls*, issued for 1966. Another girls' annual for a weekly comic was *The Mandy Book for Girls* (1971) which has also had a long run.

The favourites return

If the firm kept the female market well supplied, it was careful not to neglect the boys' publications. After all, the Thomson 'Big Five' series of boys' papers and its associated annuals had always provided the nucleus of its publications aimed at young people. But, by the early 1960s, these famous story papers and their annuals had come to an end. The weekly *Skipper* was discontinued in 1941 (annuals issued were 1932–42 and 1948); the weekly *Hotspur* was published until 1959 (with annuals issued 1935–41, 1943 and 1949); the weekly *Rover* until 1961 (annuals issued 1926–42, 1950, 1956, and 1958); the weekly *Adventure* until 1961 (annuals: 1924–41) and the weekly *Wizard* until 1963 (annuals: 1936–42 and 1949).

The *Hotspur* weekly was immediately relaunched as *The New Hotspur* on 24 October 1959, an all-picture paper. Although this was discontinued in 1963 after only 173 issues, *The Hotspur Book for Boys* was issued for 1966 and is still running. One of the delights to be savoured in this annual has been the return of *Wizard* story-paper heroes such as Wilson (the athlete) and the Wolf of Kabul. Given that the stories are today

The Victor Book (1969). © D. C. Thomson & Co. Ltd.

Below *Hotspur Book for Boys* (1979). © D. C. Thomson & Co. Ltd.

told in pictures, it soon becomes apparent that Wilson has changed little since his first appearance in the weekly *Wizard* story paper of some forty-five years ago: he still wears his all-black athletics suit and runs in his bare feet. Bill Samson, the 'Wolf of Kabul', now battles the Japanese in Burma with Chung his Himalayan assistant still by his side holding his 'clicky-ba', ready to 'crack some skulls'.

These were not the only 'Golden Age' heroes to be revived: there was also the Black Sapper (previously of the *Rover*) who travelled underground in his amazing mole machine; Bernard Briggs, probably the greatest all-round sportsman ever to grace the pages of a Thomson story paper, and the football series 'It's Goals That Count'. And there were concessions to the new age, too, in the form of superheroes. One such, 'King Cobra', was an American-style hero complete with a secret identity. The idea for another superhero comic strip, 'Spring-Heeled Jackson', obviously originated with the famous Penny Dreadful creation 'Spring-Heeled Jack'. This Jackson was a Victorian superhero, otherwise known, by the alarmed Cockney criminals he encountered, as 'the leaping Terror of the Fog'. It was an inspired approach in a field where there sometimes appears to be little inspiration left.

Another category of fiction, the war story, was featured in a new picture paper, the aptly-named *Victor*. The first issue of the weekly *Victor* was dated 25 February 1961; a *Victor for Boys Summer Special* has been issued every year since 1967 and the *Victor Book for Boys* annual was published for 1964 and is still running. The Victor diet of war, cowboy, sports and adventure stories has proved very successful, and in later years the comic has absorbed several other Thomson papers, notably the all-picture relaunched *Wizard* (435 issues, no annual), the relaunched *Hotspur* and the *Rover*.

It is evident from the pages of the *Victor Book for Boys* that the editor and his staff have also been mining the rich vein of stories which appeared in the Big Five: Matt Braddock (of the 'I Flew With Braddock' stories), Alf Tupper, 'The Tough of the Track' and 'The Fastest Miler in the World', and the Tarzanesque jungle hero, Morgyn the Mighty, had all appeared previously in the weekly *Rover* story paper.

On 28 September 1974, Thomson launched a brand new weekly, *Warlord*, the first-ever comic to be devoted entirely to war stories. Tough, action-packed, patriotic adventure was highlighted in tales such as 'Code-Name Warlord', 'Union Jack Jackson', 'Bazooka Charlie' and 'Escape From Dunkirk'. The glossy laminated covers of the *Warlord Book for Boys* (first edition: 1977) usually had explosive red and yellow backgrounds (the aftermath of aerial bombardments), with soldiers in skull-decorated patrol boats firing at unseen enemies. Again, the *Warlord* editor had borrowed from the Big Five by bringing back the Wolf of Kabul (showing Bill Samson and Chung as boyhood chums) and Matt (Bomber) Braddock.

The Thomson annuals recently on sale have been the *The Dandy Book, The Beano Book, The Topper Book, The Beezer Book, Beryl the Peril, Dennis the Menace, Bananaman, The Hotspur Book for Boys, The Victor Book for Boys* and *The Bunty Book for Girls.* Well printed and well bound, they have superb colour reproduction.

In addition, there is a sense of communication between the annuals' creators and the readership, so that each book appears to be a genuine attempt to give satisfaction and pleasure. This 'aim to please' and quality approach will undoubtedly ensure that the D.C. Thomson annuals continue to be published for many years to come.

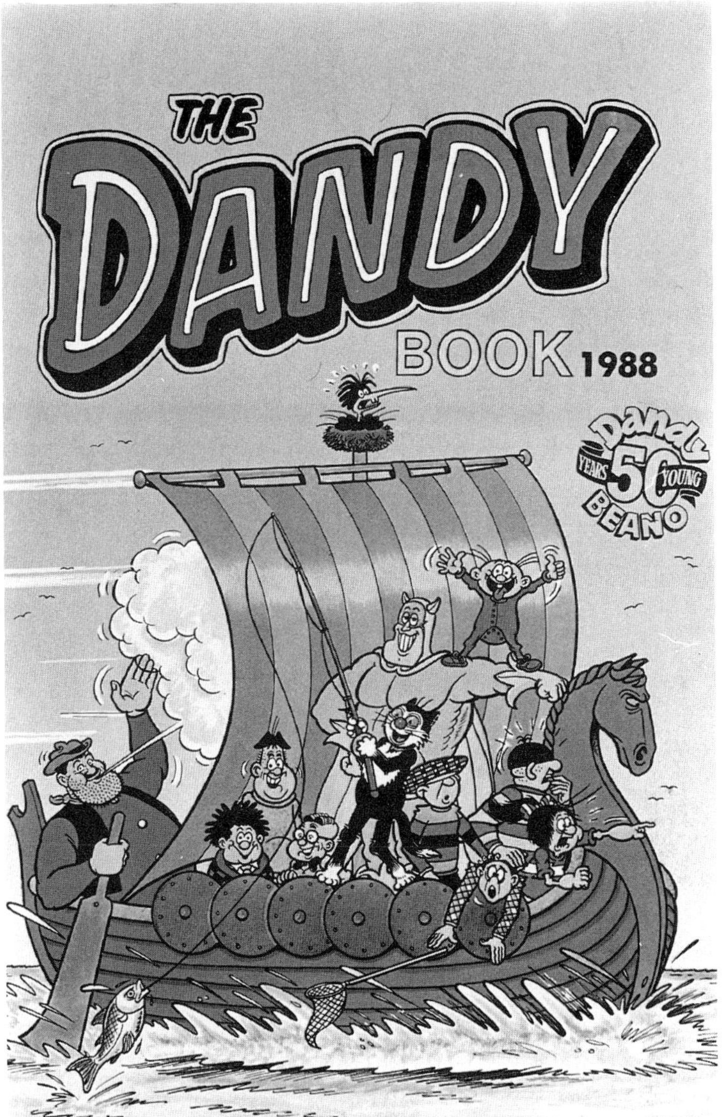

Above *The Dandy Book* (1988): fiftieth anniversary edition. © D. C. Thomson & Co. Ltd.

Warlord Book for Boys (1981). © D. C. Thomson & Co. Ltd.

CHAPTER 5

The Post-War Publishers

The Second World War decimated the publishing empires of D.C. Thomson and the Amalgamated Press. Many weekly comics were discontinued, together with their associated annuals; those weekly publications that did survive were reduced in size, and often issued less frequently, as paper restrictions came into force. The result was a dearth of reading material both during the war and immediately after the war, particularly in the field of children's publications, which were often the first to be subjected to cutbacks.

The public, however, wanted to read, and several firms stepped in to fill the gap left by the traditional suppliers. Perhaps the most remarkable of these firms was started by Gerald Swan (1902–80). In the 1930s, Swan had owned a market stall in London's Church Street Market which sold comics and magazines. Soon, he decided to start his own publishing business, Gerald G. Swan Ltd. Evidently he stockpiled what he printed so that by the time war was declared in September 1939, he had three large warehouses full of magazines. When paper-rationing was introduced in 1940, and Thomson and AP were forced to reduce their deliveries to retailers, Gerald Swan was there to supply them with his publications. Furthermore, Swan was fully entitled to his own ration of paper.

Gerald Swan had noticed that the most popular items on his market stall had been the American comics which had just begun to be shipped to England. When supplies dried up with the start of war, Swan decided to publish a line of British comics in the American style and format. His first was *New Funnies*, published in early 1940; this was followed in the same year by five more titles: *Topical Funnies, War Comics, Thrill Comics, Fresh Fun* and *Extra Fun*. In later years, some of Swan's best-known comics were *Comicolour, Cute Fun* and *Slick Fun*, which were published irregularly.

Swan called his comic annuals 'Albums'. The first to appear was the *Funnies Album* (1943–57) subtitled 'The Laughs of a Nation'. Subsequent annuals published by Swan were *Comicolour Album* (1947–55); *Cute Fun* (1947–56) and *Slick Fun* (1949–55). Encountering one of these annuals for the first time, the reader is immediately struck by the low standard of artwork in the many comic strips. Swan's albums, like all his periodicals, were crude and almost amateurish in appearance and content. Not something that a collector would want to place alongside the professionally produced comic annuals of D.C. Thomson and the Amalgamated Press, surely? And yet... there is something about the Gerald Swan publications (admittedly an aquired taste!), a certain oddness, a homeliness that is endearing.

Cute Fun: Gerald Swan (1950).

A special style

The appeal of the Swan albums to a small band of collectors is difficult to explain, but it has a lot to do with the Swan house-style: the ideas behind the poor drawings were interesting and there was none of the strict censorship applied by the big publishing houses. Murder, mayhem, death and humour parade together through the pages in a way that seems refreshing after having been accustomed to more standard fare. It sounds peculiar, but then the Swan publications *were* peculiar.

Such violence was part and parcel of comic strips such as 'Krakos the Egyptian'. Krakos was an eerie mystic who, in one memorable episode, foils the Japanese invasion of Australia by destroying their fleet; it was also to be found in the eccentric adventures of a fat private detective in 'No. 13' and in the exciting tales of 'Dr Satani – Crime Chemist'. All of these were written and drawn by William Ward, an ex-animator who had worked on the Bonzo films in the 1920s. In addition to many other strips for the Swan albums, Ward was responsible for a comic strip called 'Sheriff Fox' which mysteriously appeared years later in the *Knockout* annuals published by the Amalgamated Press.

Not all the artwork was bad. One exceptional artist, who drew in cheerful, traditional British comic style and whose work always succeeded in 'raising the tone' of the Swan publications, was Edward Henry Banger (1897–1968), who had previously worked for both AP and Thomson. Banger (pronounced Bainger) was one of Swan's most prolific artists: he drew several of the covers for the albums, and his comic strips (signed 'Bang') appeared in almost every 'funnies' comic and annual. Some of Banger's best known creations were 'Stoogie' (a vaudeville-type creation with an enormous nose); 'Skit the Kat'; 'Exploring – with Professor Peek and Phuzzy his Pygmy Guide'; 'Tornado Tom' (a cowboy) and 'Slick Sure the Detective'.

Comicolour Album: Gerald Swan (1950).

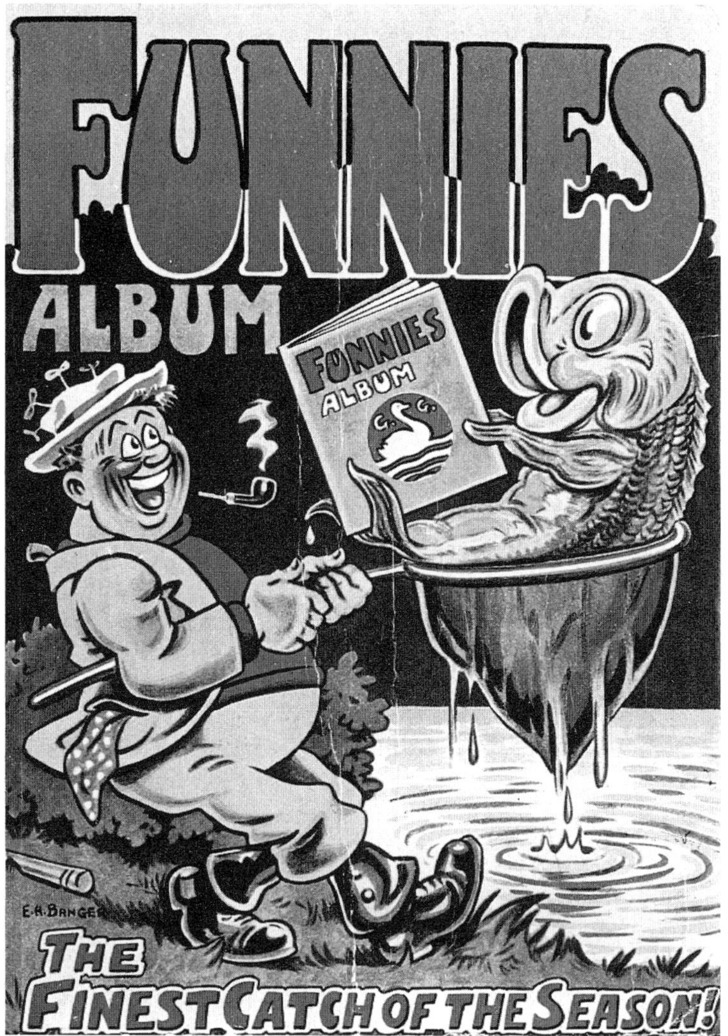

Above left *Funnies Album:* Gerald Swan (1954).

Above right *Slick Fun Album*: Gerald Swan (1953).

Swan was also able to include the output of several experienced Amalgamated Press artists who did work in their spare time. Three of the most prolific signed themselves 'Robbie', 'HEP' and 'Jack Daw'. 'Robbie' was Wally Robertson and 'HEP' was H.E. Pease; both had work appearing regularly for many years in the *Funny Wonder, Crackers, Jester* and other AP weekly comics and annuals. 'Jack Daw' was actually Percy Cocking, who drew the famous pair of tramps Weary Willie and Tired Tim for the front page of *Illustrated Chips*. All three were moonlighting in order to supplement their income, but there was more to it than that. Years later, Wally Robertson said: 'I really enjoyed working for Swan. I always had carte blanche and the pay, if I remember correctly, was slightly better than the AP. I must say that I always preferred working for companies other than the AP as I always had more scope. The AP could be very restricting at times.' Other AP artists who supplied work for the Swan albums were Frank Minnitt (who drew Billy Bunter in the *Knockout* annual) and Don Newhouse, whose work appeared in *Crackers* annual.

Regular artists also included Bert Hill (who signed himself 'B.H.'), Glynn Protheroe, whose distinctive, morose picture strips bore his surname, and 'Ron', who as Ron Embleton was to become well known in later years for his work in a variety of publications, which included the *Express Annual for Boys* (1957). Two brothers, John (Jock) and William (Ron) McCail, were also frequent contributors of many of the adventure comic strips that appeared. Two of the best known were 'Bring 'Em In Hank' (John McCail) and 'Back From The Dead' (William McCail).

During the 1940s Gerald Swan expanded his small publishing empire. Besides the four albums already mentioned, his list included: *Picture Story Album* (1944); *Kiddyfun Album* (1945–

56); *Fairies Album* (1945–57); *Schoolboys Album* (1945–58); *Schoolgirls Album* (1945–57); *Birthday Fun Album* (1946–52); *Scramble* (1948–51); *Girls' Fun* (1948–57); *Western Fun Comic Album* (1953–6); *Bible Story Album* (1950); *Babies Album* (1954); *Bunny Annual* (1953). It must be noted, however, that the dates given after each title may not be completely accurate: the range is only approximate, and it is possible that annuals were not published for particular years.

Gerald Swan's albums catered to a wide age group. One of the best, apart from the four 'funnies' albums, was *Scramble*, where the contents were mostly written stories with a few filler comic-strip pages. These were the usual boys' fare of detective, school and adventure yarns, but it has been said that many of these stories were written by hard-up, well-known authors using pseudonyms and that this also applied to the stories that appeared in *Schoolboys Album* and *Schoolgirls Album*. It is certainly possible, because the writing seemed better than the usual Swan norm.

In addition to the albums, Gerald Swan was simultaneously publishing scores of other publications: books, Yankee-style magazines, reprint American magazines and comic books (such as 'Archie' and 'Jughead'). By the late 1950s, however, large publishers such as D.C. Thomson and the Amalgamated Press had returned to normal production and were able to fill retailers' orders with smart and professional publications; it was the death knell for Gerald G. Swan Ltd. His last known publication was dated 1957. Some time afterwards he sold his company to World International Publishing who have offices in Manchester; later still, the rights to the Swan publications were purchased by the author of this book who one day intends to resurrect them in one form or another.

Bridging the gap

There were other small publishers, too, who wished to supply the young public with reading matter. Among the main ones were A. Soloway Ltd., P.M. (Philipp Marx) Productions and Paget Publications, although there were at least a score or more of others who produced dozens of comic titles (usually one-offs)

SWAN'S ALBUMS
Published Annually
OCTOBER 1st

96 pages of mirth-making and hair-raising stories for girls. (*Illustrated*). 3/6 Net.
64 Coloured Comic pages, specially for "Tinies." 3/6 Net.
Packed with New Fairy Stories and Coloured Pictures. 3/6 Net.
96 side-splitting and thrill-packed pages of schoolboy life. (*Illustrated*). 3/6 Net.
64 pages, packed with Japes, Thrills and Exciting Escapades. 2/6 Net
64 pages of Thrills and Adventure. Specially for Boys. 2/6 Net.
All Large Attractive Books CLEARLY PRINTED
Bound in Brightly Coloured Picture Board Covers
Packed with Coloured Comic Pages for boys and girls. 3/6.
96 Laughter and Thrill packed pages. 8 Colo'd Plates. 3/6.
Stories, Verses, Games, and Coloured Pictures. 3/6 Net.
Obtainable from your Bookseller or Newsagent.
Gerald G. Swan Ltd
EDGWARE HOUSE · BURNE STREET · MARYLEBONE
LONDON · N · W · 1

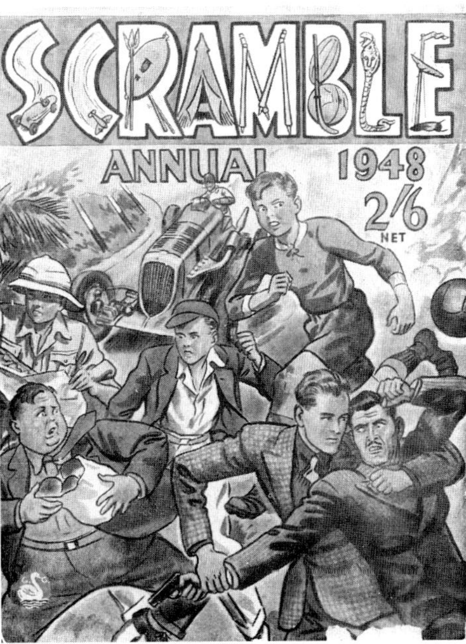

Scramble Annual: Gerald Swan (1948).

Schoolboys Album: Gerald Swan (1947).

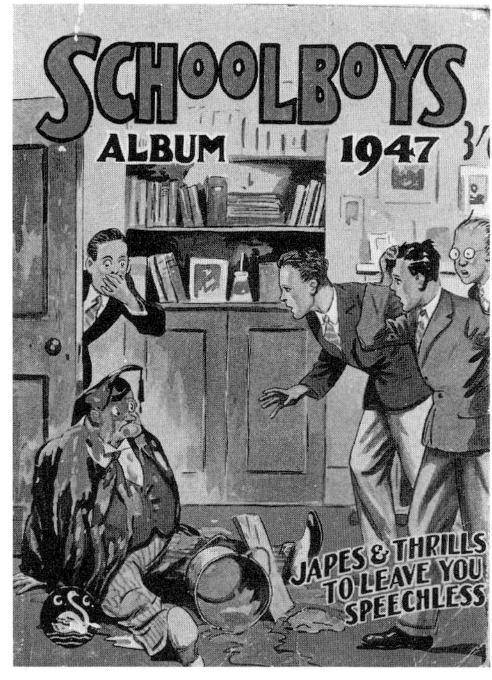

within the immediate post-war period. All of these companies produced periodicals on an irregular basis (i.e. as often as they could); annuals were a little out of their league but occasionally they were issued.

A. Soloway Ltd. was quick off the mark with two excellent titles published in paperback at five shillings apiece: *All Fun Annual* and *All Star Annual* (both 1946). These annuals bore the name of Soloway's two most popular titles: *All Fun Comic* and *All Star Comic* (27 issues of each were published between 1940 and 1949) and they were easily the best books to be issued by any small publisher at that time.

The reason for this was the superb presentation of each annual as a whole and the work of one excellent artist in particular, Nat Brand. Brand's best work was 'Halcon, Lord of the Craters' (which incorporated the best elements of Edgar Rice Burroughs's adventure tales and his Tarzan stories) and the wonderfully named 'Crash Carew, Daredevil of the Stratosphere' (obviously inspired by Buck Rogers and Flash Gordon). Nat Brand was undoubtedly an afficionado of the work of the great American comic artists Hal Foster and Alex Raymond: his stories, like theirs, were told with strikingly designed picture strips which were beautifully delineated and accompanied by Brand's own stylish hand-lettering at the foot of each panel, thus replacing word balloons in the panels. Brand's work was not merely a copy of the two American artists' work; he drew in the same style, but his drawings paid tribute to, rather than imitated, the work of Raymond and Foster.

Schoolgirls Album: Gerald Swan (1953).

Other artists could not hope to achieve such standards. Yet even when the artwork was not first-rate, the annuals were so nicely put together (good quality paper and all the comic strips in coloured inks) that it was a shame that each lasted for but a single edition.

Some small publishers simply bound together their irregularly issued comics and added a paper cover. The *Challenger Album* was one such instance: P.M. Productions stapled together the only two issues published of both *The Challenger Comic* and *Starflash Comic* to sell it for one shilling in Woolworths. With a new additional text story, its 52 pages were a bargain. P.M. Productions also published at least one hardback annual title: *The Chief Annual* (1947), comprising text adventure stories and one-page comic strips by Frank Minnitt and Wally Robertson, as well as a reprinted American newspaper strip.

Foreign comics would sometimes be stapled together, placed between boards and distributed via the newsagent chains. *The Giant Comic Album* (1950s) included issues of *Silver Starr* and *Yarmack Jungle King* comics that had originally been on sale in Australia. The artwork was by Stanley Pitt, whose style was an out-and-out copy of that of Alex Raymond; *Silver Starr* was also instantly recognisable as an imitation of Raymond's best-known comic strip, 'Flash Gordon'. But Pitt was a good enough artist to make the whole thing enjoyable, and this annual is a nice addition to any collection for his work alone.

Although Paget Publications never published an annual as such, the *Bumper Comic Album*, issued in the 1950s and published by Robert Edwards Ltd., was a 96-page collection of vintage comic strips that had previously appeared in the short-run Paget comics published in the late 1940s. Paget produced a few dozen different comics (none lasting more than eight issues) and the most frequently used artists' work was that of E.H. Banger, Wally Robertson and Jack Bridges.

Bridges, in particular, was extremely active in the Paget publications: he had a peculiar angular style which gave all his characters a somewhat wooden appearance which was very distinctive. He possessed a very nice line in typically British comic humour, and seemed to specialise in alliterative characters. e.g. Pete the Postman, Freddie Fireman, Walt the Waiter, Pete the Page, etc.

All Star Annual: A. Soloway (1946).

The London-based Featherstone Press issued between 1943 and 1948 a paper-covered biennial entitled *The Feathers Annual* (there were slight variations on this title) which was a quaint effort that must have appealed to many wartime children. Some of the stories were fantastic, to say the least. One tale by E.T. Portwin was entitled 'The Lake Under London'. It revealed that the capital city was built on a 'crust' of ground one hundred and fifty yards thick. In an adventure beneath the crust, a cavern was found and at its bottom a huge lake. Upon the walls of this cavern sprawled 'fat, white slugs' and within the lake was a hideous monster which had a 'great, white body on which swung a long, tapering neck ending in a blunt, sightless head'. Thankfully, at the end of this peculiar little tale, the entrance to the cavern was sealed forever by falling stonework. Phew! After a thriller like that, could any young Londoner ever again contemplate the ground beneath his feet in the same old way?

Another publisher of comics and annuals which were being issued in the post-war years was T.V. Boardman. Boardman's first professional contact with comics had come in the 1930s when he was the London agent for an American publisher. By 1940, he was publishing his own comics, using reprinted US material. After the war, in 1948, he issued several others, but this time with original British material: *Buffalo Bill, Swift Morgan* and *Roy Carson*. All were drawn by Denis McCloughlin, a young artist from Bolton, who was also the creator of Swift Morgan and Roy Carson. In addition, in 1949, Boardman printed UK editions of the well-known US comics *Blackhawk* and *The Spirit*, the strips being reprinted from the American originals.

T.V. Boardman again used the work of McCloughlin when he issued the *Buffalo Bill Wild West Annual* which ran for thirteen editions (1949–61), although in later years it was issued by Dean. For the *Buffalo Bill* annual McCloughlin produced some of his best work: authentic 'woodcut'-style illustrations which accompanied stories by Arthur Groom and Rex James; this annual has been described as the most authentic Western annual ever produced.

In 1954 Boardman published *The New Spaceways Comic Annual*, of which there were two editions. Although the title may have been new, most, if not all,

Below left *Ajax Adventure Annual:* T.V. Boardman

Below right *The New Spaceways Comic Annual:* T.V. Boardman (1954/55).

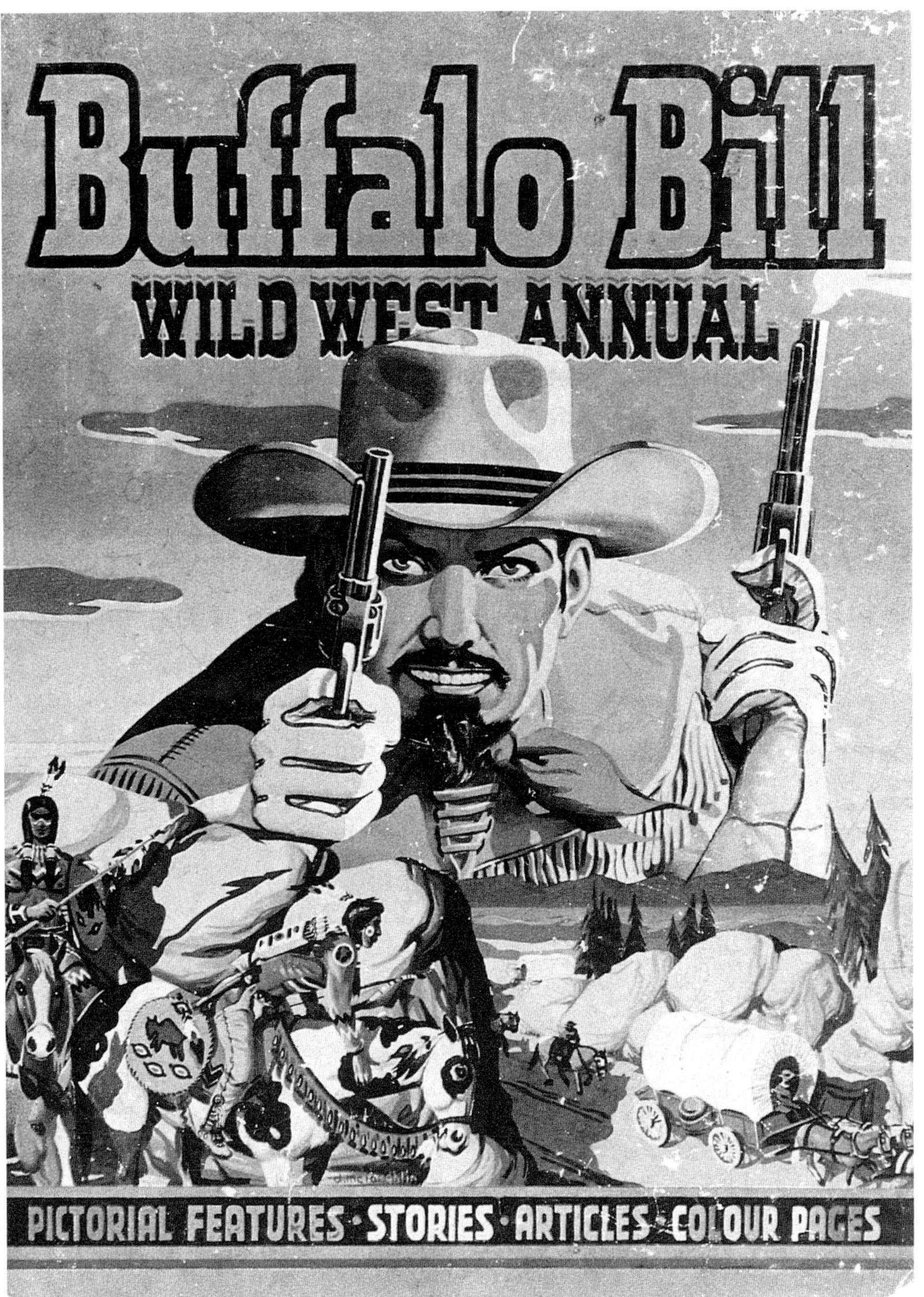

Buffalo Bill Wild West Annual: T.V. Boardman (1949/50).

of the contents were reprinted material and included earlier McCloughlin Swift Morgan and Roy Carson stories, together with US reprints of Plastic Man and other heroes.

Another annual in a similar vein was the *Adventure Annual*, published around 1953. It was issued for several years until the end of the Fifties and contained text stories as well as American reprinted comic strips 'Doll Man', 'Plastic Man', 'Blackhawk' and others. Denis McCloughlin did cover illustrations, endpapers and 'filler' illustrations for all of these books, sometimes helped by his brother, Colin. He also contributed to the three-edition *Supercolour Comic Annual* which was issued between 1949 and 1951. These also contained mostly reprinted material.

Monster Rupert: Sampson Low, Marston (1932).

The Sampson Low menagerie

The Taunton firm of Sampson Low, Marston & Co. Ltd. issued some popular titles following the war. Their excursions into the children's market had probably met with greatest success when they began to reprint in book form the adventures of Rupert Bear which had first been published in the *Daily Express* newspaper. The creator of Rupert was Mary Tourtel, whose drawings of the little bear had begun to appear in the newspaper on 8 November 1920.

Thomas Nelson had been the first publisher to reprint Rupert's adventures, but in 1924 Sampson Low took over, publishing several volumes and, commencing in 1928, a series of small yellow books entitled 'Little Bear Library' (also known as 'Rupert's Yellow Library') which were

Oor Wullie: first edition 1941. © D. C. Thomson & Co. Ltd.

The Broons: 1956
© D. C. Thomson & Co Ltd.

The Topper Book: first edition 1955. © D. C. Thomson & Co. Ltd.

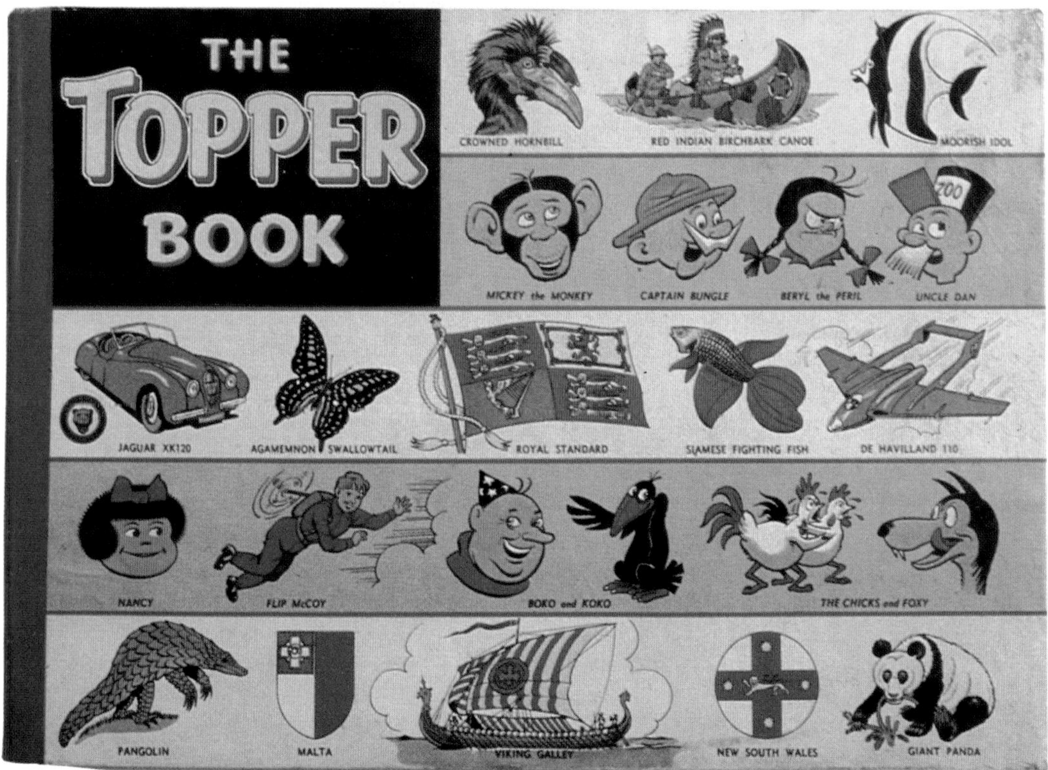

The Beezer Book: first edition 1958.
© D. C. Thomson & Co. Ltd.

Dennis the Menace: first edition 1956.
© D. C. Thomson & Co. Ltd.

Beryl the Peril: first edition 1959. © D. C. Thomson & Co. Ltd.

issued in batches over several years and numbered forty-six different titles.

Before and after the war Sampson Low also published the *Monster Rupert*; this was published in two different series, the first issued in 1931–4 (four volumes), the second in 1948–50 (three volumes). The former editions were then reissued on several occasions during the next decade. Although they were not intended as such, some collectors regard these as annuals, for each was published every twelve months at around the same time of year.

The 1931–4 *Monster Rupert* books ('monster', of course, meaning huge), if classified as early annuals, are not to be confused with the *Rupert* annual issued by the *Daily Express*. The four books were short, thick volumes containing stories that had previously appeared in the newspaper. Each had approximately 182 pages and was priced at two shillings and sixpence. For the record, as the books are undated, the cover descriptions are: Rupert watches wolf leap from bed (1931); Rupert sitting on a log (1932); Rupert being hidden by female bird (1933); Rupert and small boy in storeroom (1934).

The 1948–50 *Monster Rupert* books are larger, 7½ × 10 in (19 × 25 cm), than their 1930s predecessors, but they have less pages and, although some of the stories are the same as those in the earlier editions, there are also new ones. The cover descriptions of these three are: Rupert sitting on a log (1948); Rupert watches fox leap from bed (1949); Rupert helps small boy out of hole (1950).

When Mary Tourtel was forced by failing eyesight to retire from the newspaper feature in 1935, the *Daily Express* generously made her a gift of the copyright to her drawings. To what must have been the newspaper's later chagrin, Mary promptly sold this to her publisher, Sampson Low, for £50. That is why to this day Mary Tourtel's old Rupert stories are reprinted alongside the *Daily Express* equivalents, the former causing obvious puzzlement by their dated appearance.

The *Express* had obviously assumed that as a result of Mary Tourtel's retirement there would be no more Rupert. However, Stanley Marshall, a devoted Rupert enthusiast, managed to discover a successor, Alfred Bestall, who was to continue the feature for the next three decades (see Chapter 7).

Two popular Sampson Low annuals which began publication in 1946 were *The Nicholas Thomas Annual* and *The Toby Twirl Annual*. Both featured anthropomorphic animals: Nicholas Thomas was a cat who walked on his hind legs; Toby Twirl was a young pig who wore a type of boiler-suit, held up by braces.

It is possible that at this time the firm was seeking to create replacements for its profitable Rupert books. Mary Tourtel had ceased to draw new adventures after 1935 and, by the mid-1940s, Sampson Low probably thought that they could not keep reprinting the same stories year after year (especially as some originals had been destroyed in wartime bombing and the supply was then shorter than ever). Thus, it would have been sensible to try to establish substitutes. Little did they realise the enduring popularity of the *Daily Express* bear and the difficulty of sustaining new children's characters which did not have the added benefit of appearing each day in a national newspaper.

Although cats are undoubtedly nicer to read about than pigs, Nicholas Thomas has proved less popular in the long run. A small but dedicated group of collectors eagerly seek out the Toby Twirl annuals and related books (small hard-backed books and large, thin paper-covered booklets); Nicholas Thomas seems not yet to have found a following.

Both the Toby Twirl and the Nicholas Thomas annuals were published in a similar format to the Rupert books: three or four stories appeared in each book, and there were large pictures to illustrate scenes from the stories which were told in rhyme, just as Rupert stories were (a legacy from newspaper appearances when drawings were accompanied by verse – written by Mary Tourtel's husband, Herbert). Toby's verses were written by Sheila Hodgetts, whose stories were always imaginative and exciting, and the pictures were by E. Jeffrey who drew in a pleasant, animated style. Some colour was introduced, but in a limited fashion: drawings were printed in either all-red, all-blue, green or gold-coloured inks. There were several Toby Twirl annuals; Nicholas Thomas appeared in only one book bearing the title 'annual', but continued to be published in various formats until around 1957.

The 'Eagle' swoops

The real success story of post-war publishing was the Hulton Group with *Eagle* and its companion publications *Girl, Swift* and *Robin. Eagle*, the 'Strip Cartoon Weekly', was the brainchild of a Lancashire vicar, the Reverend Marcus Morris, and published by Hulton on 14 April 1950. Marcus

The Toby Twirl Annual: Sampson Low, Marston (1946).

Morris's first venture into journalism had been *The Anvil*, a four-page leaflet which he converted into a magazine, and for this he had some distinguished contributors who included C.S. Lewis and Harold Macmillan. He was also fortunate enough to obtain the services of a young art school student named Frank Hampson, who was responsible for the covers and cartoons.

The first comics to attract Morris's attention were the American horror comics published by Entertaining Comics, which had just begun to be distributed in Britain. He was appalled at the violence and found their contents deplorable and obscene. At the same time he recognised that the American comics were skilfully and vividly drawn and that the art of the strip cartoon was a new and important medium of communication which he felt, if used properly, could be a force for good.

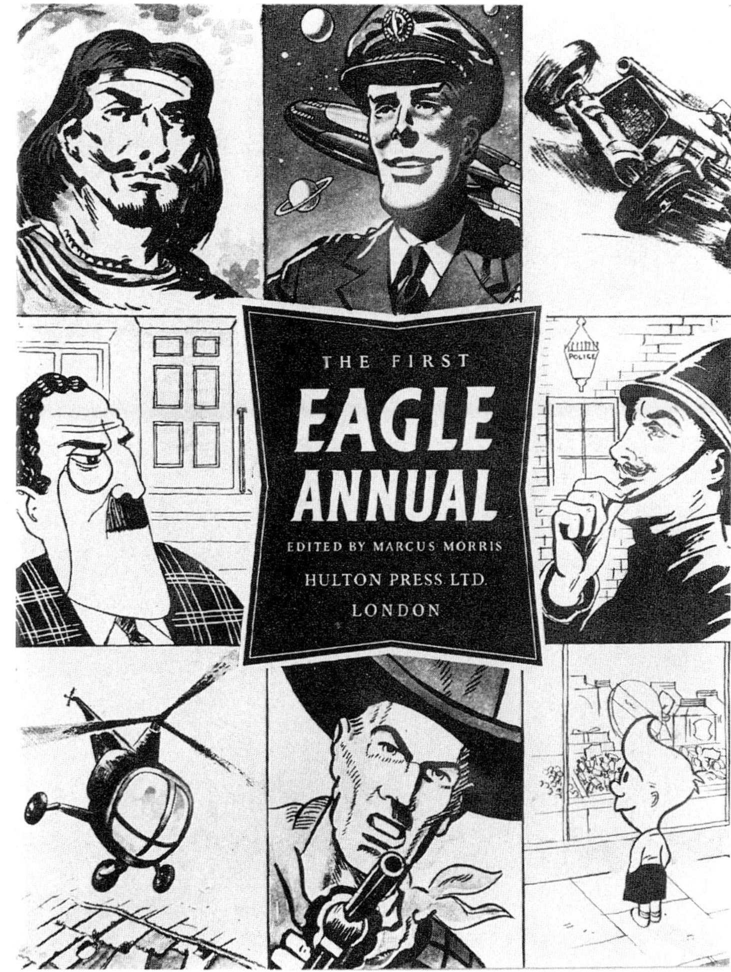

In 1949 Morris succeeded in convincing the London-based Hulton Press, publishers of *Lilliput* and *Picture Post*, that *Eagle* would be a viable proposition and the first issue of this splendidly produced comic was published the following year. It immediately sold out of its print run of 900,000 copies and its readership clamoured for more.

The front-page star of *Eagle* and the cornerstone of its success was 'Dan Dare – Pilot of the Future', a revolutionary science-fiction comic strip carefully and beautifully drawn (and sometimes written) by Frank Hampson, who had previously drawn for *The Anvil.* Dan Dare (he of the quizzical eyebrow) and his co-pilot Digby, together with Sir Hubert Dare and Professor Peabody, initially found themselves battling the green-skinned Treens, residents of Venus whose leader was the evil Mekon, 'the supreme scientist, the illustrious first one of Venus'.

Dan Dare has been called 'as real as the chap next door, as British as fish and chips or Yorkshire Pudding'. An ace pilot of the Interplanetary Space Fleet, he was no science whiz-kid, preferring a straight left rather than high-tech weapons to get him out of trouble. Throughout the 1950s he became every schoolboy's ideal, a new hero for the new Elizabethan Age.

The *Eagle Annual* was first published in 1951 for 1952, and the only thing that distinguished the first edition from those published subsequently was its number. Each had a red background, with the title of the annual printed in white; the whole of the rest of the cover was given over to the famous *Eagle* masthead: a black-and-yellow image of the bird in full flight (which, incidentally, had been adapted by the Reverend Morris from the top of a large brass inkwell he had bought from the white elephant stall at a vicarage garden party).

Robin Annual: Hulton Press (1954).

In 1960, *Eagle* came under the ownership of Longacre Press and with the 1961 edition (No. 10), the cover illustration became pictorial, showing a photo-montage of action-adventure themes; the last to be numbered (No. 12) was the 1963 edition. Between 1965 and 1969 the publisher was Odhams Press, and from 1970 to 1974 (the final edition) the International Publishing Corporation (IPC). The weekly *Eagle* was discontinued in 1969, Frank Hampson having departed some years earlier. But this was not to be the end: *Eagle*, like a phoenix from the ashes, rose again in the early 1980s, both as a weekly and as an annual.

During its run of 991 weekly publications and twenty-three annual editions the *Eagle* included the work of some of Britain's best artists: John Ryan (who drew 'Captain Pugwash' and 'Harris Tweed'); Norman Thelwell ('Chiko'); David Langdon ('Professor Puff'); Frank Bellamy (who drew the life of Churchill, 'The Happy Warrior', and, in later years, 'Dan Dare'); Reg Parlett ('Fidosaurus'); Harold Johns ('Rob Conway' and 'Dan Dare'); Frank Humphris ('Riders of the Range') and many others too numerous to mention.

There were top writers too: Charles Chilton was a successful scriptwriter for the wireless with 'Riders of the Range' (later converted into strip form for *Eagle*) and the classic serial 'Journey Into Space'. In later years Chilton was to become world famous when (Sir) Richard Attenborough filmed his stage play *Oh What a Lovely War*! Other writers included Chad Varah ('Dan Dare' and Bible stories), the distinguished journalist MacDonald Hastings (who wrote the 'Eagle Special Investigator' series) and, of course, the science-fiction writer Arthur C. Clarke, who scripted some of Dan Dare's adventures.

A string of successes

The success of *Eagle* resulted in companion publications: *Girl* (No. 1 annual published in 1953; last edition 1965); *Robin* (No. 1 annual 1954; last edition 1976) and *Swift* (No. 1 annual 1955; last edition 1963). All were edited by the Rev. Morris.

Girl was the 'sister paper to *Eagle*' and the first post-war comic aimed specifically at girls. Like *Eagle*, it was printed partly in full colour photogravure and attracted the same type of superior artwork. The annual's cover illustration, a red background with a young girl's head in white, became as familiar as that of *Eagle* throughout the 1950s before giving way to pictorial boards in the early 1960s.

Robin was a weekly picture paper aimed at the very young. It found success by including within its pages the stars of television's 'Children's Hour' ('Andy Pandy'; 'The Flowerpot Men') and adapting Kenneth Grahame's book *Wind in the Willows* into picture format. The latter was delightfully drawn by Hugh McNeill, who had years previously been responsible for 'Our Ernie' and 'Deed-a-Day-Danny' in the Amalgamated Press's *Knockout* annual.

Swift, the fourth Hulton publication to be issued, was designed for children midway between the *Eagle*, *Girl* and *Robin* age groups. Here, the opposite number to 'Dan Dare' was 'Tana the Jungle Boy' a junior version of Tarzan and drawn by the adept comic-strip artist Harry Bishop (later famous for his London *Evening News* strip, 'Matt Marriott'). Other artists were John Ryan, Roland Davies, Cecil Orr, Frank Bellamy, Don Lawrence, Peter Maddocks, Reg Parlett, Eric Parker and Derek Eyles: the list reading something like a *Who's Who* of Fifties comic artists. Both the *Robin Annual* and *Swift Annual* were of the same format as their 'big brother' and 'big sister' companions: cover illustrations featured the same red background together with a picture of the respective birds and the edition number.

All four titles, *Eagle, Girl, Swift* and *Robin*, begat a large number of 'spin-off' publications. *Eagle* had as many as thirty: everything from the *Eagle Book of Adventure Stories* and the *Eagle Book of Police and Detection* to the *Eagle Sports Annual* (1953–63). There were also the (now rare) *Dan Dare Space Book* (1953) and *Dan Dare's Space Annual* (1963) as well as the *Riders of the Range Annual* (1956–62) which featured the cowboy hero Jeff Arnold.

Girl spin-offs numbered another half-dozen with an associated series, *Girl Film and Television Annual* (1958–65); *Swift* had the *Swift Book of Pets, Swift Book of Buses, Coaches and Lorries* and several others. *Robin* had only one associated volume: the *Robin Book of Puzzles and Pastimes* (1964), later retitled the *Robin Book of Games and Puzzles*. It can only be concluded that the *Eagle* group must have proved a very profitable venture indeed for Hulton.

The 'Golden Age' of the *Eagle* group of publications was during the 1950s and represents the most triumphant of all post-war annual publishing. Marcus Morris left Hulton around 1960 to join the National Magazine Company. After this, things were never quite the same again.

However, the relaunch of *Eagle* (with a new Dan Dare!) and *Girl* in the early 1980s has reached a new readership; and although readers of the originals (now in their forties) may groan and bemoan their fate, it is true to say that the new annuals have found popularity with an enthusiastic (if smaller) audience which finds them just as attractive as the earlier versions were to their parents.

Girl Annual: Hulton Press (1953).

Dan Dare's Space Annual: Longacre Press (1963).

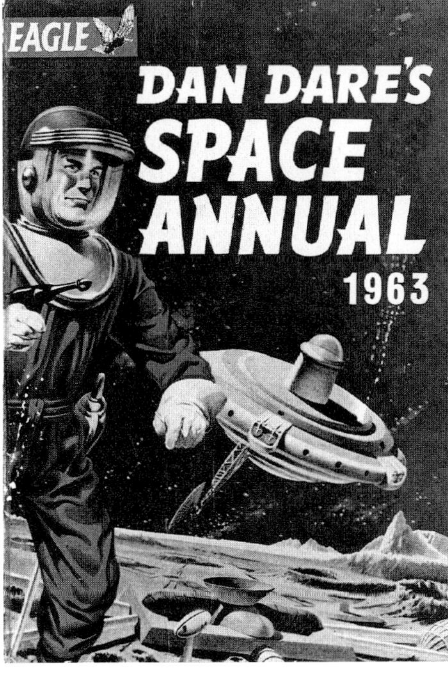

CHAPTER 6

Felix, Mickey, Donald and Flip

The first motion-picture cartoon film made in Britain was 'Hand of an Artist' (1906) by Walter Booth. It showed a hand drawing a figure which later appeared to come to life. This short film was remarkably similar to 'Phases of Funny Faces', made in the USA in the same year by J.S. Blackton. Whether Booth had heard of Blackton's film it is impossible to say, but 'Phases of Funny Faces' is acknowledged to be the earlier.

Most of the early pioneers of the animated cartoon industry were American: J.R. Bray, Earl Hurd, and above all, Winsor McCay, whose early animated short 'Gertie, the Dinosaur' is a classic of the genre. There were British animators, too, notably Dudley Buxton and Anson Dyer, who both worked for the Cartoon Film Company based in Wardour Street, London.

Although McCay's 'Gertie, the Dinosaur' became well known, it wasn't until 1919 that an American named Pat Sullivan became responsible for Felix the Cat, the first cartoon character to win worldwide popularity. Sullivan was born in Australia where he had been a newspaper cartoonist and had arrived in the USA via London, where he is said to have worked for various publications, including *Ally Sloper*.

By the end of 1921, Sullivan had signed a contract with M.J. Winkler, who would distribute the films worldwide. This led to Felix becoming more popular in Britain than anywhere else, including the United States. Felix merchandise began to appear: tableware, toys, games, dolls and, in 1923, his own annual. It was issued by E. Hulton and Co. Ltd. (a firm that would later become well known as publishers of the *Eagle* group). The *Felix Annual* was the first of what was to mark a long association between book-publishing and cartoon films.

Although Felix was said to be the creation of Pat Sullivan this was discovered in later years not to be the case. The perky and indestructible black cat was actually the brainchild of Otto Messmer, a talented and proficient artist who worked for Sullivan; and the famous name actually came from John King, a Paramount producer, who coined the name from an adaptation of the words 'feline' and 'felicity'.

Felix's main attraction was that he had personality: he also indulged in fast and furious thought (usually typified by a swift pacing with paws clasped behind his back) that was both witty and intelligent. One unique characteristic of Messmer's work was a form of surrealism lapped up by his audience: he used the artist's punctuation as it had never been used before – an exclamation mark that appeared above Felix's head would be pulled down and used as a baseball bat and ball, and a question mark became a fishing hook. It was a clever device that never failed to amuse.

Sullivan committed his studio to producing a Felix cartoon film each and every month. In time, even that hectic pace was not enough for the movie-going public who clamoured for more, and the schedule was increased to twenty-six cartoons a year. By this time, of course, the Pat Sullivan studio had become very big indeed. Before Sullivan died in 1933, several hundred Felix cartoons had been made. Unfortunately all were silent; Sullivan did not care for the new cinema technology that added voices and colour and which offered opportunities for more sophisticated animation techniques. As a result, the last Felix films to be made looked 'old hat' compared to other features released at the time (one competitor in particular, 'Steamboat Willie', made in 1928, was a 'talkie' that featured a mouse called Mickey, created by a new and exciting young talent named Walt Disney).

Felix the irrepressible

The early Felix annuals are absorbing: as well as the 96 pages of black-and-white cartoons (all lively and humorous), there were several full-page, full-colour paintings of Felix in action, and it is possible that these were specially done for these volumes. The cartoon strips, however, were not. These were reprints of American comic pages which had been previously seen in the supplements to Sunday newspapers and which had been printed in full colour in the USA. The first *Felix Annual*, containing as it did many of the Sunday pages for 1923 and 1924, is especially interesting, showing as it does the transition of the cat from a 'sharp' and 'angular' appearance in the early strips to the later, and more familiar 'rounded' look that Messmer gave Felix (although all the pages are signed by Sullivan, it was said that Otto Messmer and studio artists were actually responsible for the drawings). John Canemaker, a respected historian of animated films, has accurately described the early Felix as 'looking more like an angular dog' than a cat. 'I rounded him out after a while,' Otto Messmer is quoted as saying. 'He was much easier to draw that way, and easier to handle, in the same say that a ball is easier to turn than a box.'

During the 1920s Felix became ever more popular. In addition to the many animated 'shorts' that appeared in the nation's cinemas,

Felix, 1920s style: angular and almost dog-like in appearance. From the first *Felix Annual* (1923).

serving as an accompaniment to the main feature, *Felix* appeared in every issue of *Pearson's Weekly* from 24 November 1923 and, later, each week in the *Illustrated Sunday Herald*. The wealth of merchandising had turned Felix into a $100 million dollar industry.

The last *Felix Annual* to be issued by E. Hulton & Co. was in 1930, but the irrepressible black tom cat couldn't be kept down. Another *Felix the Cat Annual* appeared in 1956 (World Distributors), and yet another in 1962 (published by Purnell, undoubtedly brought about by the success of a new American TV series made in the late 1950s which was also shown in Britain); comic and film animation history is littered with his appearances through the years.

The popularity of Felix has extended to most countries; he still appears throughout Europe and, long after the films had stopped being produced, Felix found a new audience in Australia when a reprint series of comic books were published by Sullivan's nephew. Otto Messmer died in the early 1980s but it is more than likely that Felix will – in the words of a popular song from the 1920s – 'go on walking' until the turn of the century and beyond. If so, it is probable that the *Felix Annual* may again be seen in the nation's bookshops long before then.

Enter Mickey and Donald

Mickey Mouse had been first introduced to a cinema audience in 1928, in a brief black-and-white cartoon called 'Plane Crazy'. Shortly afterwards, a second cartoon, 'Galloping Gaucho', again featured the mouse but neither film brought satisfactory response at private showings for potential distributors.

However, it was the third film, 'Steamboat Willie', which was to make the name of Mickey Mouse world famous. Taking his cue from 'The Jazz Singer', Hollywood's first talking picture, Walt Disney decided to make a 'synchronised sound cartoon'. He achieved it by asking some of his fellow animators to work from a music and sound-effects score in accompaniment to the action in the cartoon. It worked wonderfully well and the world's first sound cartoon opened in 1928 to excited and rapturous public acclaim.

By the late 1920s, world film distribution was sophisticated enough for British audiences to see Mickey Mouse cartoons not long after their American counterparts. As in the case of Felix the Cat, merchandising soon followed, and so did a *Mickey Mouse Annual*. Published by Dean & Son in 1930 for 1931, it was the start of a long association between the firm and Walt Disney characters.

The *Mickey Mouse Annual* had only 64 pages and wasn't very big, 6¼ × 8½ in (16 × 22 cm), but it looked enormous: each page was printed on paper thick enough to give the book a depth of two inches. Mickey's adventures appeared in black and white, with several very simple comic drawings per page. Many of the pictures were probably the work of Ub Iwerks (a name of Dutch origin), Walt Disney's chief animator, who, it was said, could draw as fast as he wrote a letter. It was later revealed that Iwerks had animated the whole of 'Plane Crazy' by himself in just two weeks!

Dean & Son again capitalised on the success of Mickey Mouse by issuing other books; none was an annual, all were 'one-off' gift books for children, with agreeable artwork and stories. *Mickey Mouse in Pygmy Land, Mountaineering Mickey* and *Mickey in King Arthur's Court* were just a few of the titles Dean printed in the 1930s, all with 'the permission of Mr Walter E. Disney'.

Donald Duck, Walt Disney's other star cartoon character, made his first film appearance in 1934, in a short animated feature called 'The Little Wise Hen', but only became really well known when Disney released the classic cartoon 'The Band Concert' in 1935. By the end of the decade he had achieved the kind of worldwide popularity for a cartoon character previously enjoyed only by his stablemate, Mickey Mouse.

The first Donald Duck book was published in the USA in 1935 by Whitman Publishing of Wisconsin; with only 14 pages, it was the first of many books issued by the company. The first British book featuring Donald was more substantial: 46 pages printed on thick (but not as thick as those in the *Mickey Mouse Annual*) rough paper, with lots of text set in bold, large type, and a few black-and-white picture strips which featured both Mickey and Donald. It was published by Birn Brothers in 1936 and met with limited success: to date only one edition has been traced.

In 1939 the firm of William Collins issued for two shillings and sixpence *Donald Duck's Annual*, but it was a bad time to start new annuals: there were at least four editions, the last of which, published in 1942 for 1943, was priced at four shillings. Today this seems ludicrously cheap, for if the books were to appear now on the collector's market, they would fetch at least £60 apiece.

Donald Duck enthusiasts could nevertheless have their appetites sated by their hero's appearances in Dean's *Mickey Mouse Annual*. This ran almost continuously (no editions have been traced for the years 1944–5) until 1965, changing its format several times, from the squat volume it was in the early 1930s to the more standard size it became in the 1960s.

In the 1970s the International Publishing Corporation (IPC) issued *Walt Disney's Donald & Mickey Annual* (1973) which ran for four editions and which was superseded by *Walt Disney's*

The first *Mickey Mouse Annual* (1931).

The single-edition *Flip the Frog Annual* (1932).

Donald Duck Annual (1977), a change of title indicating that Donald had equalled if not exceeded Mickey in popularity.

A Dean & Son Disney 'one-off' issued in the 1930s was *The Snow White Annual* (1938). 'Snow White' was Walt Disney's first full-length animated cartoon film; it was released in 1937 to rapturous acclaim and still enjoys tremendous popularity whenever it is re-released. It is difficult to understand why Dean thought it could turn the subject into an 'annual'. Certainly no others were issued and it is probable that Dean were merely capitalising on both the success of the film and the vogue for anything then being labelled an 'annual'. Today, it is quite hard to find and sells for about £25, a far cry from the values of the Mickey Mouse and Donald Duck annuals.

Ub Iwerks, Walt Disney's principal animator, had known Disney since 1920, and when Disney established his own studio in 1926, Iwerks was one of the first artists to whom he offered a job. The reason was simple: Ub was the best in the business and could draw at staggering speed, a vital attribute for an animator. Iwerks designed and developed Mickey Mouse and worked on the famous 'Silly Symphonies' cartoons. In later years he also worked for Warner Brothers ('Porky Pig') and Columbia ('Colour Rhapsodies') before returning again to the Disney fold when he contributed to the perfection of the multi-plane camera, whch played such an important part in Disney's films.

Alternatives to Disney

In 1930, however, a dispute with Walt Disney led him to set up his own company and release his own independent productions. His best-known cartoons were the 'Flip the Frog' series of which he made thirty-six. These are now highly regarded by cartoon aficionados.

Dean & Son, obviously pleased with the response to the *Mickey Mouse Annual* (1930), issued the *Flip the Frog Annual* in 1931 for 1932. The title page showed Flip (looking something of a cross between Mickey and Donald) and included the dreadful pun 'annual enjoy it!'

The book, 'published by exclusive arrangement with Ub Iwerks', was full of Ub's drawings and produced in the same manner as Dean's earlier *Mickey Mouse Annual.* While Flip the Frog did not have the charm of Mickey or Donald, Iwerks's drawings were delightful.

One rare annual published probably some time in the late 1930s by Dean & Son was the *Eb' and Flo' Annual.* Eb' and Flo' were a black couple; in fact every character in the book was black, all speaking in the manner commonly attributed to negroes in the late 1930s: 'De proper place to play football am out in de yard' and 'It am no good doing dat'. Eb' was dressed as a plantation worker and Flo' wore an incongruous combination of plaid skirt, pearls and little else.

The annual (only one issue of which has been traced) looked like a spin-off from a series of cinema cartoons largely because of its similarity to the Mickey Mouse annuals: several black-and-white pictures to a page, with the occasional text story. However, no such cartoons have come to light and the resemblances in format are explained by the fact that Dean was again the publisher and that the artist, Wilfred Haughton, also drew the adventures of Mickey for the *Mickey Mouse Annual*; later, Haughton was the front-page illustrator of the *Mickey Mouse Weekly* comic from its first issue in 1936 for several years. He was, in fact, the first British professional artist to draw Mickey Mouse and, although he was never allowed to sign his Disney work, did an admirable job. His soft, rounded style instantly endowed his subjects with an endearing friendliness; Eb' and Flo' were no different, and (if readers will excuse the pun) it is a pity the tide went out after only one edition.

Pups and carthorses

Bonzo the Pup was created by ex-stockbroker's clerk George Ernest Studdy, working under the name of G.E. Studdy. After the First World War he earned a living drawing weekly cartoons about dogs, and found himself drawing one particular puppy above all others which he named Bonzo. The character became immensely popular and was extensively used for merchandising; in addition, between 1924 and 1926, no less than twenty-six animated cartoon films were made.

The first book was *The Bonzo Book* (1922) and more than a score of different titles were produced periodically before the first Bonzo annual was issued: *Bonzo's Laughter Annual* (1935), retitled *Bonzo's Annual* for the following year. A few more editions were published (using both titles) before the series was discontinued due to the material shortages of the Second World War. Studdy died in 1948 and was not to see the last short series of *Bonzo's Annual* which was published for the years 1949–52.

Animated cartoons have used every character imaginable as a source of comedy: mice, ducks, pigs, dogs; so why not a red squirrel? 'Ginger Nutt' was the chirpy

The *Eb' and Flo' Annual*, only one edition of which has been traced.

character of several David Hand cartoons produced for J. Arthur Rank.

Hand was an American ex-animator, who had worked with Disney and who had been asked by Rank to establish a British cartoon centre which would be a subsidiary of his film organisation. The company, named GB Animation, was established in 1945 and David Hand was to produce for Rank two series of highly successful cartoons: 'Animaland' and 'Musical Paintbox'. The Animaland series included the Ginger Nutt technicolour shorts, of which there were three: 'Ginger Nutt's Bee Bother', 'Ginger Nutt's Christmas Circus' and Ginger Nutt's Forest Dragon'. All were well received by film-goers and today they are still occasionally shown on television.

Around 1948, capitalising on the popularity of the films, Juvenile Productions issued the *Ginger Nutt Gift Book* which featured nearly all of the stars of Hand's cartoons. Strictly speaking, the Ginger Nutt book may not have been an annual, although it had the same shape and format. 'Gift Book' might imply that similar volumes were to be released periodically more than once a year; but there is no evidence that other editions followed the first (the front of which shows Ginger Nutt acting as ringmaster to a circus of David Hand characters), even if 'Ginger Nutt's Letter' to the readers hints at further books if this one met with approval.

After a few years, GB Animation was dissolved, an early victim of the growing popularity of television and the consequent decline of cinema audiences, and David Hand returned to the United States in 1950. Interestingly, many of those he had gathered together to work for him went on to become well-known personalities in their own right. Some were to contribute to the children's annuals. Reg Parlett, writer and artist for the Animaland series, who had contributed paintings and artwork to Amalgamated Press annuals of the 1930s, briefly continued his animation career when he worked on 'Animal Farm' (Britain's first full-length animated film) before returning to his now much-acclaimed work on the children's comics and their associated annuals. Others included Bill Holroyd and Ron Smith (whose work appeared in the Thomson annuals) and Maurice Hitchens and Roy Davis (two scriptwriters whose prolific output filled the annuals of the Amalgamated Press and IPC).

'Come On, Steve' was a weekly comic strip drawn by Roland Davies which began appearing in the *Sunday Express* newspaper in 1932. Steve was a carthorse, similar to the type Sir David Low used to depict the Trades Unions in his famous cartoons for the London *Evening Standard.* By 1936, Davies had taught himself animation sufficiently well to put together a black-and-white film cartoon of the adventures of Steve which he showed to Butcher Films of London. This distributor was keen on the idea and agreed to finance Davies so that he could provide a sound track and supply further cartoons.

The first 'Steve' film to be released was 'Steve Steps Out' (1936) and this was soon followed by five others: 'Steve of the River', 'Steve's Treasure Hunt', 'Steve's Cannon Crackers', 'Steve in Bohemia' and 'Steve Cinderella'. All were produced by his studio in Ipswich.

There were many 'Steve' books, the first being *Steve Steps Out* (1937) but only two *Come On Steve* annuals were published, one for 1948, the other for 1950. Roland Davies's work appeared in several annual titles during the Forties and Fifties. He was particularly good at depicting speed, and his drawings of racing cars, planes and trains, etc. were regularly featured in *Modern Boy Annual* (AP) and in 'spin-offs' of the *Daily*

Mail Annual such as the *Daily Mail Speedway Book* and the *Daily Mail Motorcycling Book*. Roland Davies also drew Sexton Blake picture strips for the *Knockout Annual* (AP).

The inimitable Superman

Super-horse though Steve may have been, neither he nor anyone else could ever match the snowballing popularity of that American myth 'Superman'. This costumed crusader who fought against crime appeared first in the USA in *Action Comics* in 1938 and was in the next few years stupendously successful. His popularity has endured and today, celebrating his golden anniversary, he is undisputedly the world's best-known and widely read superhero comics character.

The first Superman cartoon was made by Max Fleischer Studios and released by Paramount in 1941, with sixteen more being made until 1943 when the series was discontinued. An American non-animated television series was made in the early Fifties, followed by a cartoon series in the Sixties and yet another in the Seventies.

Superman Annual: reprinted adventures of the most famous American comic strip hero.

Although the first *Superman Annual* was not a direct result of any of these events, it is necessary to note the ready-made market that had been established for Atlas Publishing when the firm issued the first edition in 1953. The *Superman Annual* originated from comics which were reprints of the National Periodical line issued in the USA. Priced at sixpence, these 'super comics', as they were termed by Atlas, were different from the American editions in that they were printed without colour, were slightly smaller in size and had fewer pages. These reprints spawned not only the *Superman Annual* but also the *Superboy Annual* (the adventures of Superman when he was a boy) and the *Superadventure Annual* which featured other American heroes: Batman, Congo Bill, Aquaman and others.

The cover illustration for each book was always drawn by an artist commissioned by Atlas rather than by the original American artists, and it suffered considerably because of this. Each annual's 160 pages gave good value for the outlay of five shillings and was slightly cheaper compared to the home-grown products of other publishers. Today, the three titles issued by Atlas are an inexpensive means of possessing some of the vintage Superman and related stories which appeared in the 1940s and 1950s, often drawn by leading artists such as Curt Swan, Wayne Boring and Bob Kane, all of whom have

Batman Annual: reprinted adventures of the caped crusader.

in recent years been lionised by American comics aficionados. Presently, these stories in their original American editions are priced at several hundreds of pounds, beyond the reach of collectors of ordinary means. The British Atlas annuals sell for about £7.50 apiece.

Atlas continued publishing its 'super' series of annuals until the mid-to-late 1960s. It was about this time that the American comics began to be widely distributed in the United Kingdom; faced with the full-colour attractions of the originals, or of the black-and-white reprints, there seemed no competition. The Atlas comics and their counterpart annuals faded away into obscurity.

Other Superman and Batman annuals followed in the 1970s and 1980s, published by Brown and Watson, Stafford Pemberton and others; but these, although in colour and on the face of it well produced, have always represented poor value for money, being merely the equivalent of, at most, three or four monthly comics and, of course, all containing reprints.

The Marvel Comics Group, whose monthly comic publications include *The Fantastic Four, Amazing Spider-Man* and the *Incredible Hulk* have also allowed their creations to feature in annuals and these books have proved very popular, sales having been given a boost by parents who purchase them on the basis of the characters' success on television and in the cinema.

The world of Hanna and Barbera

The cinema cartoon gradually gave way to the cartoon-made-for-television; and probably no one has played a bigger role in the move from one medium to the other than the two American animators Bill Hanna and Joe Barbera. This brilliant partnership created the cat and mouse characters, Tom and Jerry, for the film studios Metro-Goldwyn-Mayer (MGM) in 1940, and continued to be responsible for fifteen years of subsequent Tom and Jerry cartoons, under executive producer Fred Quimby. Several of these won Academy Awards and found a new audience on television in later years. But Hanna and Barbera did not fall into the full public spotlight until they began to make cartoons specifically for television. Admittedly, these cheap 'limited action' cartoons were not a patch on their best Tom and Jerry features, but they found instant popularity with millions and if the strict low-cost budgets of television had not been met, the cartoon industry would have died very quickly.

Easily the most famous of Hanna and Barbera's creations

Scooby Do . . . Where Are You! Annual – based on the popular TV cartoon series.

was Huckleberry Hound, an anthropomorphous dog who spoke with a Southern (US) accent; behind him came Yogi Bear (a play on the name of a famous baseball player of the time), and two mice and a cat, Pixie, Dixie and Mr Jinks, who bore obvious similarities to Tom and Jerry. All appeared in 'Huckleberry Hound', a slapstick 30-minute cartoon show on children's TV. The jokes, animation and frequently dreadful voices of the characters caused parents to raise their eyes heavenwards, but the children loved it.

Such was the success of this slam-bang-crash series that Hanna and Barbera were able to launch several others over the next two decades. 'Top Cat' (later renamed 'Boss Cat' by the BBC), 'The Flintstones' (about a Stone-Age family) and 'The Jetsons' (a family of the future) had an appeal for adults as well as children. Despite their poor quality, all have endured and are remembered with affection by many viewers.

The first annuals produced as spin-offs from a Hanna-Barbera series, published in 1962, were *Huckleberry Hound & Yogi Bear Annual, Huckleberry Hound Comic Annual* and *Yogi Bear's Comic Annual.* Later, in 1964, the same publisher, World International, issued *Pixie, Dixie and Mr Jinks Annual.* Various editions of these were issued sporadically during the Sixties, Seventies and Eighties; all contained both colour and black-and-white comic strips whch were reprinted from American comics, together with some text which may have been especially written for the English annuals.

A *Top Cat Comic Annual* was issued by World for 1963, followed by the *Top Cat Annual* (1964). This appeared irregularly for several years. Another publisher, Brown Watson, issued for 1980 the *Boss Cat & Hong Kong Phooey Annual*, which was a coupling of the BBC-renamed *Top Cat* and a new Hanna-Barbera series.

Hanna-Barbera's Flintstone Annual was published for 1963 by World International, then intermittently for many years by World and other publishers. World also issued the *Flintstone's Comic Album* (1964) and the *Flintstone's Family Album* (1981). Again, all comic strips were reprints from American comics.

In the 1970s Brown Watson published several annuals of Hanna-Barbera cartoons: *Scooby Doo ... Where Are You Annual* (1976) capitalised on the series of the same name. Scooby Doo was a large dog who, with a group of teenagers, had adventures that always seemed to involve things that went 'bump' in the night (and often in the daytime too!): walking skeletons, Egyptian mummies, vampires, werewolves, et al. But by now children's comics and cartoons had been swept by the 'horror' craze. The theme was also apparent in the *Funky Phantom Annual* (1976), featuring the adventures of some teenagers and their pal, a 200-year-old ghost. The *Scooby Doo Annual* was initially far better produced and contained comic strips that had not appeared before; the *Funky*

Bugs Bunny Cartoon Annual (1981).

Phantom, admittedly at half the price, was very inferior, containing reprints on cheap paper.

Belatedly, a *Tom & Jerry Annual* (1968) was issued by World International (again with reprints) and this has remained in print well into the 1980s. Although it was Hanna and Barbera who created this famous duo, they received no credit on these annuals due to the fact that all were made under the copyright of MGM.

From Popeye to Bananaman

Although it may appear so to the casual observer of television annuals, Bill Hanna and Joe Barbera did not monopolise all cartoon characters. There were also the spinach-eating sailor, Popeye, the wisecracking rabbit, Bugs Bunny, and the suave, sophisticated and silent Pink Panther.

The first *Popeye Annual* was published for 1960 and has been issued periodically over many years by several different publishers. This has caused a problem for collectors in that some of the later ones give the appearance of being the first; one example of this is the Brown Watson 1973 edition which is clearly marked 'Annual No. 1'. None of the Popeye annuals has contained much original material; usually each comprises comic strips by the American artist, Bud Sagandorf, which are printed both in colour and black-and-white.

The *Bugs Bunny Annual* (1963) was published irregularly by World International for the next twenty years. All of the contents were reprints and included other Warner Bros. cartoon stars: Porky Pig, Yosemite Sam, Daffy Duck and Tweety and Sylvester. The latter pair, a canary and a black-and-white cat endowed with more personality than any other cartoon cat, were given their own title: *Tweety & Sylvester Annual* in 1974.

The Pink Panther cartoon series had been inspired by the animated title credits used in the film 'The Pink Panther' (1963) which starred Peter Sellers. The first cartoon was 'The Pink Phink' and, after success was assured when it won an Academy Award in 1964, others were produced for the cinema; later they were made exclusively for television. The *Pink Panther Annual* (1974) ran for several consecutive editions.

Conveniently, many of these cartoon characters could be found together in later editions of *TV Comic Annual*. This was first issued for 1954, being the annual for *TV Comic*, the first weekly comic to be based on television personalities, and issued in 1951 by the *News of the World* newspaper. Interestingly, the American cartoon characters were often drawn by British artists as were other strips not based on TV shows. It was then that Bugs Bunny, the Pink Panther and Popeye found themselves alongside 'The Incredible Bulk' (drawn expertly by Steve Maher, and a send-up of TV's 'Incredible Hulk'), 'Nelly and her Telly' and several other comic strips devised in Britain. The publisher of this popular annual has changed on several occasions and, although it seems to have been temporarily discontinued, if past history is anything to go by, it will doubtless be appearing again soon on some publisher's list.

The most recent cartoon character to be given his own annual is *Superted*. *Superted* is a teddy bear with super powers: he can fly and he has extraordinary strength. The character has featured in many short animated features which are beautifully produced from a small studio in Wales; the character first appeared on television a few years ago and quickly developed a large following. As well as the *Superted Annual* other books are issued periodically and there has been a good deal of merchandising.

But perhaps the most successful cartoon series of recent years has been 'Bananaman'. The first *Bananaman Annual* (1985) looks set to have a long run, although this is not directly a result of the television show. Bananaman appeared first in the weekly comic *Nutty*, published by D.C. Thomson. The comic strip itself was a parody of super-heroes: Eric Whimp, a young lad, eats a banana and is transformed into the costumed hero with big muscles and a small brain – Bananaman. Naturally, his foes are equally outlandish, and with names such as Captain Cream and Appleman they read more like a choice of dessert than serious adversaries, as is the intention. The comic strip, drawn by John Geering, became popular enough to capture the attention of television. As a result of this appeal to a wider audience, Bananaman was given his own annual. Things seemed to have come full circle.

TV Comic Annual (1980).

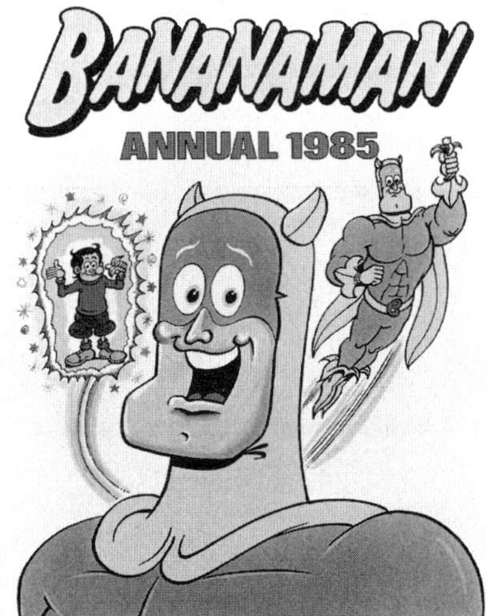

CHAPTER 7

Newspaper Publishers

Annuals issued by newspaper publishers are a separate genre in themselves. The most famous are those featuring children's characters which were created as a result of battles in the never-ending daily newspaper circulation war; the annuals came later, profitable afterthoughts to successful readership promotions. Rupert Bear of the *Daily Express*; Teddy Tail of the *Daily Mail*; Pip, Squeak and Wilfred of the *Daily Mirror*; Bobby Bear of the *Daily Herald* and many more were all responsible for maintaining large circulations and each found a following numbered in the millions. It was but a small step for newspapers to consider reprinting the popular daily features in book form once a year and thus was born the newspaper publishers' annual.

The first newspaper children's feature which later resulted in a hugely successful annual was 'Mrs Hippo's Kindergarten' which first appeared in the pages of the *Daily Mirror* in 1904 and featured Tiger Tim. However, as it was many years before a Tiger Tim annual was published (1922), and then via a different route (by a different Harmsworth company, the Amalgamated Press), this cannot be said to be the first newspaper publishers' annual.

Neither can the distinction be said to belong entirely to Teddy Tail who began appearing in the *Daily Mail* in 1915. Teddy's reprinted adventures appeared in the same year: *The Adventures of Teddy Tail of the Daily Mail* and *Teddy Tail in Nursery Rhyme Land* (both 1915) were followed periodically by several other collections over the next few years. But the key word here is periodically: there is no evidence that the publication schedule was intended to be annual, although it did, in the event, turn out to be approximately so. The Teddy Tail books were precursors of the *Daily Herald Bobby Bear Book* (1920), officially continued as *The Bobby Bear Annual* (dated the year of publication: 1922), and of the *Pip, Squeak & Wilfred Annual*, published in the same year but dated 1923.

The last edition of *Bobby Bear's Annual* was dated 1969. Leaving aside the possibility that there were one or two years when it was not published (the years 1921 and 1944 are suspect) this was a record run, equalled only recently by the *Rupert, Dandy* and *Beano* annuals.

Bobby Bear made his first appearance in the pages of the *Daily Herald* in the late 1910s, almost certainly a rival to the *Daily*

Bobby Bear's Annual (1925): 64 pages; paper covers.

Mail's Teddy Tail. The adventures of this small, brown bear who dressed in a peculiar, checked pair of short trousers held up by braces, were written for the newspaper by Kitsie Bridges ('Aunt Kitsie' to her readers) and illustrated by Dora McLaren. McLaren's drawings were, to say the least, crude but her enthusiasm for the nursery-style excitement of Bridges's stories was self-evident and her animated style found an appeal with a wide audience. The stories were told in comic strip form: large detailed pictures, with the characters' speech shown in word balloons. A more detailed description of events was told in rhyme beneath each drawing.

Early annuals were 64-page, paper-covered booklets priced at one shilling, and they reprinted adventures from the newspaper; red tint was applied to the drawings to give them some semblance of colour. The editions dated before 1931 bore the actual year of publication; it was in that year that it was decided to 'forward date' the annual: thus, the edition issued in 1931 is dated 1932, and there is no edition dated 1931.

With Bobby Bear's growing popularity, the paper-covered annuals disappeared to be replaced in the 1930s by 124-page, hard-covered books published by Dean & Son, with many of Bobby's adventures appearing in full colour. By then Aunt Kitsie had lost her credit for authorship of the stories but could console herself with having been promoted to editor. Dora McLaren was succeeded by Wilfred Haughton who did a great deal of work for Dean and who would in later years become best known for his work on *Mickey Mouse Weekly*. Haughton perfectly captured McLaren's style and provided excellent continuation.

It was common for the 1930s annuals to include an advertisement for 'The Bobby Bear Club' in an attempt to recruit new members (after all, new recruits could be expected to persuade mum and dad to buy the newspaper in order to catch up on the lastest club news). The attractions of 'The Jolliest Club In The World', so said the advertisement, were 'Adventure ... Prizes ... Mysteries ... Friendship ... Competitions ... Advice ... Secrets ... Passwords

... Codes.' The lucky member would then receive an enamelled badge and a Club Certificate together with a copy of 'the rollicking club song' which members were encouraged to sing at get-togethers.

Pip, Squeak and Wilfred

Tiger Tim was not the only popular children's character to originate within the pages of the *Daily Mirror*. On 12 May 1919 the newspaper began the most popular children's feature in England between the two World Wars – 'Pip, Squeak and Wilfred'. What was to become a nationwide phenomenon began inauspiciously in the children's section of the newspaper. 'Pip' the dog and 'Squeak' the penguin were introduced within the 'Editor's Letter' which also incorporated a single drawing showing his 'pets'. A few months later they were joined by the third member of the trio, Wilfred, a baby rabbit. The public response was overwhelmingly favourable and what had become a four-picture strip went from strength to strength.

Pip & Squeak Annual: first edition (1923).

The artist of this unlikely threesome was A.B. Payne, a Welsh cartoonist whose work had previously appeared in the comic papers of the Amalgamated Press. Soon the *Mirror* strip was increased to six pictures per day and Pip, Squeak and Wilfred were appearing in the *Sunday Pictorial* too. On 15 October 1921, the *Mirror* made them the stars of its very own newspaper comic which they called *Pip & Squeak*; it was successful enough to spawn a duplicate supplement, the *Children's Own Sunday Pictorial*. The first book of reprint strips from the newspaper was published in 1920 and the first *Pip & Squeak Annual* was published in 1922 for 1923.

'Who would have thought,' said 'Uncle Dick' (in reality the journalist B.J. Lamb) 'when I first introduced Pip and Squeak to you over three years ago, that they would have blossomed out as the founders of the splendid book you hold in your hands? It all seems ... too good to be true.' Indeed it did. But the *Pip & Squeak Annual* was a huge success and the *Mirror* soon launched a 'companion': *Wilfred's Annual* (1924). Before long the letter of introduction in that annual was saying that 'it hardly seems possible that Wilfred the baby rabbit whom Pip and Squeak adopted some time ago, should have an annual of his own, and yet here it is – *Wilfred's Annual*, a splendid book packed with delightful pictures and stories which, I am sure, will give you hours and hours of delight'. It was signed, as were all letters in both annuals, 'Your affectionate Uncle Dick'.

The two annuals were extremely similar and, although each

Wilfred's Annual: first edition (1924).

boasted that it was 'quite different in its appeal' to the other, it is likely that without the board covers, the reader would not have been able to tell them apart, although, as might be expected, rather more emphasis was placed on Wilfred in his annual, with the young rabbit enjoying the odd story of his own. Both *Daily Mirror* annuals were similar in format to APs *Playbox Annual* (heavy, good-quality paper stock, with over 200 pages, using coloured inks), which had been running for more than a decade, and the cost was also the same – six shillings – very cheap by today's standards, but expensive in 1922. Obviously the *Mirror* believed the successful *Playbox Annual* to be worthy of emulation.

Artists and writers

Austin Payne was responsible for many of the 'Pip, Squeak and Wilfred' illustrations which appeared in both books, but there were other artists who contributed drawings for the text stories: Gladys Withers, Murdock Stimpson,

Arthur Mansbridge, Will Owen, Ruth Cobb, Cyril Cowell, Harry Rountree and L. Church all supplied a highly competent level of art. There was also the work of E.E. Briscoe, which never failed to raise the tone, and that of Helen Jacobs, an artist who was in a class of her own. Her very detailed pen-and-ink drawings, used for story illustration, and her colour work for frontispieces and plates, were eminently superior to that of her immediate contemporaries. The fantasy characters that she drew with such clear and uncomplicated lines were endowed with a life and personality that made them as real as their human participants. She was in the same mould as that foremost Edwardian illustrator, Arthur Rackham, but whereas Rackham's work could at times appear frightening; Helen Jacobs' was more placid, just gentle flights of fancy into fairyland.

Other artists of quality soon joined the annuals' stable of illustrators: Charles Folkard, Anne Andersen and Alfred Bestall. Folkard (1878–1963) was already a highly respected artist (*Swiss Family Robinson*: 1910; *Grimm's Fairy Tales*: 1911; *The Magic Egg*: 1922) and obtaining his services was something of a coup. Charles Folkard is also known for his creation of the famous mouse, 'Teddy Tail', in the pages of the *Daily Mail* newspaper.

Anne Andersen contributed various pen-and-ink drawings to the *Pip & Squeak Annual* but did little colour work. However, in later years, Andersen was much sought after by publishers for her beautiful watercolour paintings, invariably executed in pastel shades, which served to accompany fairy stories: all were cosy, rosy-hued pictures delineated in classical, and very feminine, style.

Alfred Bestall was just beginning his artistic career and many of his commissions were obtained through the Byron Studios where he was then employed; by 1922 his work had appeared in magazines such as *The Cartoonist* and *Punch*. In later years his art appeared in the top magazines of the day (*The Tatler, Passing Show, The Sketch*) and he also became a well-respected book-illustrator (*The Spanish Goldfish*: 1934; *The Land of the Christmas Stocking*: 1948), and the writer and artist of the adventures of Rupert Bear which appeared each day in the *Daily Express* (a commission that continued for more than thirty years).

Unlike the *Playbox Annual*, the *Pip & Squeak* and *Wilfred* annuals allowed their writers a byline: Gwyneth Castleton, John Hunt, Florence Stimpson, Adrian Vincent, Richard Barnes, Cynthia Gordon and Raymond Lee were just some of those named. Many of these were, very probably, pseudonyms, sometimes perhaps for the editor himself who was also contributing stories, either as 'Uncle Dick' or under his real name, B.J. Lamb. The reason for a writer having an assumed name might be that he or she was also submitting work to Amalgamated Press (for instance the *Playbox Annual*) and did not wish them to know for fear of someone within that powerful company taking offence (the annuals were, of course, rivals). But whether the authors wrote under real or assumed names, the stories were by no means amateur, and many decades later these 'tiny tales' still appeal by reason of their imaginative story-lines.

Of special note were the fairy stories of John Hunt and of Florence Stimpson (very likely the wife of Murdoch Stimpson whose artwork also appeared in the annual), the adventure yarns of Richard Barnes and Grahame Hunter, and the pleasant little tales by Joyce Brisley (who sometimes illustrated them herself, and who had an artist sister, Nina Brisley).

Of interest, too, were the charming stories dealing with inanimate-objects being brought to life. Kitchen utensils, food, books, trees and plants – all, sooner or later, sprouted limbs and developed faces. Helen Jacobs was one artist who could endow a cucumber with more menace than the Queen of Hearts! In fact, there was more than a hint of the creative genius of Lewis Carroll in many of these tales. In one story angry apple kings and glaring grapes shout at the child heroine 'Off with her head!', although the ending was a happy one with the unfortunate fruit being cheerfully munched by the young 'Alice'.

A dream, a bump on the head or sheer gluttony would bring objects to life, and E.E. Briscoe was another artist who gave them a masterly treatment. 'To the oven!' shout the deliciously nasty bread-loaf family, in one story illustrated by him, as they maltreat a young lad who prefers cake: he awakens, vowing to stay away from cakes and eat up all his bread in future. A cautionary tale for little ones, not soon forgotten.

The 'Gugnuncs'

The popularity of Pip, Squeak and Wilfred increased rapidly throughout the 1920s. In 1927 the 'Wilfredian League of Gugnuncs', a 'Secret Society', was started for all aficionados of the trio. Soon, calling it 'secret' seemed to be stretching a point: in less than three months, it could claim 100,000 members and there were Gugnunc toys, pennants, games and even an official Gugnunc song. The name 'Gugnunc' was taken from Wilfred's minimal vocabulary (they were the only two words he could say: 'Gug' was baby talk and meant nothing in particular, and 'nunc' meant 'Uncle'). The size of the membership was a good pointer to the likely circulation of the annuals at the time. It was demonstrably an active group: a rally of the W.L.O.G. held at the Royal Albert Hall attracted 87,000 people!

Uncle Dick's Competition Annual: first edition (1930).

The success of competitions within the pages of the *Daily Mirror* led to yet a third volume being issued from the offices of Geraldine House, headquarters of the *Daily Mail* annuals: *Uncle Dick's Competition Annual* (1930). In the main this was, as the title implied, a book of competitions of all descriptions (although, the following year, the word 'competition' was removed from the title); these were supplemented by the occasional story, usually of the adventure variety. *Uncle Dick's Annual* was aimed at the older child, and deserved success but this was not forthcoming and it had a very short run indeed.

In the course of the 1930s, both *Wilfred's Annual* and the *Pip & Squeak Annual* lost much of their quality reproduction; the artists and writers were still of a high standard (and many were the same as those in the early 1920s) but the two books were now produced on rough, coarse, substandard paper, full-colour plates were non-existent, and the number of pages were reduced to around 176. The fact was that the peak of popularity had passed for the endearing threesome, and the *Mirror* editorship had an uphill fight on its hands as it fought to compete with the many attractive children's annuals being issued all too frequently by the Amalgamated Press. The last *Wilfred's Annual* was published for 1938; the *Pip & Squeak Annual* ceased publication with the 1939 issue.

The three characters were revived after the war in the *Pip, Squeak & Wilfred Annual* (1953–5) but, regrettably, they were now 'old hat'. That generation preferred the new comics of the day; the age of the Gugnuncs had faded from view.

The Oojah Annual: first edition (1923).

Oojah, the amazing elephant

The *Daily Sketch* was impressed by the immediate success of Pip, Squeak and Wilfred and the effect the strip had on the circulation of the *Daily Mirror*.

The *Sketch* decided it needed a children's feature of its own and, on 8 October 1921, it became the first British newspaper to issue a children's supplement (scooping the *Daily Mirror*: its *Pip & Squeak* supplement was published the following week). Entitled *The Oojah Paper* (later retitled *The Oojah Sketch*), its star was 'Oojah', an elephant – albeit a forgetful one – who walked on his hind legs and could perform magical tricks.

The following year, in 1922, E. Hulton & Co. issued *The Oojah Annual* – 100 pages of 'Stories, Pictures and Games for Little People'. The annual, edited by 'Uncle' Oojah, reprinted some of the weekly *Oojah Sketch* cartoons; in addition there were Oojah text stories and other 'funny animal' features.

The *Daily Sketch* had been very fortunate in obtaining the services of a good writer and a fine artist: Flo Lancaster began her writing career just before the First World War and her work included many stories for girls' and women's magazines. There is no evidence that she created Oojah but it is more than probable that she did.

Thomas Maybank was a distinguished illustrator who, it is said, had contributed 'a number of startling fairy designs to *Punch* between 1902 and 1904', all of which took their inspiration from the gifted Victorian cartoonist and illustrator, Richard Doyle (1824–83). Maybank had also drawn extensively for *The Tatler, The Sketch, The Strand* and *Pearson's* and contributed to the Ward Lock series of *Wonder Books*. He depicted 'Flip-Flap, the Great Oojah' (as 'Uncle' was called in the early adventures), in fine style: his large and detailed drawings, while very humorous, still managed to retain the elephant's dignity. Similarly, his companions Don (the little Hum-Jum-Jarum) and Snooker (a cat who wore boots) were beautifully drawn and never failed to amuse.

Sadly, Thomas Maybank died in 1925 and, although his work continued to appear for a short time after his death, another artist was soon recruited. It was, fortunately, an able successor, H.M. Talintyre. Where Maybank's drawings had been humorous, Talintyre's were often downright funny and his comic style served to make the characters instantly lovable, yet he still managed to put a great deal of care and detail into his art.

In 1927 the *Daily Sketch* itself took over the publishing of the Oojah annual and named it *Uncle Oojah's Big Annual*, which was somewhat deceptive as it contained fewer pages than the last Hulton edition. Then, shortly after, the firm of William Collins took up the option of issuing the annual. Collins continued to publish the book until the last consecutive edition in 1942. The combination of Flo Lancaster's stories and Talintyre's art have made these annuals the best of all in the eyes of many collectors.

The book reverted to its first title of *The Oojah Annual* in the late 1940s, this time published by Peter Pitkin. The several volumes produced were similar in style to the Collins annuals but in a slimmer and taller format once again, like the first. Flo Lancaster's stories and rhymes were illustrated by Talintyre throughout.

Laughs and thrills

The *Daily Sketch* also featured the famous strip cartoon. 'Pop'. Pop, a short, fat, nearly bald little man whose popular cartoons also appeared in the *Illustrated Daily Herald*, made his first appearance in the *Daily Sketch* on 21 May 1921, drawn by a Scotsman, John Millar Watt, whose work had previously appeared in both the *Daily Chronicle* and *The Sphere*.

The first *Pop Annual*, dated 1925 and priced at two shillings and sixpence, was hardbacked, as was the 1926 edition. The following twenty-two editions were paperback, the last appearing in the early 1950s; this, incidentally, was the only edition with artwork other than by J. Millar Watt (it was by the artist Gordon Hogg, who continued to draw the strip long after Millar Watt's retirement). Collectors should note that no editions were published for 1940 and 1941.

The humour in 'Pop' was, for the most part, too sophisticated for children but the annual was often read by the whole family, which is the reason for its inclusion here. Millar Watt was an extremely talented artist whose art was rivalled only by the quality of his writing: the 'Pop' strip cartoon, in its near forty-year run and twenty-four annuals, observed and commented upon most aspects of British life in an original and intensely funny way. Testimony to Millar Watt's work came in practical form from the USA when 'Pop' became one of the very few British strips to be syndicated there. In the sophisticated and highly competitive American market, this was no small tribute.

The Pop Annual: first edition (1925).

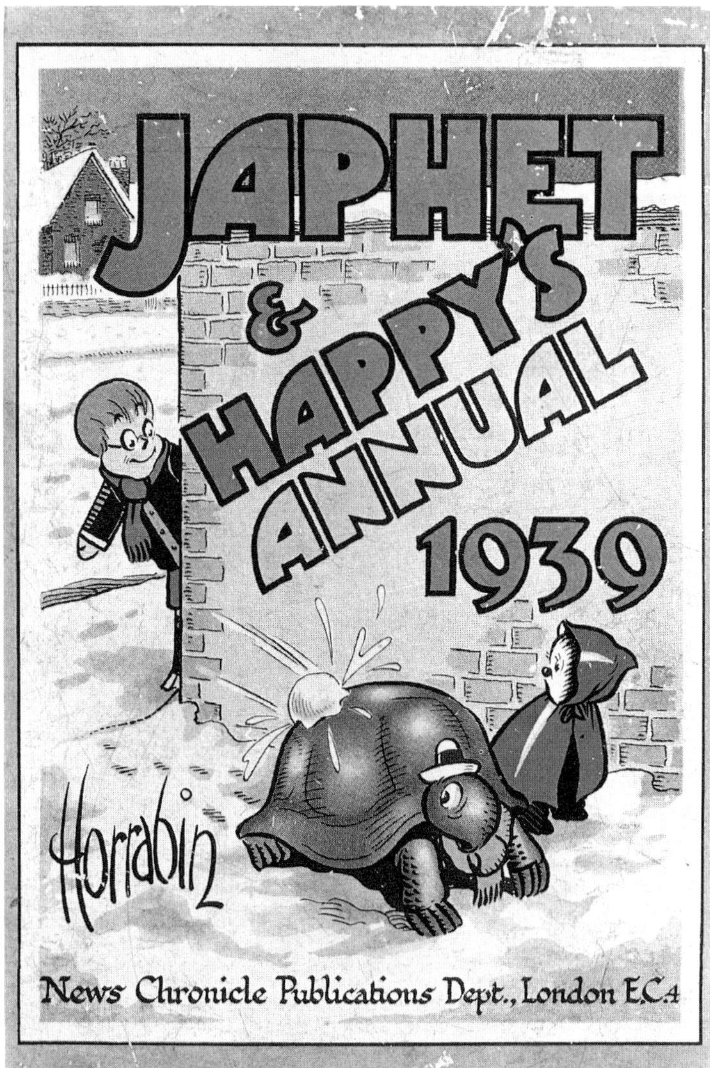

Japhet & Happy's Annual (1939).

Not all newspaper publishers' annuals were based on existing features. Very occasionally, one would be issued as a straight commercial proposition, relying on the strength of the book's contents and the promotion by the parent newspaper to build a healthy readership. One such was the immodestly titled *World's Best Boys' Annual* (1926–37) published by Allied Newspapers in Manchester.

Immodestly titled it may have been, but certainly during its twelve-year run there was little room for complaint. The stories were strong, exciting tales of the schoolboys' favourite fare: western, science fiction, detective, sporting and historical yarns together with tales of adventure from far-flung corners of the globe. Gunby Hadath, who had written for the *Boy's Own Paper*, and Major Charles Gilson, a popular *Chums* contributor, were only two of the many authors who wrote for this annual. The stories were also well illustrated by leading artists: D.C. Eyles (sport and adventure), Fred Bennett (humour and school stories) and T.H. Robinson (adventure) were a few of those commissioned to provide pen-and-ink drawings or paintings for colour plates. The *World's Best Boys' Annual* is typical of the many excellent 'adventure' annuals that were issued in the years before the Second World War.

Noah and Nipper

Some of the gentlest of comic strip humour was to be found in *Japhet and Happy's Annual* (1933–53). This featured the adventures of the Noah family and their pets: characters made of wood but endowed with considerable life.

'The Adventures of the Noah Family' began as a one-panel cartoon in the *Daily News* in 1919 and continued for many years in that newspaper before transferring to the *News Chronicle* in 1930 where the feature continued to be published until the late 1940s. During that time the name of the feature was changed twice: firstly to 'Japhet and Happy' and, later, to 'The Arkubs'.

The daily strip was created and subsquently written and drawn by the prolific artist James Francis Horrabin (1884–1962), at one time the art editor of the *Daily News*. Horrabin was also a cartographer whose maps of both World Wars were used by many newspapers; in addition, he provided illustrations for books and magazines. A man of many parts, Horrabin was Labour MP for Peterborough (1929–31), a lecturer, and also familiar to pre-war television audiences as a 'Quick-Draw Cartoonist'.

'The Adventures of the Noah Family' was quickly reprinted, the first such paperback volume being

'Some Adventures of the Noah Family', published in 1920, and followed by others at approximately yearly intervals. All of these booklets were published by the *Daily News* until the feature was transferred to the *News Chronicle*, which then continued the reprintings.

Japhet and Happy's Annual, thick hardbacked books, also contained reprints from the daily newspaper and a selection of the best of J.F. Horrabin's pictures which were supplemented by stories also written by him. 'Japhet', it should be explained, was the small son of Mr Noah; an endearing little chap whose manner of handling the everyday implements of life must have been a constant mystery to readers: being wooden, his arms were mere pointed stumps – he had no hands. 'Happy' was a small bear cub, one of the many animals that lived with the Noahs on their ark. These included a goat named Gerald, a parrot called Polixenes and an ostrich named Adelaide.

The newspaper started a club, which was advertised in the annuals: with the resounding title of the 'Grand United Order of Arkubs', it promised all the benefits of other newspaper children's feature clubs, such as challenges and secret codes, with the extra attraction of a special card to be sent to each member at Christmas and on birthdays. To join, the reader was asked to send in twelve 'Happy' badges which were printed at the rate of one a day in the *News Chronicle*. In an additional promotion, the *Chronicle* seemed to go wild when it promised that every Arkub who enrolled six new members would be sent as a gift a splendid Arkub breakfast set of best-quality china. *Japhet and Happy's Annual* was one of the small number of annuals which continued to be published during the war years.

The *Daily Mail Nipper Annual* (published in the years 1934–41) was a series of eight large paperback books reprinting the popular *Daily Mail* comic strip 'Nipper', which began in the newspaper in 1933 and ran until 1947.

Nipper was a very young lad (obvious because he still wore a nappy) and the creation of the artist Brian White who, it is said, based him on his own son. White was a talented cartoonist who had a nice line in humour which was

Daily Mail Nipper Annual (c.1934). Comic strips without word balloons are particularly hard to do; but Brian White, Nipper's creator, always managed it beautifully. The strip shown below is a typical example.

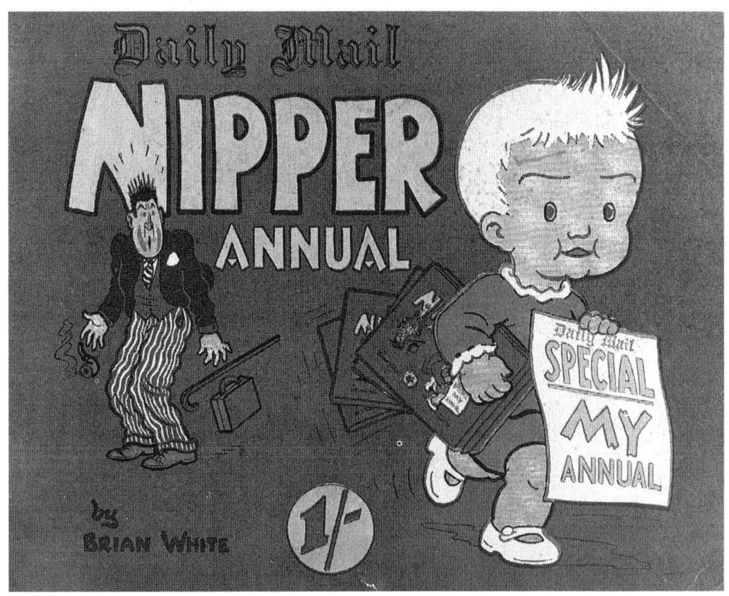

pleasantly consistent in its quality. It was also to White's credit that he never fell into the trap of making Nipper's adventures merely 'cute': the daily one-to-four panel 'gags' had a sophistication quickly appreciated by adults, which contributed to its longevity.

One of the most amusing aspects of the Nipper strip was the reactions of Nipper's father. Here, Brian White seemed to borrow more than a little from H.M. Bateman: after a particularly shocking 'Nipperism' Dad's brylcreamed, smoothly combed-back hair would literally stand on end, his body shaking and trembling, looking for all the world like a man in a Bateman 'The Man Who...' type of drawing.

All of the annuals contained reprinted material, some having the advantage of a colour section in the centre of the book; and White also had a hand in some of several advertisements that appeared in each book. For collectors, the last two Nipper annuals (published in the years 1940 and 1941) are the hardest to find: both were reduced in size and subject to the usual wartime cutbacks.

Teddy Tail and Jolly Jack

The *Daily Mail's* premier children's feature was 'The Adventures of Teddy Tail' (subtitled 'The Diary of the Mouse in your House'), which began on 5 April 1915, and was Britain's first daily newspaper strip. Two slim, 32-page, hardcover books reprinting the first adventures were published in the same year by A. & C. Black Ltd. and these were followed by several others over the next few years.

For anyone who had spent their formative years in the period between the wars, 'Teddy Tail of the *Daily Mail*' was a famous and much-loved institution. And judging by the millions of members it boasted, few people could not have been members of 'The Teddy Tail League', the club for Teddy Tail aficionados. Each member was given a badge, plus the usual club paraphernalia, and was sent a coloured postcard on their birthday.

Teddy Tail was also referred to as 'the mouse with the knot in his tail' but few people are aware of the knot's origins, for the story has seldom been retold: Teddy's friend, Dr Beetle, had fallen into a hole and in order to help him out, the mouse tied a knot in his tail and lowered it down for the doctor to hold on to. Once Dr Beetle was free, to quote Teddy '... a dreadful thing happened. We couldn't get the knot undone.' And so it remained, firmly tied, for Teddy's entire forty years of publication.

Initially, the Teddy Tail feature was drawn by Charles Folkard who later left to pursue his career as a book illustrator (his work in that field is now much collected). His brother, Harry, then took over and continued to draw the feature until the early 1930s. Harry Folkard was the artist responsible for Teddy's picture on the 'Teddy Tail League' badge; Herbert Foxwell did a series of paintings (around six in number) which were used for the birthday cards sent to League members.

In April 1933, the *Daily Mail* decided to publish a weekly comic supplement, *The Boys and Girls Daily Mail*, and Teddy Tail naturally was the first choice to be its front-page star attraction. This boost to Teddy's career was further supplemented by the addition to the newspaper's staff of Herbert Foxwell, formerly of the Amalgamated Press. Foxwell was one of AP's top artists; he had been mainly responsible for developing Tiger Tim from a quaint, somewhat scrawny character into the resplendent, fully developed megastar of five annuals and three weekly comics (see Chapter 3).

Herbert Foxwell took to drawing Teddy Tail with obvious enthusiasm: his first work for the supplement appeared in November 1933 and he continued to submit both front page and inside drawings for the two editions a week.

Foxwell was also asked to supply work for *Teddy Tail's Annual* which was published by Collins for the *Daily Mail* for the years 1934–42. He painted the covers and many of the interiors for the 1934–40 editions before joining the army (he was later killed in action). The 1941 and 1942 editions were drawn by different artists. Foxwell's cover paintings were every inch as splendid as those he had done for the Tiger Tim annuals. Never very good at drawing people (all his renditions were quite wooden and lifeless), he showed something approaching genius when it came to depicting comic animals: he breathed fresh life into Teddy Tail and his friends, just as he done years earlier for Tiger Tim.

Due to the war, the Teddy Tail newspaper strip stopped in 1940 and was resumed around 1946, ending for good in 1960; the *Teddy Tail Annual* recommenced publication with an issue for 1949 which ran until 1962. This 'second series' of the annual (with drawings by Roland Davies) was published by Juvenile Productions Ltd. (London).

'Hallo, my Hearties! Shiver my timbers if I haven't come to the end of my annual. My first annual too! Just think how excited I feel about it!' wrote Jolly Jack in his letter to the readers which appeared on the last page of the first *Jolly Jack's Annual* (1935). Printing the letter at the back of the book rather than at the front was a tradition previously peculiar to AP's Tiger Tim annuals; perhaps it was no surprise, then, to discover that the leading contributor to *Jolly Jack's Annual* was Herbert Foxwell.

Jolly Jack and his chums, Captain Bowsprit and the rest, were the comic characters who appeared every week in the *Sunday Dispatch*. Unfortunately, Jack and half the crew on the 'Fun

Above *Teddy Tail's Annual:* first edition (1934). Cover art by H. S. Foxwell.

Left *Jolly Jack's Annual:* first edition (1935).

Ship' were human rather than animal and Foxwell was not at his best with the human form. Admittedly, he managed to slip in the occasional comic animal here and there, but Jack was a poor replacement for the kind of central character that was needed, as exemplified by AP's Tiger Tim which he had now abandoned.

The 1935 edition is interesting for 'Jolly Jack's Theatre', a several-page pull-out drawn by Foxwell, and for which readers were encouraged to cut pictures from the *Sunday Dispatch* in order to supplement those in the book. This and subsequent editions also printed the work of some other well-known 'annual artists', among them S.J. Cash, L. Church, Walter Bell and Ruth Cobb.

Jolly Jack's Annual continued to be published by Collins for the *Sunday Dispatch* every year until 1940, when the last edition was issued dated 1941.

Rupert – the perennial favourite

The *Daily Express Children's Annual* was undated but published for the years 1930–4. Edited by S. Louis Giraud, this series of five (all but the first are numbered) short, thick annuals are today much sought after by two different groups of collectors.

The annual was one of the earliest – perhaps the first – to introduce 'self-erecting models to illustrate the stories'. These were what are known today as 'pop-ups' and, although sometimes crude in appearance, were cleverly designed. 'Pop-up' collectors pay high prices for copies in good condition with all models complete. The editor also made it a point always to include a Rupert Bear story in each edition. Despite the fact that these stories were reprints (and often shorter than their original length), all editions of the *Daily Express Children's Annual* are eagerly hunted by Rupert collectors. The two annuals that are especially interesting are the first and second editions (1930 and 1931): both contain a 'pop-up' Rupert, the second, incidentally, being better than the first.

In the autumn of 1935, for 1936, the *Daily Express* published another new annual, *The Boys' and Girls' Book of the Year*, a truly mammoth volume with 296 pages, 11 × 8¾ in (28 × 22 cm), containing exciting stories and practical articles. This was a replacement annual for the *Daily Express Children's Annual*, the last edition of which had been published two years earlier. Subsequent books in this new series always included the year in the title: *Boys' and Girls' Book for 1937*, followed by *Boys' and Girls' Book for 1938 and 1939*. Today, this set of four annuals would be of little interest were it not for the inclusion in each of at least one original Rupert Bear story: the 1936 and 1937 editions had twelve one-page stories of six pictures apiece; the 1938 edition had 'Rupert and the Travel Machine', and the 1939, 'Rupert and the Red Box'. All were written and drawn by Alfred Bestall.

As is evident, there is now and has been for some years considerable interest in Rupert Bear: the *Rupert* annual, now in its fifty-third edition, is one of the most collected of all annuals. But Rupert's history extends further back than the annual, the *Daily Express Children's Annual* or *The Boys' and Girls' Book of the Year*: Rupert first appeared in the *Daily Express* in 1920. The little bear's creator was Mary Tourtel, and she was succeeded in 1935 by Alfred Bestall who continued to write and draw the feature for twice as long again.

Mary Tourtel's first newspaper work had been a one-panel-a-week feature for the *Sunday Express* in 1919 called 'In Bobtail Land'; this was followed by a similar series for the *Daily Express* entitled 'When Animals Work'. Her contact with the *Express* newspapers was a natural one, for many years

The dustwrapper of the first *Rupert* Annual issued in 1936.

earlier she had married Herbert Tourtel who was an editorial executive at the *Daily Express*.

In 1920, R.D. Blumenfield, the editor of the *Express*, having observed the success of 'Teddy Tail' in the *Daily Mail* and 'Pip, Squeak and Wilfred' in the *Daily Mirror*, asked Herbert Tourtel if his wife could come up with a suitable rival. Mary submitted a series of pen-and-ink drawings which was called 'Little Lost Bear' and this began in the morning newspaper on 8 November 1920. In a short time other children's features had been dropped and Rupert has appeared almost continuously ever since.

A Rupert annual did not appear for some years. The firm of Thomas Nelson & Son Ltd. was the first to reprint Rupert's adventures in a series of four small books issued in 1921 and 1922. Sampson, Low, Marston & Co. Ltd. (later Purnell) then reprinted the stories with two books issued in 1924 and 1925. Later, Sampson Low published the successful 'Little Bear Library' series and, in the 1930s, the *Monster Rupert* books (see Chapter 5).

After Mary Tourtel retired in 1935, Stanley Marshall, who was editorially responsible for the Rupert feature, recruited Alfred Bestall, talented former contributor to *Punch*, whose work had also appeared in *Tatler, Strand* and other leading magazines.

Alfred Bestall's first Rupert story for the *Daily Express* appeared on 28 June 1935 (in the same year that he supplied drawings to the *Boys' and Girls' Book of the Year*). The following year Stanley Marshall decided that there should be a Rupert annual. Because Bestall's work (and the story-lines, as directed by Marshall) was different to that of Mary Tourtel, Marshall titled the annual 'The New Adventures of Rupert' (although the stories were all reprints of the past year) and it was issued in the autumn of 1936. As this annual has never included the following year's date on the cover, it has similarly never been 'forward-dated' in the minds of collectors, all of whom refer to the first edition Rupert annual simply as 'the '36'. This annual is extremely rare (especially bearing in mind the number of collectors who wish to acquire it) and a mint copy, complete with dust-wrapper, is alleged to have recently changed hands for £700.

The next three Rupert annuals (published in 1937, 1938 and 1939) were of a similar format to the first, although with a full-colour picture (from a painting by Bestall) pasted down on to the boards, instead of the dust-wrapper of the 1936 edition. The inside was printed in black and red.

The 1940 issue was the first to be printed in full colour and this and the 1941 editions are highly prized by collectors, one reason being that the colour process used was unusual: the colours were bright and gentle and complemented the artwork in a fashion that later 'flatter' colours did not. The 1942–9 editions all had paper covers and were all labelled 'Economy Standard'. Naturally, the earlier these are, the rarer they tend to be: the 1942 edition is difficult to find in good condition.

In 1950, the annual became a hardback once again and the book also lost its 'Economy Standard' motif. With this edition a tradition was established that has become a part of the Rupert annual ever since: pasted inside each book at both front and back was a beautifully executed set of endpapers – reproductions from paintings by Bestall.

Many of Alfred Bestall's endpapers – not many of which actually featured Rupert – are captivating. Paul McCartney was so taken with the endpapers for the 1957 edition, titled 'The Frog Chorus', that he composed music and produced a short animated film based on the picture. A long-established Rupert 'fan', McCartney has long expressed his affection for the *Daily Express* character.

Alfred Bestall retired from newspaper work in 1965 but continued to contribute work for the annual until 1973; and there lies a short story. Rupert had always been pictured on the cover as a brown bear, despite the fact that on the inside he was shown as white. Allegedly, following a direction by Sir Max Aitken, the son of Lord Beaverbrook, and at the time owner of the *Express*, Rupert's traditional colouring on the front of the book was changed to white. Unfortunately, the amendment was made without reference to Alfred Bestall who was considerably annoyed when he saw the result. In consequence, Bestall refused to submit any more Rupert artwork for the cover of the annual. However, his contributions to the interior went on until 1983.

A few examples of the brown-Rupert annual were printed and at least one is known still to exist, making it by far the rarest of all Rupert annuals and the ultimate 'collectors' item'. The *Daily Express* obviously realised its mistake and the following year, in 1974, reinstated a brown-faced bear on the cover and has continued to do so ever since.

When Alfred Bestall retired, the task of writing Rupert stories was taken over by Fred Chaplain who had been Rupert's editor since 1952. When Chaplain retired, in 1978, the job of editing Rupert was passed to the capable James Henderson who has also written many of the stories that have since appeared.

Henderson has been responsible for some major changes to the annual: he has used new artists, introduced new characters and has changed the size of the book to make it larger and more visible in the bookshops.

The leading Rupert artist at present is John Harrold who paints the pictures used for the covers. At the suggestion of Henderson, Harrold included Alfred Bestall among the characters depicted on the cover of the fiftieth anniversary edition issued in 1985, which has rapidly become a collectors' item. The annual reprinted stories from each decade of a half-century of Rupert stories, many of them by Bestall. A short time before this, Alfred Bestall had been awarded the MBE for his Rupert work. He died in 1986 aged 93.

Provincial annuals

Annuals came predominantly within the realm of the national newspapers, but there was the occasional exception produced by the provincial Press: in 1939 the *Manchester Evening News* published *The Adventures of Fudge the Elf*, a now extremely rare annual-style book which was followed in later years by similar volumes.

'Fudge' was the first creation of Ken Reid (1919–87) who was later to become best known for his work on 'Roger the Dodger' and 'Jonah' for the *Beano* (see Chapter 4). Fudge the Elf made his first appearance on 7 April 1938. *The Adventures of Fudge the Elf* (Hodder & Stoughton), the first Fudge book, contained original material which had not previously appeared in the newspaper; but not so the second volume, *Frolics with Fudge*, published in 1941 by the University of London Press, which featured material first printed in the newspaper in 1940.

Because of the Second World War, no further books were published before 1947, when a book a year was printed until 1951. All were published by the University of London Press and were *Fudge's Trip to the Moon* (1947), *Fudge and the Dragon* (1948), *Fudge in Bubbleville* (1949), *Fudge in Toffee Town* (1950), and *Fudge Turns Detective* (1951). All comprised reprint material, with some additions and deletions of artwork. Like the early editions, they are all very hard to find in any condition. The 1948 and 1949 editions were republished (in paperback) in 1981 by Savoy Books of Manchester.

The character of Fudge and his adventures were aimed at quite young children but Ken Reid's work was sophisticated enough to build up a large readership among adults too. Reid turned to the children's comics in the early 1950s; first for the Amalgamated Press and later for D.C. Thomson, publishers of the *Beano* and *Dandy*. Despite this extra workload, he continued to draw Fudge's adventures for the *Manchester Evening News* until 1961 when he was forced by illness to retire.

Another star of the provincial Press was 'Gloops', the cheerful cartoon cat of the *Sheffield Telegraph* and its associated newspapers. Gloops – whose catchphrase was a lispy 'Thmile!' – appeared regularly in the Northern newspaper for almost thirty years, from 1928 to 1957. The cat's popularity in the region was helped by the establishment of an official 'Gloops Club' which ran for almost as long as the newspaper strip itself. Nearly forty books were published, some associated with the club, others were annuals issued in either the summer months or just prior to Christmas.

Fudge and the Dragon (1948): facsimile edition (1981).

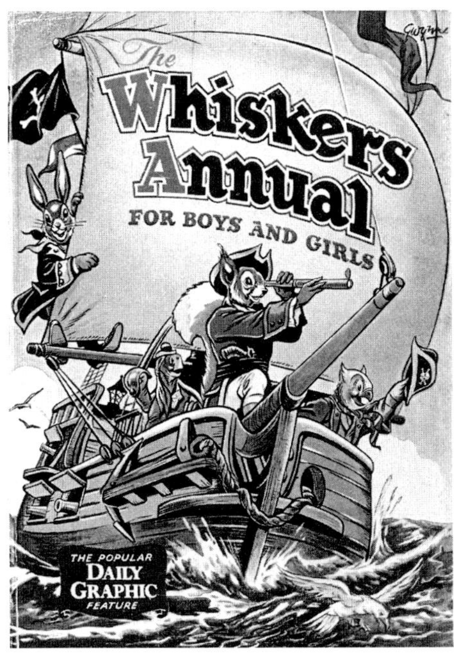

The Whiskers Annual (1950).

The Whiskers Annual was 'the book of the popular and world famous children's feature appearing every morning in the *Daily Graphic*' and was published for the years 1948 to 1952, the first edition being smaller in size than the others. The daily 'Whiskers' feature was by Cyril Price (signing himself 'Gwynne'), an artist who specialised in drawing animals (he had also contributed to the children's comics), and the annual was a lively presentation of his art in full colour.

The Whiskers characters were Whisk the Squirrel, Toodles the Tortoise, Hank the Hare, Mr Owl, Flop the Frog and Ben Brock the Badger. All were splendidly drawn although Gwynne frequently made no concession to the bodies of his animals: Whisk the Squirrel had a man's body except for head and tail, as was also the case with some other incidental characters. But the pictures were drawn with strong, bold lines and Gwynne's page designs were visually exciting.

The *Sunday Express* was one of the very few weekend newspapers to publish an annual. Edited by S. Louis Giraud (who had also been responsible for the *Daily Express Children's Annual*), the *Choktok's Annual* (1933) was issued for all those who read the 'Children's Corner' in the *Sunday Express* and who were members of the 'Choktok Club'. This club was divided into five chapters, all named after wildlife: the 'Striped Tigers' were members who lived in England; the 'Crested Eagles' were Scottish, and so on. As a result, the *Choktok's Annual* was unique in that it had no less than five letters – one to each reader group – from 'Uncle Mack', the editor of the Children's Corner. Page 128 of this annual signs off with the rousing message, 'This is the end of the first Choktok's Annual but the Choktoks go on forever!' Alas, this turned out to be the only edition; today, without the inclusion of even a Rupert Bear story, the annual is of such minor interest it is almost valueless.

In 1954, Beaverbrook newspapers, publishers of the *Daily* and *Sunday Express*, decided to set their sights on the youth market, issuing a tabloid newspaper for boys and girls entitled *Junior Express*. In less than a year this had been revamped into a comic and renamed *Junior Express Weekly* and, in 1956, still battling for a niche in the comic market, was renamed simply *Express*. Annuals were issued for 1957–60.

Perhaps the best artists that the annual attracted were Harry Bishop and Ron Embleton. Bishop drew 'Gun Law', the comic strip of the American television series 'Gunsmoke', which starred James Arness as US Marshal Matt Dillon. Embleton's contribution was 'Wulf the Briton' (the front-page feature of the weekly comic): stories set in an ancient Britain occupied by Rome. Sadly, both artists' work was spoiled in the annuals by what appeared to be an inferior colouring process. The weekly was later retitled yet again to *TV Express*, an annual being published for 1962.

'A Boys' and Girls' Annual should be a book that is fun to

read. There is plenty of fun in this book. There is also much information to be picked up in the pleasantest way.' These truisms appeared on the flyleaf of *The Daily Mail Annual for Boys and Girls* (1947–55) which was, from a parent's point of view, a superb annual in every way: a small gem which brought together some of the best talents in the business but, nowadays, undeniably one of the least collected of all annuals and worth little.

The Daily Mail Annual for Boys and Girls was edited by the journalist, Susan French, and each volume was a blend of written stories by popular children's authors and illustrations and comic strips by fine artists. Writers included Percy Clarke, Molly Chappell, Marjorie Whitaker, Susan French and others; and there were illustrations by Eric Parker, 'Spot' (the artist Arthur Potts), and comic strips by Brian White ('Nipper') and Roland Davies ('Come On, Steve!'). Arthur Potts also contributed drawings of Teddy Tail.

Why, then, should the book be so ignored by collectors? The answer must lie in the fact that, despite the wealth of its contributors, overall it appears intrinsically dull: an annual to be purchased by gift-buying parents, aunts and uncles for their young relations. And without the help of a companion periodical purchased weekly by children on their own account, the annual was dead on its feet, supported at the time by adult purchasers but neglected in later years because it was not something the recipients would have bought themselves or, in the end, found appealing.

Copies of the annual can today be found in second-hand bookshops for less than £1 each, usually without their attractive dustwrappers which (as they were by quality artists like Leslie Islingworth) are well worth having if they can be found. After 1955 the annual became two editions: *The Daily Mail Annual for Boys* and *The Daily Mail Annual for Girls*; both of these ran for several years, well into the Sixties.

Most national newspapers have issued annuals at one time or another; those dealt with in this chapter are the best known but there have been many others, too, including those published by the *Daily Mirror, Daily Record* and *News of the World*; even the *Daily Worker* at one time issued its own annual.

The *Daily Mirror* in particular has had considerable success with its daily comic strip 'Garth'. Garth is a thick-necked muscleman drawn initially by Stephen Dowling and, in later years, by other artists, including the late Frank Bellamy. It is Bellamy's work that has more than once been collected together and issued in annual format; the first of these (paperback) was in 1975, published by IPC.

As well, there have also been those perennial favourites beloved both of children and adults: 'Fred Bassett' (*Daily Mail*); 'Bristow' (London *Evening Standard*); 'The Gambols' (*Daily Express*) and, of course, the 'Giles' book of reprinted *Sunday* and *Daily Express* cartoons which have for so many years (since 1943, in fact) encapsulated and epitomised the British way of life. All these annuals, and more, remain an additional and valuable source of revenue for newspapers. Fleet Street, as it has been known, may disappear but 'newspaper publishers' annuals will remain with us as long as the Press itself does.

Title page from *Garth Annual (1976)*.

Chapter 8

Wham! Smash! and Frankie Stein

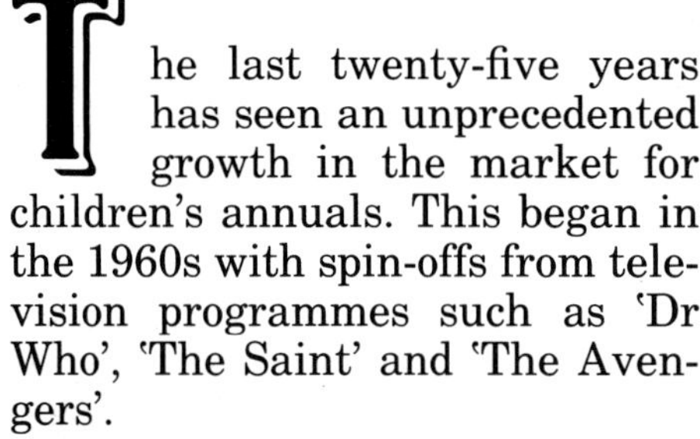

The last twenty-five years has seen an unprecedented growth in the market for children's annuals. This began in the 1960s with spin-offs from television programmes such as 'Dr Who', 'The Saint' and 'The Avengers'.

The *Dr Who Annual* is the most collected of all the television spin-offs. Devotees of the series will pay up to £40 for certain editions (1967, 1968 and 1969). 'Dr Who' was first shown on the BBC in 1964 and the first annual was published in the autumn of 1965. It pictured on its cover the first Dr Who, the late William Hartnell, and was written by the then script editor of the series, David Whitaker. Although it is the first, it is not the most valuable and is relatively easy to find. The second, due to a low print run, is much more difficult, and that too features William Hartnell.

Several actors have accepted the role of Dr Who, and the annuals, which have been published every year since, reflect these personalities – from Patrick Troughton, who succeeded William Hartnell, through Jon Pertwee, Tom Baker, Peter Davidson and Colin Baker. Four Dalek annuals (the Daleks, of course, are Dr Who's arch-enemies) were also published for the years 1976–79. Another associated book was the *K9 Annual* (Dr Who's dog), issued for 1983. Other television spin-offs are at present worth little and can be picked up very cheaply indeed. However, this may not always be the case, and the wise collector would do well to bear this in mind.

Several television series using puppets instead of live actors (unkind critics said they couldn't tell the difference in the acting from that on some regular television shows!) have resulted in a range of 'spin-off' titles. The man responsible for these television programmes was Gerry Anderson. Anderson was the co-founder of Pentagon Films, a company set up in order to make commercials for both the cinema and television. However, he soon moved on to making half-hour shows for children's TV (but which also had a large adult following). His first hit series for television was a Western, 'Four Feather Falls', which, like many of those that followed, was enacted entirely with a puppet cast. Anderson's next series was one of his most popular and possibly the one he is best remembered for. This was 'Supercar', which was first shown on ITV in 1959/60. The Supercar was a flying and amphibious vehicle driven by 'Mike Mercury', and the cast included his fellow puppets.

Gerry Anderson made several more series, each of which was equally successful, if not more so: 'Fireball XL5', 'Stingray', 'Thunderbirds', 'Captain Scarlet', 'Joe 90', 'The Secret Service' (which, usually mixed live actors and puppets), 'UFO', 'Space 1999' (with live actors) and 'Terrahawks'. Later, Anderson's 'Thunderbirds' was popular enough to be followed by two full-length feature films for the cinema.

Annuals associated with almost all of these series have been issued; in addition, one of the 'Thunderbirds' characters, 'Lady Penelope', was awarded her own annual. The following identifies the first edition of each and how many were in the series: *Supercar Annual* (1962: two); *Fireball XL5 Annual* (1963: four); *Stingray Annual* (1965: two); *Thunderbirds Annual* (1966: three); *Captain Scarlet and the Thunderbirds Annual* (1969: one); *Thunderbirds Annual* (1966: five); *Lady Penelope Annual* (1967: three); *TV21 Annual* (1965: three); *Captain Scarlet Annual* (1967: two); *Joe 90 Annual* (1968: two); *Space 1999 Annual* (1975: five); *Terrahawks Annual* (1983: three). Current prices of Gerry Anderson 'spin-off' annuals range from two to twelve pounds. There have also been books and periodicals relating to most series.

The Baxendale touch

There were other new developments in the Sixties. In 1964, Odhams Press decided to issue a new weekly humour title, *Wham!*, based on the work of Leo Baxendale who had previously drawn Little Plum, the Three Bears, Minnie the Minx, the Banana Bunch and other characters for D.C. Thomson (see Chapter 4). Baxendale had decided to leave Thomson and look for a new publisher which might offer fresh opportunities. He was received with open arms by Alf Wallace, managing editor of the Odhams group of comics: Baxendale was offered a contract which effectively doubled his annual income.

The Dr. Who Annual: first edition (1965). The 'Doctor' portrayed here is the late William Hartnell.

Odhams were no strangers to comics publishing: they had earlier inherited the Eagle group (which, as well as *Eagle*, included *Girl, Swift* and *Robin*) from Longacre Press when Hulton had been taken over by Longacre in 1960. But they wanted to expand their small empire: in 1963 Odhams had commissioned a market research survey which revealed how Thomson comics dominated the market; Odhams were keen to compete, and they sought Baxendale's help to recruit other top Thomson artists.

In the event, Baxendale's only recruit was Ken Reid (who had drawn 'Roger the Dodger' and 'Jonah' for the *Beano*), but it was enough. Reid was a first-class artist and writer. To say 'only' in relation to Ken Reid is the equivalent of talking about 'only one atomic bomb': Reid's effect was devastating. For *Wham!* he both wrote and drew 'Frankie Stein', a superb comic creation who had the staying power to be regularly published in weekly comics and annuals for the next twenty-five years.

A companion paper for *Wham!* entitled *Smash*!, was launched in February 1966. Both weeklies featured many of Leo Baxendale's creations and several by Ken Reid. Baxendale's best-known were: 'Grimly Feendish', 'General Nitt and His Barmy Army', 'George's Germs', 'Bad Penny' and 'The Nervs'. Reid excelled himself not only on 'Frankie Stein' but also on 'Queen of the Seas' and 'Jasper the Grasper', the last being something of an innovation in humour strips for, instead of being set in modern times, events took place in Victorian England.

The first *Wham!* annual was published in 1965 for 1966 and the first *Smash!* annual (a paperback, today quite rare) was issued in 1966 for 1967. Simultaneously, Odhams were issuing reprinted stories from American comic books originally published by Marvel Comics. These reprints were included in the weeklies *Pow!*, *Fantastic!* and *Terrific*, all of which were discontinued after about a year. However, these titles were issued with annuals: *Fantastic* (1969) *Terrific* (1969) and *Pow!* which was published for 1968–72 before being amalgamated with *Wham!* to become *Wham! and Pow! Annual* (1973). Work by both Baxendale and Reid was published in at least two of these titles.

Wham! and *Smash!* were bold ventures and, by today's standards – where a weekly comic is thought to have done well if it lasts a year – each was a qualified success. *Wham!* lasted three and a half years and *Smash!* over five. But readership fell and, as a result, they were discontinued. But long before this Baxendale had departed for Fleetway Publications which published, with many other titles, *Buster*.

Wham! Annual (1967).

The many faces of Buster

Fleetway Publications was formerly the Amalgamated Press and was still based in Fleetway House, Farringdon Street. The first weekly comic title to be published by the new company was *Buster*, a 16-page tabloid which featured a combination of both humorous and adventure comic strips.

Buster was blessed with an excellent editor, Jack LeGrande (1920–86), who had joined the Amalgamated Press in the 1930s as office boy to the editor of *Film Fun*, Fred Cordwell (see Chapter 3). Throughout the 1960s Jack LeGrande gathered together an impressive array of artistic talent: Eric Parker, Hugh McNeill, Arthur Martin, Reg and George Parlett, Leo Baxendale and many others. Even the legendary Roy Wilson, whose work had appeared in so many of AP's top titles during the 1920s and 1930s, was recruited. It was for *Buster* that

Left *Smash!* companion to the successful *Wham!*

Right *Pow!* – another title originated by Odhams Press.

Wilson drew his last comic page ('Morecambe and Wise') before he died in 1965.

Buster also included the work of another artist who had begun his comics career working for Odhams Press. This was Terry Bave, whose first comic strip was 'Sammy Shrink' for *Smash*! Terry and his wife Sheila have proved to be two stalwarts of the industry: for over twenty years Terry's drawings and Sheila's scripts have appeared in almost every humour title published by both Fleetway and IPC. 'Sammy Shrink', the adventures of a small boy about ten inches high, has been one of the most popular characters in humour comics; the feature is still running today in IPC's *Whizzer & Chips*.

Bave has always had a simple style which gets very little appreciation from comic art aficionados but is undeniably popular with children: his features always come near the top in readership polls (readers are regularly asked to cast a postal vote for their favourite comic strips, allocating them a position between 1 and 10) and he is in great demand to visit local schools.

Brian Walker is another prolific artist whose work has filled the pages of IPC annuals. Walker is a traditionalist who takes every opportunity to emulate the work of the leading comic artists of the Thirties. And he is also capable of striking originality too: 'Scream Inn', a popular feature he drew for *Shiver & Shake* ran for years, appearing regularly at the top of the readership polls.

The first Buster annual, entitled *The Buster Book*, was issued for 1962. Until the 1979 edition, it was published as a paperback in varying sizes; since then it has been published in hardcover, although again in different sizes. *Buster's* central character is 'Buster', a small boy who wears a green-checked cap and who is usually to be found up to his ears in gentle mischief. Initially, when the weekly comic began, Buster was billed as the 'Son of Andy Capp' (the famous *Daily Mirror* comic strip character) and his cap is indeed a model of the one worn by his 'dad'. However, this relationship was soon dropped and Andy has not been mentioned since. Buster, who has always appeared on the front page, has had several different artists in his twenty-eight-year history, but the best known is Reg Parlett who both drew and wrote the feature for more than ten years.

Reg Parlett is one of the great names in British comics. He began his career in 1923 drawing for the Amalgamated Press's weekly *Merry & Bright*. Soon his work was being enthusiastically sought by editors for the front pages of several top titles and, in the 1930s, when the AP began issuing annuals for popular comics such as *Crackers*, *Jingles*, *Jester*, *Funny Wonder* and *Radio Fun*, it was Parlett who was called upon to contribute paintings for covers and frontispieces as well as submit comic pages (some of them in full colour) for the interiors.

In the late 1940s he supplemented his comic work by working for a cartoon studio and then returned to comics on a full-time basis in the 1950s. His work has appeared in every major AP, Fleetway and IPC comic since then and it is difficult to find a humour title which does not contain his drawings. Reg Parlett is still drawing comic pages for *Buster* and *Whizzer & Chips*, both weeklies and annuals. He is aged 83 and his career (thus far!) has spanned an incredible 65 years.

The present 'Buster' artist is Tom Patterson, who is in the Leo Baxendale 'school' of illustrators. Patterson's work is brilliant: where once he appeared simply to be an imitator of Baxendale's style, he has now surpassed him in the sheer visual creativeness of his drawings. He is innovative and has a superior ability to 'improve' a written script with his drawings in a manner that is outrageously funny and even surrealistic in its content. Just as good, too, is Patterson's other major feature, 'Sweeny Toddler', which appears on the front page of the weekly *Whizzer & Chips* and its associated annual.

Whizzer & Chips, contrary to its name, is not an amalgamated title (two comics joined together when one has been discontinued). It was launched as a weekly in October 1969 on the clever premise that it was 'Two Comics in One!' The characters in the first comic, *Whizzer*, are purportedly rivals of those in the second, *Chips*. The editor since its inception has been the very able Bob Paynter, who still oversees its production. In the uncertain publishing conditions of today, its longevity is something of a triumph.

The first *Whizzer & Chips Annual* was dated 1971. Both the weekly and the annual featured the work of many of the artists who drew for *Buster*: Leo Baxendale, Reg Parlett, Terry Bave et al. But there were new contributors, too, in the shape of Mike Lacey and Sid Burgon, both of whom are extremely prolific and professional.

The IPC annuals

IPC published a string of weekly humour titles during the 1970s and 1980s: *Cor!!; Knockout* (1971), a revival of the old AP title; *Shiver & Shake*, another 'two in one' title; *Whoopee!; Monster Fun; Cheeky; Jackpot; Wow!; School Fun; Oink* and *Nipper*.

Nearly all of the above weekly humour comics have had annuals issued, and several were still being published long after the weeklies had been discontinued. Dates of the first editions are as follows: *Cor!!* (1972); *Knockout* (1973); *Shiver & Shake* (1974); *Whoopee* (1975); *Monster Fun* (1977); *Cheeky* (1979); *Jackpot* (1980); *Wow!* (1984); *School Fun* (1986); *Oink* (1988) and *Nipper* (1988).

One of the more interesting of these was *Monster Fun* (weekly issued: 1975; annual: 1977). This was in the tradition of '*Fun*' titles that had been published in years past by IPC's predecessor, AP: *Film Fun* (weekly: 1920; annual: 1938); *Radio Fun* (weekly: 1938; annual: 1940); and *TV Fun* (weekly; 1953: annual: 1958). *Monster Fun* was published at the height of the children's 'horror craze': traditional character types were replaced by vampires, werewolves, ghosts, mummies, monsters and other nightmarish creations. Subjects that were once only for the stout of heart became lovable figures of fun and objects of children's laughter.

The premier artist of *Monster Fun* was Robert T. ('Bob') Nixon who drew 'Kid Kong' (a spoof comic strip based on 'King Kong') and 'Frankie Stein' (the character created by Ken Reid for Odhams Press). Bob Nixon is one of the best humour artists to have emerged during the last twenty years. His cheerful style has a vitality and exuberance which is essentially British. Nixon contributed paintings for many of the annuals published during the 1970s. The *Monster Fun Annual* was issued for the years 1977–85; Nixon was responsible for the covers on the 1977–80 volumes and his work appears in every edition.

So well received in the readership polls was Bob Nixon's version of 'Frankie Stein' that IPC issued, for two years running (1976 and 1977), the *Whoopee! Book of Frankie Stein*. Both editions were paperback and both had covers reproduced from paintings specially commissioned from Bob Nixon. In future years it is very likely that these books will be 'collectors' items': in addition to Nixon's covers and interior art, each volume contains work by some of Britain's leading comics illustrators.

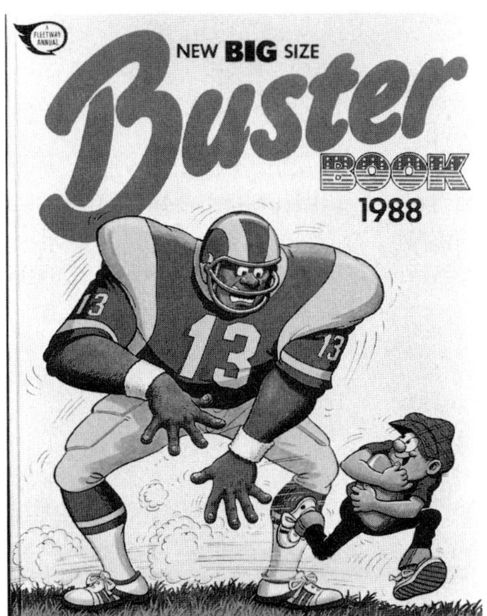

Buster – after 28 years, the longest-running Fleetway character and title.

Ken Reid was also contributing a lot of work to the IPC comics of the Seventies and Eighties, and he drew several long-running features for *Monster Fun*. But the feature in *Buster* with which he became particularly identified was 'Faceache', a small boy who could, at will, transform himself into hideous monsters. Reid began to draw 'Faceache' in 1970 and was still drawing the feature for *Buster* when he died in 1987. 'Faceache' pages by Reid that are reprinted in Christmas annuals are usually his best efforts and are well worth having on the basis of his art alone.

Nipper was originally issued as a pocket-sized comic and published early in 1987. Newsagents quickly complained of the small size and, as a result, IPC obliged by making it larger. Initially, there were plans for an equally small-sized annual but, in the event, the *Nipper Annual* (1988) was issued in a standard size.

Autumn 1987 also saw publication of the *Oink Annual* (1988). *Oink* was a bi-weekly (now weekly) comic with 'pigs' as its main theme: punny jokes are made relating to bacon, ham, gammon, pork, etc. The humour is often crude, often funny and frequently both. The *Oink Annual* (a paperback) is an apt reflection of the contents of the periodical: there is an anarchic streak running through it which appeals both to children and an older age group. Indeed, so 'anarchic' was the bi-weekly that it caused W.H. Smith to reclassify it and move it from the children's comic section to the shelf for satire magazines.

Like its huge publishing rival, D.C. Thomson, IPC has long issued 'Summer Specials': thick, paper-covered, extra editions of weekly comics which are also known as 'Holiday Specials'. These appeared once a year and contain half-reprint and half-

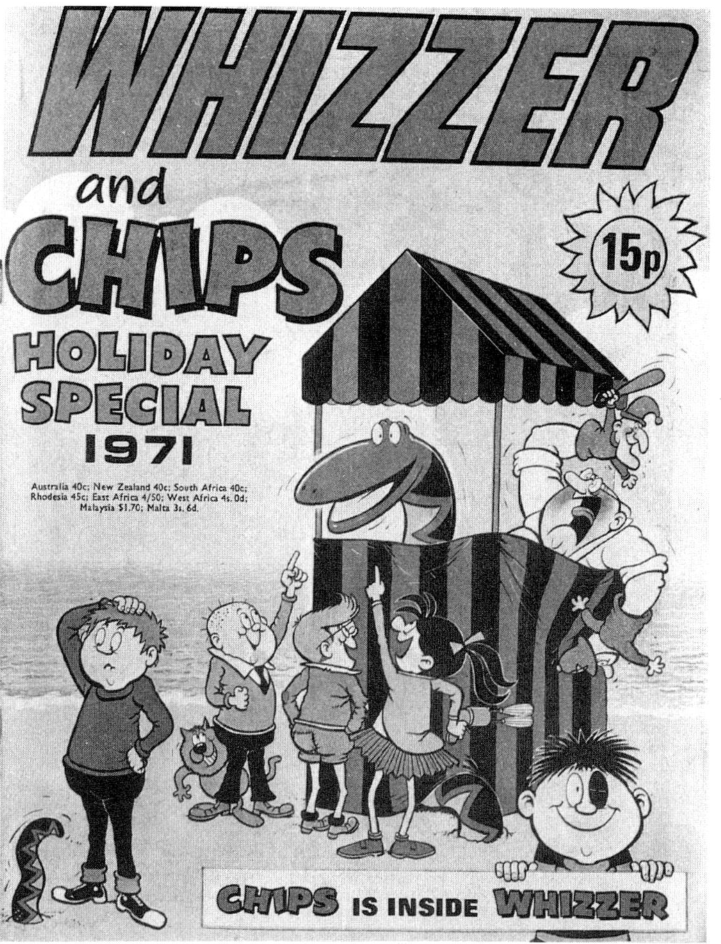

Whizzer & Chips Holiday Special (1971) – an IPC Summer annual.

original material. The first 'Summer Special' published by IPC was the *Whizzer and Chips Holiday Special*, published in 1970. Like their Thomson equivalents these should not be overlooked by the serious collector. Because of the less substantial format, compared to the hardback Christmas annuals, the Summer annuals are inevitably harder to find in the years following publication.

Glimpses of the future

Not since 'Dan Dare' in the *Eagle* of the 1950s had the readership of a weekly comic been as inspired as they were in 1977 when 'Judge Dredd' made his first appearance. Dredd was introduced in the second issue of *2000 AD*: he was a lawman of the future, equipped with body armour, gun and a super-bike which could, if need be, operate by itself.

Dredd was a member of a genetically bred force of crimefighters, the Judges, who rigidly enforced the law in Mega-City One, one of three enormous cities which between them occupied the entire Eastern seaboard of the United States. The setting was the year 2070, following the first Atomic War which had devastated the rest of North America. The stories, many of which were written by John Wagner and Pat Mills, were quirky and often weird in their concepts.

Several artists have contributed to Dredd's success, but the two best known are Mike McMahon and Brian Bolland. Both are extremely popular, with a huge following of fans. McMahon's drawings are sketchy and crude but full of action; Bolland's art has clarity, his characters are beautifully delineated and his drawings are more in the American style of comic art. In the USA the character, in particular Brian Bolland's version, has become exceedingly popular via black-and-white reprints published by Titan Books and monthly comics in the American all-colour comic book format. Bolland has now extended his career into American comics, drawing for long-established super-hero comics like *Green Lantern* and a brand-new tour de force, a series entitled *Camelot 3000*. He is widely acknowledged to be one of the finest British practitioners of adventure comic art in decades.

The weekly *2000 AD* comic spawned other series and heroes too, including a revamped version of 'Dan Dare' which was drawn by another talented illustrator, Dave Gibbons. Gibbons's version did not, however, take hold and it was not until 1982 that another version of Dare would prove sufficiently popular to sustain reader interest. This new Dan Dare (actually a descendant of the great space hero of the Fifties) was initially the work of B.J. Tomlinson, who wrote the stories, and Gerry Embleton, who drew it. The feature appeared in full-colour in the centre pages of the new *Eagle*. This is another comic which has found success with its formula of science fiction and adventure and recently celebrated its sixth anniversary.

No mention of *2000 AD* would be complete without reference to Alan Moore, a scriptwriter of extraordinary abilities. He has written many stories for *2000 AD* and has, for the last few years, contributed to American comic book titles for which he has become one of the top writers and won several awards.

Annuals have been issued for *2000 AD* (1978–); *Judge Dredd* (1981–); *Eagle* (1985–) and *Dan Dare* (1979–80), as well as for another weekly in a similar vein, *Starlord* (1980–1), which did not find equal success and was discontinued.

The driving force behind *2000 AD* was Pat Mills, the editor who had earlier been involved with two other IPC comics, *Battle Picture Weekly* and *Action* (later amalgamated in one title as *Battle Action*). *Battle*, as might be guessed from its title, was an out-and-out war comic in broad competition with rival publisher D.C. Thomson's *Warlord*. *Action* catered to a variety of tastes. Both *Battle* and *Action* could be very violent but occasionally the stories showed the kind of flair that made for exciting reading.

Some other IPC 'adventure' annuals have been *Hurricane* (1965–74); *Thunder* (1972–4); *Vulcan* (1977) and *Tornado* (1980–1), as well as extensions of some of the old Amalgamated Press annuals like *Lion* and *Tiger* (the former sometimes published in softcover). *Scorcher* (1971–), which uses football as a main theme, has also been a successful title.

All of these contained much the same type of material – good knock-about boys' stories, told both in text and pictures. Due to the amalgamation of some weekly comics, the best characters sometimes turn up in more than one title. This is true of 'The Spider', 'Robot Archie', 'Adam Eterno', 'The Steel Claw' and 'The Steel Commando'. The annual that is hardest to find is *Vulcan*, a one-off edition with paper covers published for 1977. This contained reprints of all the comic strips just mentioned and is a good representation of the best modern adventure strips produced by IPC. Indeed, some of the potential of these features is still being realised today: the adventures of the 'The Steel Claw' are being published in American comic book format on both sides of the Atlantic, and are rapidly finding a whole new readership.

It is astonishing how some of the older children's favourites survive; but doubtless it only proves how good many of them were in the first place. 'Biggles', the intrepid aeroplane pilot created by Captain W.E. Johns more than half a century ago, has recently been issued with an annual (1980) by Hodder & Stoughton. Even the comedians of the silent cinema have not been forgotten: in 1974, Brown & Watson published the *Charlie Chaplin Annual* (1975). As history has proved, the range and subjects for children's annuals is seemingly endless, and while there are children and publishers, it seems inevitable that the twain shall meet.

Capt. W. E. Johns' famous hero of the 1930s is still flying high a half-century on.

Children's Annuals Collectors' Price Guide

There follows a list of 100 collectable annuals. Prices given are for copies in very good to excellent condition.

YOP = Year of Publication

Adventureland
1924–1941
1924 £25–30
1925 15–20
1926–1935 12–15
1936–1941 8–12

Ally Sloper's Christmas Holidays
1884–1913 (YOP)
1884 £10–15
1885–1913 8–10

Ally Sloper's Summer Number
1880–1887 (YOP)
1880 £10–15
1881–1887 8–10

Arthur Askey's Annual
1940
1940 £20–25

The Beano Book
(1943–1950: **The Magic Beano Book**)
1940 to the present day
1940 £400–700
1940–1942 300–500
1943–1945 300–400
1946–1950 50–150
1951–1959 15–25
1960–1969 10–15
1970– 5–10

The Beezer Book
1958 to the present day
1958 £15–20
1959–1969 5–10
1970–1979 3–7
1980– 2–5

Beryl The Peril
1959 to the present day
(*published biennially; uneven in later years*)
1959 £15–20
1961–1965 10–15
1967–1977 5–10
1979–1988 2–5

Big Budget For Boys
1930–1943
1930 £8–10
1931–1943 4–6

Big Budget For Girls
1930–1943
1930 £8–10
1931–1943 4–6

Black Bob – The Dandy Wonder Dog
1950–1965
(*published biennially 1953–1959; no edition issued for 1963*)
1950 £10–15
1951 7–12
1953–1959 5–10
1961 5–8
1965 4–7

Bobby Bear (Daily Herald Book/Annual)
1920–1969
(*possible some years not issued*)
1920 £10–15
1921–1925 8–12
1925–1939 7–10
1940–1949 5–8
1950–1960 3–5
1961–1969 2–3

Boy's Own Annual
1879–1940 (YOP)
1879 £20–25
1880–1915 15–20
1916–1925 10–15
1926–1940 8–10

British Boys Annual
1912–1934
1912 £8–10
1913–1934 3–5

British Girls Annual
1912–1934
1912 £8–10
1913–1934 3–5

British Legion Annual
1934–1935
1934–1935 £2–3

The Broons
1940 to the present day
(*published biennially but no editions issued for 1944 and 1946*)
1940 £250–400
1942 150–300
1948–1956 50–75
1958–1964 15–25
1966–1988 5–10

Bruin Boys Annual
1927–1940
1927 £20–25
1928–1933 10–15
1934–1940 8–12

Bubbles Annual
1924–1943
1924 £20–25
1925–1929 10–15
1930–1943 8–12

Buffalo Bill Wild West Annual
1952–1962
1952 £8–12
1953–1962 6–10

The Buster Book
1962 to the present day
1962 £5–10
1963–1969 4–8
1970–1979 3–5
1980– 2–3

Butterfly Annual
1939–1940
1939–1940 £20–25

Champion Annual For Boys
1924–1956
(*not issued 1943–1946*)
1924 £15–20
1925–1929 10–15
1930–1942 8–12
1947–1956 5–10

Chick's Own Annual
1924–1957
1924 £20–25
1925–1939 10–15
1940–1945 8–10
1946–1947 3–5

Chips Annual
1939–1941
1939–1941 £20–25

Chums
1893–1940 (YOP)
1893 £20–25
1894–1915 15–20
1916–1925 10–15
1926–1940 8–10

Comicolour Album
1947–1955
1947 £7–10
1948–1949 5–10
1950–1955 4–8

Cor!! Annual
1972–1986
1972 £3–8
1973–1979 2–4
1980–1986 1–3

Crackers Annual
1933–1941
1933 £15–20
1934–1941 12–15

Cute Fun Album
1947–1956
1947 £7–10
1948–1949 5–10
1950–1956 4–8

The Dandy Book
(*see: Dandy Monster Comic*)

The Dandy's Desperate Dan
1954
1954 £20–25

The Dandy Monster Comic (*from 1953:* **The Dandy Book**)
1939 to the present day
1939 £400–700
1940–1942 300–500
1943–1945 300–400
1946–1950 50–150
1951–1952 20–25
1953–1959 15–25
1960–1969 10–15
1970– 5–10

Dandy-Beano Summer Special
1963 (YOP)
1963 £10–15

The Dennis The Menace Book
1956 to the present day
(*published biennially*)

1956 £20–25
1958–1962 15–20
1964–1972 5–10
1974–1988 3–7

Dr Who Annual
1966 to the present day
1966 £10–12
1967 30–35
1968–1970 20–30
1971–1975 5–10
1976–1982 2–5
1983– 1–2

Eagle Annual
1952–1974
1952 £7–12
1953–1959 5–10
1960–1964 3–7
1965–1974 2–5

Every Boy's Hobby Annual
1927–1937
1927 £8–10
1928–1937 6–8

Felix Annual
1923–1930
1923 £20–25
1924–1930 15–20

Film Fun Annual
1938–1961
1938 £75–100
1939–1940 60–75
1941–1945 30–40
1946–1949 25–30
1950–1955 15–20
1956–1960 8–10
1961 5–8

Frankie Stein (Whoopee! Book of)
1976–1977
1976–1977 £5–10

Funnies Album
1943–1957
1943 £10 15
1944–1949 5–10
1950–1957 4–8

Funny Wonder Annual
1935–1941
1935 £20–25
1936–1940 15–20
1941 20–25

Girl Annual
1953–1965
1953 £5–10
1954–1959 4–8
1960–1965 2–5

Girl's Crystal Annual
1940–1976
(*1943 issue not traced*)
1940 £10–15
1941–1950 6–10
1951–1960 4–6
1961–1976 2–3

Golden Annual for Girls
1925–1939
1925 £8–10
1926–1933 5–8
1934–1939 3–6

Golden Fun and Story Book
1939–1940
1939–1940 £20–25

Greyfriars Holiday Annual for Boys and Girls
1921–1941
(*see also: Holiday Annual for Boys and Girls*)
1921–1930 £15–20
1931–1941 £10–15

Holiday Annual for Boys and Girls
1920
(*see also: Greyfriars Holiday Annual*)
1920 £20–25

Hotspur Book For Boys (*first series/ undated*)
1935–1949
(*not issued for some 1940s years*)
1935 £20–25
1936–1943 15–20
1949 8–10

Jester Annual
1936–1940
1936 £20–25
1937–1940 15–20

Jingles Annual
1936–1941
1936 £20–25
1937–1940 15–20
1941 20–25

Jolly Jack's Annual
1935–1941
1935 £7–10
1940–1941 4–8

Judge Dredd Annual
1981 to the present day
1981 £5–7
1982–1986 3–4
1987– 2–3

Knockout Fun Book
(*continued as* **Knockout Annual**)
1941–1962
1941 £60–65
1942 40–50
1943–1945 30–40
1946–1949 25–30
1950–1955 10–15
1956–1961 8–10
1962 5–9

Lion Annual
1954–1981
1954 £7–10
1955–1959 4–7
1960–1969 3–5
1970–1981 2–3

Mrs Hippo's Annual
1926–1940
1926 £20–25
1927–1933 10–15
1934–1940 8–12

The Magic-Beano Book (*see: The Beano Book*)

Mickey Mouse Annual
1931–1965
1931 £150–175
1932–1940 75–150
1941–1945 30–50
1946–1949 15–20
1950–1959 8–15
1960–1965 5–8

Modern Boy's Annual
1931–1940
1931 £8–10
1932–1940 6–8

Monster Fun Annual
1977–1985
1977 £3–5
1978–1980 2–4
1981–1985 1–3

The Monster Rupert
1931–1934 (*first series*)
1948–1950 (*second series*)
1931–1934 £35–45
1948–1950 10–15

My Favourite Annual
1933–1935
1933 £10–15
1934–1935 8–10

Okay Adventure Annual
1956–1958
1956 £5–8
1957–1958 3–5

Oor Wullie
1941 to the present day
(*published biennially but no editions issued for 1945 and 1947*)
1941 £250–400
1943 150–300
1949–1955 50–75
1957–1965 15–25
1967– 5–10

Pip and Squeak Annual
1923–1940
1923 £20–25
1924–1929 15–20
1930–1940 10–15

Playbox Annual
1909–1956
1909 £30–35
1910–1930 10–15
1931–41 20–25
1942–46 15–20
1947–1956 5–10

Puck Annual
1921–1941
1921 £20–25
1922–1934 15–20
1935–1941 10–15

Radio Fun Annual
1940–1960
1940 £60–75
1941 50–60
1942–1943 40–45
1944 35–40
1945–1949 25–30
1950–1955 10–15
1956–1960 8–10

Rainbow Annual
1924–1957
(*some 1940s issues not traced*)
1924 £25–30
1923–1933 12–17
1934–1945 10–15
1946–1957 4–8

Robin Annual
1954–1976
1954 £2–4
1955–1959 2–3
1960–1976 1–2

Rover Book For Boys
1926–1959
(*not issued for some 1940s years*)
1926 £25–30
1927–1942 15–25
1950–1959 5–10

Roy of The Rovers (Tiger Book of)
1960 to the present day
1960 £3–5
1961–1969 2–3
1970– 1–2

Rupert
1936 to the present day
1936 £400–700
1937–1939 150–400
1940–1941 150–300
1942–1944 100–250
1945–1946 60–75
1947–1949 30–45
1950–1955 20–30
1956–1959 15–20
1960–1973 10–15
1974–1984 4–6
1985 5–8
1986– 3–4

School Friend Annual
1927–1981
(*some 1940s issues not traced*)
1927 £12–15
1928–1935 8–12
1936–1942 10–15
1943–1949 8–10
1950–1960 5–7
1961–1981 2–3

Schoolgirls Own Annual
1923–1942
1923 £15–20
1924–1932 10–15
1933–1942 8–10

Sexton Blake Annual
1938–1942
1938–1942 £20–25

Shiver and Shake Annual
1974–1986
1974 £3–5
1975–1979 2–3
1980–1986 1–3

The Skipper Book
1932–1948
(*not issued for some 1940s years*)
1932 £20–25
1933–1942 15–20
1948 10–12

Slick Fun Album
1949–1955
1949 £8–10
1950–1955 4–8

Smash! Annual
1967–1976
1967 £5–10
1968–1970 4–8
1971–1976 1–3

Sparkler Annual
1936–1940
1936 £20–25
1937–1940 15–20

Sparky Book for Boys and Girls
1968–1980
1968 £5–10
1969–1980 2–7

Swift Annual
1955–1963
1955 £2–4
1956–1959 2–3
1960–1963 1–2

TV Fun Annual
1957–1959
1957 £4–7
1958–1959 3–5

Teddy Tail's Annual
1934–1962
(*some 1940s editions not issued*)
1934 £8–12
1935–1942 5–10
1949–1956 3–5
1957–1962 2–3

Tiger Annual
1957–1981
1957 £7–10
1958–1959 4–7
1960–1969 3–5
1970–1981 2–3

Tiger Tim's Annual
1922–1957
(*some 1940s issues not traced*)
1922 £20–35
1923–1933 15–20
1934–1945 10–15
1946–1957 5–10

Tip Top
1937–1955
(*some 1940s issues not traced*)
1937 £15–20
1938–1947 10–15
1948–1955 6–10

The Toby Twirl Annual
1946–1947
1946 £3–5
1947 2–4

The Topper Book
1955 to the present day
1955 £20–25
1956–1959 15–20
1960–1969 5–10
1970–1979 3–7
1980– 2–5

Triumph Annual
1937–1941
1937 £15–20
1938–1941 10–15

Uncle Dick's (Competition) Annual
1930–1931
1930–1931 £10–15

Victor Book for Boys
1964 to the present day
1964 £5–10
1965–1975 3–7
1976– 2–5

Wham! Annual
1966–1972
1966 £5–10
1967–1970 4–8
1971–1972 1–3

Whiskers Annual
1948–1952
1948 £8–10
1949–1952 5–8

Whizzbang Comics Annual
1942–1943
1942–1943 £20–25

Whizzer and Chips Annual
1971 to the present day
1971 £3–8
1972–1979 2–4
1980– 1–3

Whoopee! Annual
1975–1987
1975 £3–4
1976–1979 2–3
1980–1987 1–2

Wilfred's Annual
1924–1939
1924 £15–20
1925–1929 10–15
1930–1939 8–12

Wizard Book for Boys
1936–1949
(*not issued for some 1940s years*)
1936 £20–25
1937–1942 15–20
1949 8–10

Wonderland Annual for Boys and Girls
1921–1926
1921 £10–15
1922–1926 8–10

Index

This is an index of the titles of the children's annuals featured in this book.